Effective Delegation Skills

Bruce B. Tepper

WITHDRAWN
by Unity Library

UNITY SCHOOL LIBRARY
UNITY VILLAGE, MISSOURI 64065

American Media Publishing
4900 University Avenue
West Des Moines, IA 50266-6769 U. S. A.
800/262-2557

Effective Delegation Skills

Bruce B. Tepper
Copyright ©1995 Richard D. Irwin, Inc.

This publication is designed to provide accurate and authoritative information in regard to the subject matter covered. It is sold with the understanding that neither the author nor the publisher is engaged in rendering legal, accounting, or other professional service. If legal advice or other expert assistance is required, the services of a competent professional should be sought.   4/03

Credits:
American Media Publishing: Arthur Bauer
                               Todd McDonald
Managing Editor: Karen Massetti Miller
Designer: Gayle O'Brien
Cover Design: Polly Beaver

Published by American Media Inc.
4900 University Avenue
West Des Moines, IA 50266-6769

Library of Congress Catalog Card Number 95-79760
Tepper, Bruce B.
Effective Delegation Skills

Printed in the United States of America
ISBN 1-884926-45-2

Introduction

Delegation is a problem for new supervisors, new managers, and experienced professionals alike. It is one of the greatest challenges we face in supervising others.

If you are new to supervision or management, you must learn a number of seemingly overwhelming tasks. Delegation is one of those tasks often put aside to be dealt with in the future because it is difficult to accomplish and carries with it many emotional implications.

Delegation is a skill that can be learned and developed. It is a skill that is critical to your growth as a supervisor or manager. You must know how to delegate if you want to have time to do your job properly and to motivate your subordinates to do their very best.

The easiest way to learn any skill, like delegation, is to break it down into its components and deal with each one separately. This book does just that. New supervisors or managers will gain helpful insights and ideas on setting up their own programs of delegating work. Seasoned veterans will learn some new ideas and have their efforts to be better supervisors reinforced.

Delegation is one of the most valuable tools available to make your job a success. It can bring you greater loyalty from subordinates and senior management. Good delegation skills can go a long way in helping you reach your own personal and business objectives.

Self-Assessment

The following self-assessment will help you to determine how sharp your delegation skills are and will suggest areas where improvements can be made. Using the following key, circle the number next to each statement that reflects how often you identify with the statement. Score yourself at the end of the self-assessment.

4 = Always
3 = Usually
2 = Sometimes
1 = Rarely
0 = Never

1. I make a point of not doing work assigned to employees.

    0 1 2 3 4

2. I give clear directions regarding tasks that need to be done.

    0 1 2 3 4

3. I do not feel threatened by good employees.

    0 1 2 3 4

4. My sense of influence and success comes from the success of my subordinates.

    0 1 2 3 4

5. I feel in control—even with projects I've delegated to others.

    0 1 2 3 4

6. I feel confident about my direction and role as a supervisor.

    0 1 2 3 4

7. I trust my subordinates to do a good job.

    0 1 2 3 4

8. I take the time to teach my subordinates how to do tasks I have delegated.

    0 1 2 3 4

9. I believe that delegating as many tasks as possible is in everyone's best interest.

    0 1 2 3 4

10. I recognize the difference between being a supervisor and performing the tasks my employees perform.

    0 1 2 3 4

11. I feel confident leading and directing others.

    0 1 2 3 4

12. I am patient in allowing employees to
complete tasks and to learn from their mistakes.   0 1 2 3 4

13. I give employees additional time to do a task
correctly if it isn't done correctly the first time,
rather than take the assignments away from
the employees to do them myself.   0 1 2 3 4

14. Before delegating work, I break each task
down into its basic components to see
what skills will be needed.   0 1 2 3 4

15. I make sure employees have adequate
training to perform each task.   0 1 2 3 4

16. I allow adequate time for employees to
perform each task.   0 1 2 3 4

17. I examine obstacles employees may face
in performing each task.   0 1 2 3 4

18. I try to match tasks to employees' personality
traits, thinking styles, and capabilities.   0 1 2 3 4

19. I do a profile on each employee and his or
her capabilities.   0 1 2 3 4

20. I provide written instructions to employees
for each new task they are to perform.   0 1 2 3 4

21. I review the instructions and details of the
task and make sure the employee understands
what is required.   0 1 2 3 4

22. I have contingency plans for delegated tasks to
make sure the tasks get done.   0 1 2 3 4

23. I have developed and implemented an evaluation
plan to monitor how well employees do with each
task.   0 1 2 3 4

24. I encourage employees to make their own
decisions and to solve problems related to
new tasks.   0 1 2 3 4

25. I encourage employees to set their own
performance objectives.   0 1 2 3 4

26. I maintain a very supportive posture
for all of my subordinates.   0 1 2 3 4

27. I avoid harsh criticism of an employee's
performance of new tasks.   0 1 2 3 4

28. I solicit feedback from employees on how
they feel they are doing with new tasks.   0 1 2 3 4

29. I try to determine employees motivational
needs when delegating tasks.   0 1 2 3 4

30. I enlist the support of my supervisor
or manager for the delegation plans
I implement.   0 1 2 3 4

31. I treat delegation as a productivity
maximizer and as a method of
developing employee skills.   0 1 2 3 4

32. I see my role as that of a general
contractor or conductor; I see the
big picture while orchestrating
the activities of others.   0 1 2 3 4

33. I try to challenge my subordinates
to extend their own capabilities.   0 1 2 3 4

34. I am open and receptive to new
ways to handle old tasks that may
come from my employees.   0 1 2 3 4

35. I believe that delegation is an essential
element of good management, and it
is important to me, my employees,
my supervisor, and our customers.   0 1 2 3 4

Score Yourself

Total the number of points you have circled for all 35 statements.

Scoring 110 points or more means you are pretty comfortable with your role as a supervisor or manager and understand and accept the need to delegate work in performing your role. Although there is always room for improvement, you are close to being the kind of supervisor motivated employees like to work for. This book will help reinforce the skills you are using effectively.

A score of 80 to 109 points means you accept the need to delegate work and try to do so. Some weaknesses remain that need a little extra attention. This book will help you to strengthen those weaknesses.

Less than 80 points indicates that you are a relatively new supervisor or manager just beginning to delegate work or that you are battling obstacles to delegation. This book will give you the skills you need to become an effective delegator. In the process, you will become a better supervisor or manager.

Good luck!

● Table of Contents

Chapter *One*

Why Work Should Be Delegated

Chapter Objectives

▶ Appreciate the need to delegate work.

▶ Understand the impact of delegation on your supervision and management effectiveness.

▶ Recognize how important delegation is to your subordinates.

Case Study

Tómas Garcia is one of the hardest-working people employed by a tax consulting firm. He believes that his diligence and attention to detail are the main reasons he has been promoted to supervisor in the marketing department. Tómas has always been the top performer in every category, but now he is concerned about staying on top of the workload and maintaining the kind of quality that is necessary. He also is concerned about his new management duties and how he can handle everything.

As a supervisor, Tómas has a staff reporting to him. He is concerned that they will not be able to do their jobs, so he is inclined to do everything himself. That way he knows the tasks will be done correctly. Tómas says, "There just isn't time to teach the staff all they need to know." He believes he can delegate work later on, when he is more established.

1

Take a Moment

1. Is Tómas likely to succeed if he does not delegate job tasks and instead performs all the tasks himself? Why or why not?

_____

_____

2. How might Tómas overcome his fear of delegation?

_____

_____

Why Delegating Work Is So Important

One of the most critical keys to successful management and supervision is the ability to delegate work to others. Delegation of work offers major advantages to the supervisor, employees, and the company:

> **Delegation of work offers major advantages to the supervisor, employees, and the company.**

◆ As a supervisor or manager, you will have time to manage, which is a job totally different from any job done by the people who work for you.

◆ You will have time to develop management and supervision skills that will add to your productivity and, consequently, improve the company's performance.

◆ You will help develop other people and improve their skills.

◆ You will be able to identify talent and ability more clearly among your subordinates by allowing them to become more involved in a greater variety of tasks.

◆ You will demonstrate respect and appreciation for those who report to you. By delegating work, you let your employees know that you trust them and want them to be successful.

Take a Moment

Do you need to delegate?

Take this brief quiz to determine how pressing your need is to delegate work.

	YES	NO
1. Do you feel overwhelmed with work?	❑	❑
2. Do you find yourself working too many hours?	❑	❑
3. Do you leave tasks unfinished?	❑	❑
4. Do you fail to meet deadlines?	❑	❑
5. Is the quality of work from your department as good as it should be?	❑	❑
6. Do your employees regularly ask for additional assignments or more responsibility?	❑	❑
7. Are you having difficulty organizing assignments and tasks?	❑	❑

If you answered "yes" to more than two of these questions, you probably are having major problems doing your job as a supervisor or manager.

If you fail to delgate work, you will never learn and apply the necessary skills of supervison and management.

The Effective Supervisor or Manager

Management skills are distinct from frontline skills and tasks. In many businesses, it is common practice to promote the best "task performer" to manager. Frequently, there is an attitude of benign neglect: If you are good at your job, you probably will be a great manager or supervisor. Unfortunately, the skills needed to supervise are totally different from those required to perform job-specific tasks. If you fail to delegate work, you will never learn and apply the necessary skills of supervision and management.

Take a Moment

Are you a good supervisor?

Take a moment to evaluate your supervision skills. Complete each statement by checking the appropriate blank.

	Excellent	Good	Poor (Needs Improvement)
1. My ability to give clear direction to other people is	_____	_____	_____
2. My management skills are	_____	_____	_____
3. My leadership skills are	_____	_____	_____
4. My decision-making skills are	_____	_____	_____
5. My ability to introduce and handle change is	_____	_____	_____
6. My ability to manage my time effectively is	_____	_____	_____
7. My ability to use praise and criticism is	_____	_____	_____
8. My ability to set goals and objectives and meet them is	_____	_____	_____
9. My ability to generate a positive attitude among my subordinates is	_____	_____	_____
10. My ability to focus on the big picture and not get bogged down in doing the job of my employees is	_____	_____	_____

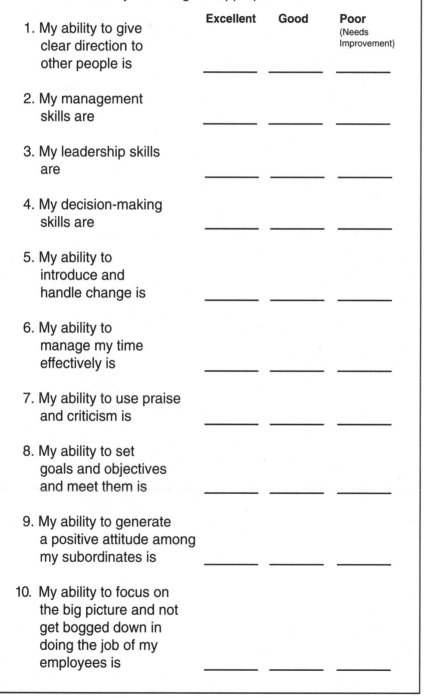

These statements reflect the essential elements of supervision and management. If you are not good or excellent in every category, failure to delegate work may be one of the main reasons. Delegation frees up your time and allows you to focus on what you were hired to do: manage and supervise.

Delegation and Your Subordinates

Delegation is also important to the people who work for you.

Delegation demonstrates your faith and trust in your employees' abilities.

◆ It demonstrates your faith and trust in their abilities.

◆ It allows them to develop and improve their skills.

◆ It creates greater involvement for them in their company.

◆ It is a sign of respect for their capabilities.

◆ It helps you to evaluate them on a much broader basis. You see their potential in many areas.

◆ It builds morale. Think back to the days before you were a supervisor. Didn't you seek out tasks to demonstrate your capabilities and sense of responsibility? Don't deny that aspect of the job to the people who work for you.

Take the following quiz, duplicate it, and give copies of it to your subordinates. Ask each of them to complete the quiz anonymously and return it to you. At the same time, take the quiz yourself and see how closely the answers of your subordinates match your own.

After you and your group have taken the quiz, step back for a moment. How far apart are the opinions of you and your employees on your delegation skills and willingness to delegate work?

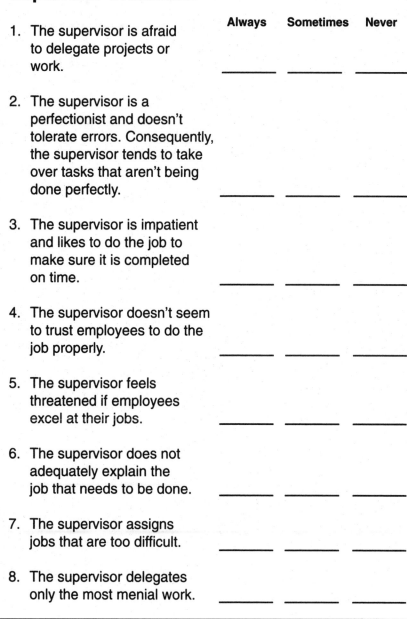

Take a Moment

Supervisor evaluation

	Always	Sometimes	Never
1. The supervisor is afraid to delegate projects or work.	_____	_____	_____
2. The supervisor is a perfectionist and doesn't tolerate errors. Consequently, the supervisor tends to take over tasks that aren't being done perfectly.	_____	_____	_____
3. The supervisor is impatient and likes to do the job to make sure it is completed on time.	_____	_____	_____
4. The supervisor doesn't seem to trust employees to do the job properly.	_____	_____	_____
5. The supervisor feels threatened if employees excel at their jobs.	_____	_____	_____
6. The supervisor does not adequately explain the job that needs to be done.	_____	_____	_____
7. The supervisor assigns jobs that are too difficult.	_____	_____	_____
8. The supervisor delegates only the most menial work.	_____	_____	_____

1

Chapter Summary

◆ You must believe that the need to delegate work is crucial.

◆ Subordinates must be trusted to do their jobs properly.

◆ You must be patient enough to teach subordinates what they will need to know to do their jobs properly.

◆ Be sure to delegate work to give yourself the chance to learn new supervisory management skills.

Chapter*Two*

Overcoming Obstacles to Delegation

Chapter Objectives

▶ Understand the obstacles to delegating work.

▶ Overcome delegation obstacles and begin the process of delegation.

Case Study

Rosemary Weissgarten has been a supervisor at a publishing company for several months. She is becoming more firmly established in her job, but she still does most of the work herself. By doing the work rather than delegating it, she ensures quality and, quite frankly, she enjoys many of the tasks she has to perform.

Intellectually, Rosemary knows she must make a more concerted effort to delegate tasks. But emotionally, it is very difficult for her to do so. "When you've done certain types of work for a long period of time, you get used to doing it yourself," says Rosemary.

Take a Moment

Questions to consider:

1. How can Rosemary let go of the tasks she no longer needs to perform?

_____

_____

2. How can Rosemary ensure that the tasks she does so well will be performed as well by her subordinates?

_____

_____

2

Understanding the Obstacles

Supervisors and managers find it difficult to delegate work to other people for several reasons.

◆ After working in a job for some time, much of your sense of confidence and, for that matter, power, comes from your knowledge of the job. If other people do your work, you truly feel a sense of loss. Consequently, when moving into a supervisory job, you want to continue doing the work you did before becoming a supervisor.

> **Loss of control is an obstacle that keeps some supervisors from delegating.**

◆ You may sense a loss of control. Someone else will do the tasks you used to do, and that person may do them better! That person might become a recognized authority in the office, just as you might have been in the past. Recall Tómas Garcia from Chapter 1. Prior to being promoted, he was the best at his work. He may experience a true sense of loss if someone else learns his former tasks and uses his expertise.

◆ You may sense a loss of direction and focus. When you begin work as a supervisor or manager, you must learn new tasks. In a sense, you are starting all over. Your confidence level may drop because you are a "student" again. After becoming very proficient at a job, you may find it difficult to walk away from it.

◆ You may lose your sense of accomplishment. When you perform tasks and complete them, you often sense great satisfaction. As a supervisor, you oversee others who get the sense of accomplishment instead.

Take the following quiz to determine your sensitivity to these issues.

Take a Moment
Are you able to let go?

	Always	Sometimes	Never
1. Since I'm responsible for the results, I have an obligation to handle tasks others may not be able to do.	_____	_____	_____
2. I find it very difficult to trust others to do things as well as I do.	_____	_____	_____
3. I find it difficult to trust others to do things as quickly as I do.	_____	_____	_____
4. It bothers me to see someone else do my old job differently from the way I did it.	_____	_____	_____
5. Without doing my old job, I feel somewhat lost.	_____	_____	_____
6. I enjoy the tasks of my old job more than the new tasks I'm supposed to do.	_____	_____	_____
7. I find it emotionally draining to give up what I've done for so long.	_____	_____	_____

Even one "always" is too many on this quiz, although an "always" answer for statement 6 may be understandable for a short period of time.

In time, you will build confidence as you learn new tasks. However, there is no reason to wait. By facing the change squarely and moving quickly into learning new tasks, you can accelerate your elimination of these sensitive issues.

2

Overcoming the Obstacles

Several steps can help you overcome the obstacles to delegation.

1. Accept delegation as inevitable. Stop fighting it. You cannot do your job properly as a supervisor or manager without delegating work to others.

2. Develop your new skills of supervision. Focus on how quickly you can learn new skills and how quickly you can set up a delegation plan as described in Chapter 5 of this book.

3. Think about when you first started your last job. The fear of the unknown and the knowledge that you had much to learn undoubtedly were part of your thoughts. You mastered the old job and did it well or very likely you would not have become a supervisor. Your new challenges are much the same. Don't let new responsibilities intimidate you. Break down the tasks and learn them one by one. In time, you will find that supervision will be just as rewarding, if not more so, as your old job.

Don't let new responsibilities intimidate you.

4. Take any additional steps. You may find it necessary to learn more about supervision and management and to increase your comfort level with your new roles.

Complete the following Delegation Progress Chart and set a timetable for completing every step.

Delegation Progress Chart

Task/Goal	Date Completed
1. I have complete confidence in my ability to lead others.	_____
2. I have developed the necessary skills to supervise and direct the activity of others.	_____
3. I have identified five tasks that I used to do that should now be done by others. I am comfortable delegating the following tasks that I used to do:	_____

a. _____

b. _____

c. _____

d. _____

e. _____

| 4. I have identified three key tasks I must learn and will learn them by the date listed. | _____ |

a. _____

b. _____

c. _____

| 5. I have overcome all fears of being shown up by subordinates or replacements on my old job. | _____ |

6. I am able to teach others without jumping in and finishing tasks. _____

7. I have the patience to allow others to make mistakes and learn their jobs. _____

2

There is no correct numerical score. Your objectives are to:

♦ Step into your new role and supervise others. Don't do the tasks yourself.

♦ Step back and allow others to develop and learn even if they make mistakes.

♦ Step up and start learning new skills that will help you do your job better and enhance your career.

Overcoming the obstacles to delegation requires a mind-set that permits you to grow. You must think of yourself as a new person with new responsibilities. Do not let fear or insecurity hold you back. You can develop new skills as you have done before. Delegation does not come naturally. Make it a part of your conscious thoughts until it becomes a little more routine.

Chapter Summary

♦ Accept your role as a supervisor and make a conscious effort not to do tasks others should do.

♦ Develop an attitude of wanting to develop the skills of others without stepping in and doing their jobs for them.

♦ Recognize the sense of loss that can occur when delegating work, but welcome the challenge of learning new tasks.

♦ Accept the fact that others may do your old job differently than you, better than you, or both.

♦ Recognize that your new role of supervising others includes developing the talents of your subordinates.

Chapter*Three*

Choosing the Right Tasks to Delegate

Chapter Objectives

▶ Review your area of responsibility.

▶ Determine which tasks are most suited to delegation.

▶ Develop a priority list of tasks to be delegated.

Case Study

James Watson has just been appointed supervisor of the menswear department of a large department store. His responsibilities include supervising a staff of 15 people who cover all the hours the store is open, selecting merchandise to display and where to display it (except for promotions developed by the store's marketing and advertising department), and reviewing inventory to make recommendations to management on trends and client interests. James knows that it is essential to delegate some of the work to his assistants, but he is not sure where to begin.

Take a Moment

Questions to consider:

1. Which tasks should James control? Why?

_____

_____

2. Which tasks should James delegate? Why?

_____

_____

Areas of Responsibility

Let's begin by separating the issues of responsibility and delegation. James may choose to delegate any variety of tasks he wishes. However, he still remains responsible for their completion.

One obstacle to delegation that was not discussed in Chapter 2 is the fear of being responsible for someone else's work and having that work fail to live up to expectations. Supervisors and managers cannot delegate responsibility for work under their direction. Consequently, James must choose his tasks carefully to make sure they will be done properly. In many cases, he should continually review the work of others to make sure it is up to acceptable standards.

3

Getting Started in Task Selection

Choosing tasks to delegate begins with breaking down a job into small components. The best place to start is with your job description. If you have a formal job description, list the tasks described, then break them down into their smallest possible components.

Choosing tasks to delegate begins with breaking down a job into small components.

The following breaks down work for James Watson:

Supervision of Staff

◆ Determine work schedules.

◆ Conduct employee reviews.

◆ Provide ongoing skills and sales training/support.

◆ Mediate employee disputes.

◆ Assign work.

◆ Cover counters as a backup salesperson in busy times.

◆ Review daily invoices for commission reports.

◆ Motivate salespeople to work harder.

◆ Handle customer service problems/complaints.

Merchandising

- ◆ Review each shelf and display area to make sure they are adequately stocked and neatly arranged.

- ◆ Replace display stock as needed or rearrange displays as necessary.

- ◆ Review displays for appeal and reorganize as necessary.

- ◆ Maintain cleanliness of display areas.

- ◆ Make sure all marketing department displays are set up and maintained.

Inventory Control

- ◆ Review invoices on a daily basis to make sure control tags have been removed from garments and attached to the store copy of the receipt.

- ◆ Complete the daily inventory report, listing items sold by category.

- ◆ Check stock daily to make sure adequate supplies of popular items have been ordered from the store's warehouse and are in the stockroom.

- ◆ Complete the trend report for store buyers on items customers ask for that are unavailable or out of stock and on items that are moving up or down in popularity.

In looking through James's list, there are a number of items that clearly can be delegated (for example, checking stock daily). This is a starting point for James to determine where to delegate.

Now it's your turn. Compete the chart on the next page using your job description as a basis for general categories. Under the General Categories column, list your primary responsibilities. There probably will be less than four or five. (James's were supervision of staff, merchandising, and inventory control.) In the center column, list specific tasks in a manner similar to those on James's list.

Task Selection and Responsibilities Chart

General Categories	Specific Tasks	Delegate
_____	_____	_____ yes _____ no
	_____	_____ yes _____ no
_____	_____	_____ yes _____ no
	_____	_____ yes _____ no
_____	_____	_____ yes _____ no
	_____	_____ yes _____ no
_____	_____	_____ yes _____ no
	_____	_____ yes _____ no
_____	_____	_____ yes _____ no
	_____	_____ yes _____ no

Which Tasks Are Best Suited to Delegation?

Now move to the third column to the right of each specific task labeled "Delegate." In this column, check yes or no after answering the following questions:

1. Is the task one that logically should and could be done by someone else? (That is, the task is not clearly a management or supervision task, such as conducting employee reviews.)

2. Do I feel comfortable turning this task over to the right person knowing I'm still responsible for the results? (Remember, you cannot do everything yourself, so it will be necessary to delegate work.)

3. Are any of my staff trained and/or capable of handling this task?

4. Will the person chosen to handle this task have adequate time to perform it effectively?

5. Can I present this task as an important one to make sure the individual who carries it out does it properly?

Developing a Priority List

Not every task that should be delegated can be delegated all the time.

♦ There may not be anyone qualified to do the task when you need it done.

♦ It may be necessary to provide training, which you may not have time to provide immediately.

♦ Some tasks are seasonal and do not require permanent work assignments.

With these thoughts in mind, complete the following table, listing in the left-hand column each task you have decided can be delegated under the right circumstances. Next to each task, list any obstacles to delegating the task right now. In the right-hand column, list your target date for delegating the task—one that gives you time to overcome obstacles listed in the middle column.

Priority List: Tasks to Delegate Chart

Task	Obstacles	Implementation Date
_____	_____	_____
_____	_____	_____
_____	_____	_____
_____	_____	_____
_____	_____	_____
_____	_____	_____
_____	_____	_____
_____	_____	_____
_____	_____	_____
_____	_____	_____

3

Delegating Work to Your Supervisor

In some cases, it makes sense to delegate work upward to your manager or supervisor.

If a situation occurs that may involve procedural change that could affect other departments, it may be more logical to delegate the decision and implementation to you supervisor. He or she may be in a better position to get things done more quickly.

If you feel you can improve your boss's comfort level by involving him or her, do so. Like you, your boss may suffer from anxieties about delegating work and responsibility.

If delegation of certain assignments is likely to meet resistance, you may want the extra authority your boss's position brings to the table. Be careful, though: You do not want to risk undermining your own authority as a supervisor.

If you feel apprehensive about delegating a task, you may want your boss to make the decision for you. Again, be careful. You do not want to appear weak or indecisive.

Chapter Summary

◆ Create a clear and concise job description for your position.

◆ Break down each main area of responsibility into small tasks.

◆ Review each task and determine whether you must do it or whether it can be done by someone else.

◆ Create an implementation timetable for every task that can be delegated.

◆ Note tasks that may involve policy changes so you can enlist the help of your supervisor or manager.

◆ Constantly evaluate each task to make sure it still is worth doing, and recommend eliminating tasks that are no longer necessary.

Chapter *Four*

Delegating Tasks to the Right People

Chapter Objectives

▶ Determine who is capable of handling delegated tasks.

▶ Select which tasks should be delegated to each of your subordinates.

Case Study

The hotel reservations center where Sonia Owens works as a supervisor recently reorganized, giving her new areas of responsibility. She now supervises telephone operators handling inbound calls for two hotel chains; the operators are required to use different procedures for each chain.

The increased workload brought on by new responsibilities has convinced Sonia that she must delegate a number of tasks to handle her job efficiently. She has selected the tasks to be delegated; her problem now is to decide who is best suited to handle those tasks.

Take a Moment

Questions to consider:

1. Why is Sonia's decision a difficult one to make?

_____

_____

2. What steps can Sonia take to make her decision?

_____

_____

Determining Who Is Capable of Handling Delegated Tasks

Theoretically, every employee should be capable of taking on additional responsibility as needed. Realistically, other considerations must be taken into account.

The first step in deciding whether or not a person is capable of handling a new assignment is to answer the following six questions:

1. **Will the person have time to do the task?**
   This is a basic question, but one that must be considered. The supervisor must determine whether the task interferes with the subordinate's ability to do his or her primary job.

2. **Does the person have the ability to do the task?**
   If the task requires physical strength, a great aptitude for math, a highly creative mind, etc., the individual may not be up to handling the task.

3. **Is the person trained to do the task?**
   Even though an individual is capable of doing the work, he or she may not have the training to do it.

4. **If the person lacks the skills to do the tasks, can he or she be taught those skills in a reasonable period of time?**

5. **Is the person generally reliable?**
   In an ideal world, all of your employees are reliable, but in real life they may not be. Reliability can be a key factor if you need the task done in a timely manner.

6. **Is the person seeking out new responsibility?**
   One of the reasons for delegating work is to develop your employees. If for some reason individuals do not want additional responsibilities or duties, do not force extra tasks upon them. Try to find someone who will benefit from helping you.

Ideally, you can answer "yes" to all of these questions about delegating a task. In some situations, however, it may be absolutely necessary to delegate tasks when you cannot answer

4

> Even though an individual is capable of doing the work, he or she may not have the training to do it.

"yes" to all six questions. In such cases, be prepared to monitor closely the tasks you delegate. Do no wait until they are completed before checking progress.

At the hotel reservation center, Sonia is likely to be faced with having her employees handle calls for both hotel chains, not just one. Each chain's procedures may be very different, and her employees may not have been training for both.

Sonia would be wise to consider reliability and willingness to help above some of the other characteristics. Most likely, the necessary skills can be taught fairly quickly and the employees should, in all cases, be capable of doing the work unless they are so busy in their present jobs that they have no more time.

Matching the Tasks to the People

Not everyone who works for you will be capable of doing every task you want to delegate to him or her. To help determine who is best suited, take each task and determine the skills and aptitudes necessary to do the job.

For each task you plan to delegate, complete the following chart. Circle those traits that are required for each task, and add to each category as appropriate. The results will give you a profile of what the task requires. You may want to make copies of this chart for future use.

Task Profile Chart

Task: _____

_____

◆ Thinking Styles

    Quick decision making   ❑

    Creative thinking   ❑

    Ability to see the "big picture"   ❑

    Other: ❑

◆ **Personality Traits**

Patience   ❏

Empathy and understanding   ❏

Friendliness   ❏

Sensitivity   ❏

Intensive style   ❏

Relaxed style   ❏

Perseverance   ❏

Forceful   ❏

Individualistic   ❏

Team player   ❏

Other: ❏

◆ **Existing Abilities**
(that do not require time to learn or develop)

Physical strength   ❏

Math aptitude   ❏

Language aptitude
   (good communications skills)   ❏

Manual dexterity   ❏

Pleasant telephone voice/vocal skills   ❏

Other: ❏

The next step is to match your employees to the task requirements. You want to determine who can do what.

Complete the following chart for each of your employees. Again, you may want to make extra copies.

4

Employee Profile Chart

Employee name: _____

1. **What adjectives describe this person's personality?** (Forceful and decisive, timid and indecisive, etc.)

   _____

   _____

2. **What is this person's style of thinking?** (Creative and innovative, able to see the "big picture" of our company as a whole, good at implementing ideas of others, narrowly focused on his or her own job/department, etc.)

   _____

   _____

3. **What special skills or aptitudes does this person possess?** (Physical strength, a whiz at math, etc.)

   _____

   _____

Putting People and Tasks Together

The next step is a fairly obvious one: Finding the best fit between the tasks and the people available. This is not a contest, however. While the best fit is always desirable, circumstances may cause you to select someone else. For example, you may have one person who is the best fit for every task you want to delegate. But it would not be reasonable or fair to assign all of those tasks to that person.

To create your delegation plan, you will need to put the attributes and skills that you have already identified into some sort of order for each task. Use the following chart to organize them.

Task-Employee Fit Chart

Task	Attributes/ Skills Needed	Order of Importance*
_____	_____	_____
_____	_____	_____
_____	_____	_____
_____	_____	_____
_____	_____	_____
_____	_____	_____
_____	_____	_____
_____	_____	_____
_____	_____	_____

*1 = highest need/essential
2 = very useful
3 = helpful, but not vital

By now you have determined what skills each task requires, the order of importance of those skills, and the individuals best suited to handle those tasks.

Chapter Summary

- Identify all key tasks to be delegated.

- Determine the capability of each employee to take on new tasks.

- Determine skills and aptitudes required for each task that you have decided to delegate.

- Determine each employee's skills and aptitudes in relation to the tasks you plan to delegate.

- Prioritize the skills required for each task you plan to delegate.

- Recognize the possibility for errors in judgment and review your appraisals regularly to make sure they are correct.

Chapter *Five*

Creating and Using a Delegation Plan

Chapter Objectives

▶ Establish a delegation plan.

▶ Put your plan into action.

Case Study

William Jafir is a supervisor for an auto parts manufacturer. He has accepted the need to delegate many of the tasks he is responsible for handling. He has gone through his work carefully and identified and prioritized the tasks he is prepared to delegate. He also has taken a close look at his staff and has a pretty good idea of their capabilities, time limitations, and so on.

The challenge for William now is to get a plan up and running—to start assigning work in some logical fashion. William wants to implement a program that will be accepted by his employees and ensure a reasonable balance of work for everyone.

Take a Moment

Questions to consider:

1. How should William go about creating his delegation plan?

_____

_____

2. How can William gain the acceptance of his employees to the plan?

_____

_____

5

Establishing a Delegation Plan

To establish a delegation plan, look at your task list from Chapter 3. Determine how long each task takes you to complete, and consider whether each task might take longer for someone else to complete.

Determining How Much Time Is Needed

The best way to determine the amount of time needed to complete a task is to fill out a time log and track how much time you spend on the task. In traditional time logs, you track only the total time needed, not when the activity occurs.

Set up the time log to cover a sufficient period of time. This depends on how often you perform each task. If each task is repeated within five days, a weekly log will be sufficient. You should be able to track most tasks within a month.

Time Log

Task	Time Needed to Complete	
	By Me	*By Employee*

After tracking you own tasks and time, estimate how long it will take your employee to complete the tasks. With some direction from you, they eventually should be able to complete them as quickly as you did.

Now it's time to go back and pick up some of the information you completed in Chapters 3 and 4. To establish your delegation program, you need to create a grid of tasks, skills, and people. This is a key step in building a successful delegation program.

For each task, complete the following chart. Fill in the names of your employees on the lines provided. In the left-hand column, list all the skills, personality traits, aptitudes, etc., that you believe are required to complete the task. In order of their match to each of those skills, rank your employees, with *1* being the top rank.

Task Skills Requirements Chart

Task: _____

Employee Names

_____   _____   _____

Ratings

Skills:

A. _____   _____   _____   _____

B. _____   _____   _____   _____

C. _____   _____   _____   _____

D. _____   _____   _____   _____

E. _____   _____   _____   _____

F. _____   _____   _____   _____

G. _____   _____   _____   _____

H. _____   _____   _____   _____

I. _____   _____   _____   _____

The following chart is a sample for you to follow:

Sample Task Skills Requirements Chart

Task: Weekly Inventory _____

Employee Names

	Mary	Tom	Teresa
	Ratings		
Skills:			
A. Accuracy	1	3	2
B. Math	1	2	3
C. Handwriting	2	3	1
D. Product Knowledge	2	1	3
E. Patience	3	2	1

5

In this example, Mary probably should be your first choice for doing the weekly inventory if she has the time. She has the lowest total score (which in this case is the best) and ranks strongest, or at least average, in four of the five categories. Of course, if patience is your most important priority, you might want to reconsider using Mary.

If you believe patience is of the greatest importance, you can weight the average. For example, you might decide that everything is equal except patience. Perhaps you believe patience is worth 50 percent more than any other characteristic. In this case, you would add another category that would also be called *patience* and assign values of 0.5, 1.0, and 1.5 respectively, instead of 1, 2, or 3. That adds the 50 percent difference into your rating system.

This approach is not foolproof. It can, however, help clarify priorities in assigning tasks.

Use the information you developed in Chapter 3 to determine the requirements of each task and the information from Chapter 4 to determine the skills and abilities of each employee. Keep all the data in your files to help you when new tasks need to be assigned in the future.

Putting Your Plan into Action

Now you have got a list of what it takes to do every task and the capabilities of each of your employees. At this point, you are ready to start assigning.

Using the information from your list, take a look back at the six questions in Chapter 4 and determine if your first choice to handle the task will have the time to complete it. If not, you may have to go to your second choice.

Once you have decided which task to assign to what person, you need to prepare the person. Follow these steps to help ensure the smooth implementation of your program:

1. **Write out instructions for each task.**
   Make sure they are simple and direct and they cover every aspect of the task. To gain your employee's acceptance in taking on the task, you need to make it as easy as possible for the employee to get started and to know how to complete the task properly. Written instructions provide start-up information and a reference to help the employee continue doing the task until he or she is completely comfortable with it.

2. **Meet with the employee and review the instructions.**
   Make sure he or he understands clearly what is expected. Invite questions to clarify any points of concern.

3. **Establish criteria for evaluating each task (see Chapter 6).**
   Let the employee know what those criteria are. Be open to discussion on these points; your employee may have some good ideas for different and possibly more meaningful evaluation criteria.

4. **Create a contingency plan.**
   Be prepared for the employee who lacks time to get the task done when needed, for the employee who doesn't understand clearly what has to be done, and for the employee who doesn't have the ability or skill to do the task properly. Your contingency plan could include:

   ◆ Turning the task over to your second choice

   ◆ Completing the task yourself

   ◆ Seeking some other way to do the task

   ◆ Seeking some other task that would accomplish the same or similar results

5

Finally, create one last chart—one that allows you to keep track of who is responsible for what—so that duties are clearly defined.

Take Responsibility Chart

Task	Name	Date Assigned
_____	_____	_____
_____	_____	_____
_____	_____	_____
_____	_____	_____
_____	_____	_____
_____	_____	_____
_____	_____	_____
_____	_____	_____
_____	_____	_____
_____	_____	_____

Chapter Summary

◆ Set up your time log to determine how much time each task requires.

◆ For each task you plan to delegate, create a chart listing the necessary tasks and match those tasks to the skills and abilities of your employees.

◆ Select an employee (as your first choice) for each task you plan to delegate.

◆ Develop a contingency plan for each task you plan to delegate.

◆ Set up a reminder system to check on employees.

◆ Create written instructions for each task and review them with the employee.

5

Chapter *Six*

Evaluating Your Plan

Chapter Objectives

▶ Monitor your delegation assignments.

▶ Monitor the performance or results of your delegation.

▶ Evaluate your delegation assignments continually.

Case Study

Carol Swam works in the marketing department of a real estate development firm. She has established her first delegation program. She has followed the instructions in this book and now has three subordinates in her department doing new tasks. For the first time, Carol can take the time to plan future activities for her department.

Since she started her plan several months ago, a couple a problems have occurred. Some of her employees have asked about swapping assignments. One wants to change the procedures as well. One employee has not lived up to Carol's expectations, and Carol is concerned about having to reassign work or even take it back and do it herself.

Carol needs a tool to monitor the effectiveness of her delegation program.

Take a Moment

Questions to consider:

1. What should Carol do to ensure the effectiveness of her delegation program?

_____

_____

2. How can Carol avoid slipping back to a nondelegating way of supervision?

_____

_____

Monitoring Delegation Programs

In Chapter 5, you learned how to set up an implementation program. You assigned tasks based on the best possible information available: Matching employee skills to task requirements.

6

In some cases, the match will not work out as well as you think it should. The three most common reasons for this are:

◆ The task requirements turn out to be different from what you thought they would be, and the employee does not have the requisite skills or abilities.

◆ The employee is not as skillful as you thought and is unable to do the task correctly or effectively.

◆ The employee dislikes or resents the task and deliberately does a poor job.

Regardless of the reason, the results will be less than you expected. You can start to evaluate the problems by looking back at the assignments themselves. Are the assignments still the most logical choice?

Determine the reasons why each task is not being performed as well as it should be. Complete the following chart to help you do so.

Monitoring Task Delegation Chart

Task: _____

	Yes	No
1. Does the employee appear to clearly understand the task?	❏	❏
2. Does the employee clearly understand the expected results?	❏	❏
3. Does the employee have the proper training to complete the task?	❏	❏
4. Does the employee have the time to do the task properly?	❏	❏
5. Does the employee have a positive attitude about performing the task?	❏	❏
6. Is the employee physically capable of performing the task?	❏	❏
7. Is the employee mentally capable of performing the task?	❏	❏
8. Has the employee received proper recognition and support from his or her supervisor for doing the task?	❏	❏

Any "no" answers should be cause for concern.

Monitoring Performance Results

There is a difference between doing a job properly and doing the bare minimum to get by. As a supervisor or manager, you are responsible for the output of your department or unit. Consequently, employees who take the bare-minimum approach can hurt everyone's efforts.

When you assign tasks, you need to clearly define how well the task is being performed. The following chart is designed to help you monitor performance. Feel free to add any elements that are specific or unique to your needs.

The chart uses a numerical ranking system to help you analyze performance. Since more than one person may be assigned to perform a task at different times, the chart allows you to compare the efforts of different people. Write the names of people to whom tasks are assigned in the blanks to the right and enter a numerical score next to each name.

If one person always has performed the task, consider offering someone else the opportunity to perform the task and learn another element of the company's business.

> **As a supervisor or manager, you are responsible for the output of your department or unit.**

Monitoring Employee Performance Chart

Task: _____

1 = Excellent, 2 = Good, 3 = Acceptable but needs improvement,
4 = Unacceptable

**Names of People Assigned
to Perform the Tasks**

1. Task completed on time   _____ _____ _____

2. Task completed properly   _____ _____ _____

3. Work is done efficiently   _____ _____ _____

4. Positive attitude about assignment _____ _____ _____

5. Willingness to take responsibility
   for his or her work   _____ _____ _____

6

6. Has clear understanding of
   the task   _____ _____ _____

7. Takes pride in taking on
   responsibilities   _____ _____ _____

Take a look at the performance rankings. Possible results of using this chart may include:

◆ Assigning the task all the time to one person who performs well on all the criteria

◆ Reassigning tasks to different people

◆ Restructuring the task so it can be delegated (that is, breaking a task into smaller parts and dividing the work among more employees)

◆ Helping the individual do certain parts of the task

◆ Providing additional training to help the person perform the task

It is usually unwise to take a task back and do it yourself.

Completing the chart should not be a one-sided exercise. Ask employees for their feelings as well. Discuss privately with the employees any less-than-acceptable situations. Ask the employee what he or she feels is the cause of the unacceptable work and what you both can do, as a team, to improve the task.

It is usually unwise to take a task back and do it yourself. Such action demonstrates a lack of faith in and support for the employee. If an employee feels unable or incompetent to handle the task and suggests you take it back, you might consider doing so on an interim basis. Your company is still counting on you, and the work must be done.

Continual Evaluation of Tasks

Once a task is assigned and the work appears acceptable or better, do not assume things will always continue on an even keel. A variety of things can occur that may affect how well the delegated task continues to be done on a long-term basis.

You also should expect your employees to show continued improvement in doing new tasks. Improvement is part of their learning process. For example, after teaching an employee how to perform a task, you may find that within two weeks the work is acceptable and the employee can do it alone. You feel, based on your own experience and that of other employees in the company, that the employee should be doing a good to excellent job within six weeks. At the end of six weeks, you find no improvement. The key is to stay on top of employee performance on an ongoing basis to make sure there is improvement. The following chart is designed to help accomplish ongoing performance.

> **Stay on top of employee performance on an ongoing basis to make sure there is improvement.**

In the left-hand column, fill in the time periods appropriate for your company and the task. You might start in days or weeks and then move to a monthly or quarterly time period. Your chart should cover the period of time you think it takes to perform the task at an excellent level.

In the right-hand column, next to the time period, fill in the criteria or characteristics that show where performance should be at that time. In a sense, this chart is an extended job description for one particular facet of the job.

Use this chart as a comparative tool. Is the employee where he or she should be at a particular point in time? Use the Monitoring Performance Chart on page 49 along with employee interviews to determine reasons the employee may not be at the optimum performance level.

Ongoing Performance Chart

Task: _____

Time Period	Level of Performance
_____	_____
_____	_____
_____	_____
_____	_____

Chapter Summary

◆ Define exactly what is expected of each employee in performing a delegated task.

◆ Monitor each employee's performance in handling delegated tasks on an ongoing basis.

◆ If tasks are not performed properly, take steps to determine why.

◆ For improperly performed tasks, develop an action plan to accomplish them correctly.

◆ Monitor performance over a period of time to make sure there is continued improvement.

Chapter *Seven*

Developing New Employee Skills

Chapter Objectives

▶ Test employee capabilities.

▶ Get employees to accept new tasks.

▶ Develop new employee skills.

Case Study

As a supervisor at a software development and manufacturing company, Van Lljenski knew he needed to upgrade the skills of this employees. Changes in technology and methods necessitated the constant improvement of his employees' skills. New responsibilities and methods frequently were assigned to Van. His challenge was to make sure that his employees could keep up with those changes and learn new skills as needed to accomplish their work. He also had to be concerned with employees accepting new methods and new responsibilities.

Van is looking for ways to test the limits of his employees and to help them develop new skills to perform their jobs as effectively as possible.

Take a Moment

Questions to consider:

1. How can Van test his employees' capabilities?

_____

_____

2. How can Van gain his employees' acceptance of new tasks?

_____

_____

Testing Employee Capabilities

Before delegating tasks, be sure that your employees are capable of doing those tasks.

In Chapter 4, you learned how to test employees' knowledge, desire, and general capabilities to handle assignments. The purpose was to determine how good a match you could make between an employee's general aptitude and the requirements of the task.

In order to test employee capabilities, you must know what the job requires now or will require in the future.

In as much detail as possible, outline in the following chart the skills that are needed now and in the future to perform the task you wish to delegate. List those tasks in the left-hand column.

In the right-hand column, indicate the skill level of the employee. This will help you to identify areas where the employee needs help. Consider discussing this chart with the employee to make sure your opinions are accurate and are shared by the employee.

> **Before delegating tasks, be sure that your employees are capable of doing those tasks.**

7

Employee Proficiency Scale Chart

Skill Rankings for Employees

1 = Excellent
2 = Good
3 = Adequate
4 = Needs assistance

Employee Name: _____
Task: _____

Skills Required Now	This Employee's Level of Proficiency	Skills Likely to Be Required in the Future
_____	_____	_____
_____	_____	_____
_____	_____	_____
_____	_____	_____
_____	_____	_____
_____	_____	_____
_____	_____	_____
_____	_____	_____
_____	_____	_____
_____	_____	_____

Be as specific as possible. For example, if the task currently requires excellent wordprocessing skills, it is likely that part of the work will soon require more advanced computer knowledge. Try to determine as best as possible what new skills will be needed. Then go back to your evaluations from Chapters 4 and 6 to see which employee is best suited to the task in question.

If an employee lacks the necessary skill to perform a task, you have two choices:

◆ Don't delegate the work to that employee.

◆ Provide the training needed so that employee will be capable of doing the work.

The second option is generally more desirable so long as the employee has the aptitude to do the task and has the willingness to learn how to do the task. If your company has a training department, use their help in developing needed employee skills.

Getting Employees to Accept New Tasks

Once you have decided to assign a task:

◆ **Do not take tasks back unless absolutely necessary.** To do so can be demoralizing to the employees who are trying their best. It also can serve employees as an escape from learning how to do the task in the first place. Employees must assume they will have to learn how to do the work you have assigned in the best possible manner they can.

Do not take tasks back unless absolutely necessary.

◆ **Check employees' performance periodically.** Make sure they are learning what is needed to do the task properly.

◆ **Encourage employees to make their own decisions about how to do their tasks better.** Rather than imposing your ideas on them, let your employees see whether they can find solutions to their task problems. There are two important reasons for doing this:

1. Employees may come up with new ideas or methods that work better for them than those imposed by their supervisor.

2. Employees are more likely to use and retain solutions they find than solutions that are imposed on them.

◆ **Challenge employees to do the best job they can.** Appeal to their sense of pride and accomplishment and take advantage of any available company-sponsored incentive programs.

7

◆ **Involve your employees in setting performance objectives for themselves.** It is much easier for employees to reach goals they have helped set.

◆ **Explain how delegated tasks and their efforts fit into company objectives as a whole.** It is much easier to motivate employees who see the results of their work and the impact it may have on others than to motivate employees who see an isolated task and who may not understand its relevance.

Use the following Monitoring Delegated Tasks Chart to help an employee who is resisting a delegated task or who is unsure of how to handle the task. To help you fill in the chart, a sample version is shown first.

Sample Monitoring Delegated Tasks Chart

◆ Task:
To complete the inventory update form and enter it into the central computer system daily.

◆ Measurement Criteria:
1. Understanding the form.

2. Knowing the part numbering system and where the inventory number is located.

3. Accuracy of data entered on the form.

4. Proper entry of form data to central computer.

◆ Action Steps:
1. Review the forms with the employee.

2. Review the part numbering system with the employee.

3. Review where part numbers are located.

4. Conduct a brief test with the employee on the part numbering system and location of part numbers by asking the employee to locate and retrieve specific parts.

5. Check accuracy on a daily basis for several weeks. For any inaccuracies, ask the employee to suggest a solution to prevent them in the future.

6. Teach the employee how to enter data into the central computer system. Have the employee print out entries to check accuracy against the original form.

◆ **Follow-Up Plan:**
Weeks 1–2: Check results daily.

Weeks 3–8: Check results weekly.

Every 90 days: Meet with the employee and review processes and methods to maintain accuracy. Reinforce the reasons this report is important to the company.

Monitoring Delegated Tasks Chart

Task: _____

_____

_____

Measure Criteria: _____

_____

_____

Action Steps: _____

_____

_____

Follow-Up Plan: _____

_____

_____

7

Promoting Employee Growth

One of the objectives of delegating work is to develop employee skills. When employees lack necessary skills, they can drag down productivity and may feel frustrated in their efforts to be productive workers.

As you delegate tasks, make a list of skills that employees seem to lack. (You can use the chart that follows as a starting point.) The skills probably will fall into one of three categories:

◆ Basic skills, such as language, math, or reading.

◆ Attitudinal/personality traits, such as attention to detail, patience, or empathy.

◆ Higher job-task skills, such as knowing how to use a piece of machinery or understanding basic accounting.

All of these can be addressed with training, although some are easier to improve than others. As you see trends emerging with your employees, determine the areas where they need improvement. Take the steps yourself or with your human resources department to make the necessary improvements.

Employee Skills Improvements Chart

Time Period	Level of Performance
_____	_____
_____	_____
_____	_____
_____	_____
_____	_____
_____	_____
_____	_____
_____	_____
_____	_____

Chapter Summary

◆ Test employee knowledge before assigning skills.

◆ Rank employee skills in relation to task requirements.

◆ Identify key areas where individuals and your department need to improve.

◆ Involve your employees in the process of determining how to do a given task most efficiently.

◆ Make a point of developing new employee skills as their need becomes apparent.

7

Chapter *Eight*

Delegation and the Supportive Supervisor

Chapter Objectives

▶ Understand the role of a supervisor or manager in the delegation process.

▶ Identify employee needs as they relate to delegation.

▶ Work more closely with your manager or supervisor.

Case Study

As a supervisor with a fair amount of experience at a Big Eight accounting firm, Janelle Littlejohn developed the habit of delegating work as much as possible. In most cases, the work was done well and her employees responded enthusiastically to the opportunities she provided them. In some cases, however, her employees did not do as well as they could; in other words, after some period of time, performance declined with the new tasks.

Janelle's superior is beginning to wonder if Janelle is delegating too much work or if she is delegating the wrong tasks to the wrong people. Janelle is also concerned.

Take a Moment

Questions to consider:

1. Does Janelle understand her role in the delegation process?

_____

_____

_____

2. What can Janelle do to be more supportive of her employees?

_____

_____

_____

3. What can Janelle do to gain more support from her supervisor?

_____

_____

_____

The Role of the Supervisor

Delegating work to others involves many key decisions. Which tasks do you delegate? To whom do you delegate? When do you delegate? How is delegated work evaluated?

In addition, the human element plays a role in the delegation process. As a supervisor, you need to support your employees in their efforts to learn, develop, and apply new skills and to help them advance their careers.

Take the following test to see how you do in supporting your employees with delegated work.

8

Support your employees in their efforts to learn, develop, and apply new skills and to help them advance their careers.

Do You Support Your Employees with Delegated Work?

	Always	Sometimes	Never
1. I delegate work as much as possible.			
2. I delegate every task that reasonably can be delegated.			
3. I carefully match tasks to the appropriate people.			
4. I try to challenge employees and expand their capabilities.			
5. I provide careful training for a delegated task.			
6. I test the employee's knowledge to make sure he or she understands the task.			
7. I provide coaching and assistance as needed while the employee performs the task.			
8. I am available to answer questions as needed.			
9. I am patient with employees learning new tasks.			
10. I avoid harshly criticizing an employee who is handling a delegated task.			
11. I give the employee a second chance (or more if needed and time permits).			

12. I ask for feedback on how
the employee feels about
doing the task.   _____ _____ _____

13. I encourage employees to
be creative and come up
with new ways to do the task. _____ _____ _____

Give yourself 3 points for each *Always,* 2 points for each
Sometimes, and 1 point for each *Rarely.*

If your score is over 30, you are a relatively sensitive and caring
supervisor who wants your employees to succeed. If your score
is between 20 and 30, you have some good ideas and good
intentions, but you need to get more involved with your
employees in helping them improve their skills. If your score is
under 20, rethink your role as a supervisor. Delegation is a
critical part of supervision, and you may want to look back at
your general handling of employees as well as how and why you
delegate work.

Delegation and Identifying Employee Needs

As a supervisor, you have the following needs:

◆ Producing the work assigned to you

◆ Coordinating and supervising your staff

◆ Determining which tasks to assign to which people

◆ Helping employees to improve their skills and perform their
tasks as effectively and efficiently as possible

◆ Providing support and feedback to employees

◆ Coaching employees as needed

◆ Evaluating employees' performance

Employees also have needs, and they vary from person to
person. As a supervisor, you should make the utmost effort to
be sensitive to those needs.

8

Employees often want to know "What's in it for me?" when they are asked to perform a delegated task. The answer to their question can include any of the following:

◆ Pride and responsibility

◆ Career advancement

◆ Pay raise

◆ Public recognition

◆ Increased power and influence

◆ Acquisition of new skills

Use the following chart to determine employee motivations and needs. Wait until you have assigned a task and have seen how well the employee handles it before completing this chart.

Determining Employees' Needs Chart

Employee name: _____

Task: _____

Performance level of employee (circle one):

Excellent   Good   Fair   Needs Improvement

If "Fair" or "Needs Improvement," what are the most likely causes? (Lacks training, doesn't understand, doesn't like to do it, etc.)

Ask the employee for an explanation of why his or her performance is not up to your standards. List the top three reasons given by the employee.

1._____

2._____

3._____

After you have identified a problem, complete the chart below. List the problem in the left-hand column. In the right-hand column, write out your planned course of action. Your plan may include assigning the task to someone else or disciplining the employee if the reasons are attitudinal in nature.

Action Plan Chart

Employee name: _____

Task: _____

Problem	Plan of Action (including date to implement)
_____	_____
_____	_____
_____	_____
_____	_____
_____	_____
_____	_____
_____	_____
_____	_____
_____	_____

8

Working More Closely with Your Own Supervisor

Delegation is a part of the job of supervision. It is one of your duties. Most supervisors are accountable for delegation as well as other managerial and supervisory performance skills. In addition, you clearly need support and a good relationship with your own superior.

Here are some tips to help you build a better relationship with your supervisor or manager and gain support for your efforts:

◆ **Keep your supervisor informed.** Let the supervisor know that you are delegating certain tasks and to whom they are delegated.

◆ **Keep your supervisor appraised on how your delegation efforts are going.** Which employees are responsive and which are not? Which tasks are being handled well and which are not?

◆ **Ask your supervisor for help when needed.** Your supervisor may be able to offer excellent advice about which tasks to delegate and how to handle the delegation process.

◆ **Ask for your supervisor's feedback as well as advice.** Find out how well you are doing as a delegator.

◆ **Make sure you have your supervisor's support for your efforts.**

Chapter Summary

◆ Take a personal interest in how well your employees handle deleted tasks.

◆ Provide support, guidance, and instruction.

◆ Ask employees how they feel about handling newly delegated tasks.

◆ Involve your manager or supervisor by informing him or her of your delegation decisions and asking for input when needed.

8

Chapter *Nine*

The Positive Results of Delegation

Chapter Objective

▶ Appreciate the positive results gained by delegating work to others.

Case Study

Mark Johnson's employer, a plastics company, recently cut back the number of supervisors as a cost-saving measure and asked each remaining supervisor to take on additional work. The only way Mark can handle the new workload is by delegating as much of it as possible and as quickly as possible.

In the past, Mark has found that in some cases, it is still faster and certainly more reliable to do a job himself. Delegating takes time. Employees need to be motivated to take on more work, and often they need to be taught what to do, how to do it, and then closely monitored to make sure the task is done right.

Take a Moment

Question to consider:

1. Mark sees the obvious advantages to his employees of having work delegated to them. But what's in it for Mark?

_____

_____

Positive Results for the Supervisor

Delegation requires a lot of up-front effort. But if delegation is done properly, you will see many clear results that will make your life as a supervisor easier and will help you advance your own career.

> **Delegation requires a lot of up-front effort.**

◆ **Time**
Without delegating work, most supervisors would be overwhelmed. By definition, a supervisor "supervises" tasks, people, or both. It is good "management" of your time to delegate work whenever possible.

◆ **Sense of accomplishment**
Work gets done—more work than most supervisors could ever do alone. Your output is maximized by delegating.

◆ **Pride**
Helping others improve their skills and learn new tasks creates pride in the accomplishments your employees achieve.

◆ **Recognition**
Good performance often leads to recognition by superiors and other employees. Delegating work often creates recognition because of increased output and the development of people skills.

◆ **New methods and techniques**
Assigning work to subordinates may stimulate their thinking. In their efforts to save time, reduce efforts, etc., they may create or discover new ways to handle the task. A new method might turn out to be a tremendous time/effort/cost saver for the company. A fresh perspective may cause you to take another look at whether the task is still needed or useful. Subordinates who have never performed a task have not vested interest in how the task has been done. They frequently can bring a fresh perspective that will change and improve the way the task is performed.

◆ **Improved management skills**
Your own career as a supervisor or manager depends on ever-improving management skills. Delegating work is one of the most difficult and most critical skills leading to success.

9

71

Positive Results for the Company

Delegating work also provides the company with some positive results.

♦ **Greater efficiency**
By managing the people and processes in your areas of responsibility, you match the tasks to the people. You help ensure the most efficient use of talent, which in turn results in greater productivity.

♦ **Finding and developing new supervisory talents**
Delegation of work may involve several employees. Their abilities to handle new challenges or respond to difficult situations may help identify new leadership talent. Growing companies are always in need of new supervisory talent. Therefore, it is an extremely positive reflection on you when responsibility is given to your subordinates.

♦ **A way to test your overall management skills**
Because the primary skills of management and supervision are managing people and processes—not doing individual tasks—your ability to delegate work becomes a key measurement by which your manager or supervisor will evaluate how well you are doing.

♦ **More stable workforce**
Employees who are challenged and recognized for their efforts are more likely to stay on the job and continue to grow. Supervisors who do not entrust any responsibility to their subordinates are inviting frustration and lack of interest.

Positive Results for the Employee

Delegating work provides positive results for the employee, too.

- **Sense of accomplishment**
  Employees who are entrusted with new responsibilities take pride in their ability to handle the work.

- **Sense of career development**
  Employees working under supervisors who entrust work to them see a company that is employee-oriented and happy to help employees improve themselves.

- **Greater job interest**
  Variety and change on the job can greatly stimulate interest. Greater interest usually means higher productivity. Giving employees new challenges often leads to a renewed interest in their work and a desire to expand their knowledge and improve their skills to an even greater degree.

- **Pride**
  Learning new skills and impressing one's boss can instill a lot of pride. Giving your subordinates that opportunity through delegation of work can help them take greater pride in their contribution to the company.

Learning new skills and impressing one's boss can instill a lot of pride.

9

Positive Results for the Customer

All businesses and organizations have customers. Delegating work affects the organization's customers as well as the organization itself in positive ways.

◆ **Lower costs**
   The most efficient use of talent by your organization means lower costs and better value for your customers. Customers will not have to pay for inefficiencies caused by supervisors who want to do everything themselves and, consequently, turn out fewer products or services and those of poorer quality.

◆ **Greater access to information and help**
   Being the only one who knows how something is done does not make you irreplaceable to the company. It encourages your company to find someone to replace you who is more open to helping other employees grow on the job.

   Customers want help and information as quickly as possible. If you are the only one who can provide it and you are on vacation, out sick, or just too busy to respond, your company runs the risk of losing customers. Well-run organizations try to have multiple resources for information, products, and services. Well-trained subordinates, therefore, are invaluable to you.

◆ **Reliability**
   Customers want to know that you deliver a consistent level of service and quality. Delegating work to some extent requires standardizing methods and ideas; the result is that customers see consistent quality no matter who they talk to in your organization. Knowledge is shared and a smoother-running business is the result.

Chapter Summary

◆ Take a big picture view of your role as a supervisor and avoid getting bogged down in details that should be the concern of your employees.

◆ Focus on the importance of maximizing efficiency and productivity.

◆ Be open to innovation and new ideas that result from delegating.

◆ Take pride in seeing your subordinates develop new skills, including leadership.

9

Posttest

You have just taken another step in your professional development by completing *Effective Delegation Skills.*

This posttest is provided to reinforce the material you have just covered. If you have difficulty with any question, go back to the book to review key concepts.

1. List the ways your subordinates will benefit from your use of delegation.

   _____

   _____

   _____

2. Identify the primary reasons that supervisors and managers find it difficult to delegate work to other people.

   _____

   _____

   _____

3. What can you do to overcome the obstacles you identified in Question 2?

   _____

   _____

   _____

4. List the questions you should ask yourself when deciding whether a specific task should or should not be delegated.

   _____

   _____

   _____

5. List the questions you should ask yourself when determining whether a particular person is capable of handling a delegated task.

   _____

   _____

   _____

6. To establish a successful delegation program, it is helpful to

   create a gird of _____,

   _____, and _____.

7. What steps should you follow to ensure the smooth implementation of your delegation plan?

   _____

   _____

   _____

8. List the most common reasons that a supervisor's matches of employee skills to task requirements may result in failure.

   _____

   _____

   _____

9. What questions should you ask yourself when determining why a delegated task is not being performed well?

   _____

   _____

   _____

10. What role should your supervisor play in your efforts to delegate work to subordinates?

_____

_____

_____

11. Identify the positive customer-oriented results of delegating tasks to subordinates.

_____

_____

_____

Critical acclaim for *The French Mathematician*

"An engaging historical drama: the political and religious tumult of early-nineteenth-century France seethes behind the life of a prodigiously gifted mathematician, Evariste Galois. Petsinis . . . develop[s] a sense of Galois' France with great fluency and obvious knowledge."
— *Kirkus Reviews*

"Mathematical geniuses are as unworldly and strange as they are rare. Tom Petsinis has convincingly re-created the life and intellectual ambiance of the brilliant and vulnerable Evariste Galois at one of the most turbulent moments in French history, managing to relate with stark simplicity a tale that is by its very nature romantically colorful."
— Guy Davenport

"In these days of political folly, what better literary escape than the history of mathematics?" — *Los Angeles Times Book Review*

TOM PETSINIS

THE FRENCH MATHEMATICIAN

BERKLEY BOOKS, NEW YORK

THE FRENCH MATHEMATICIAN

A Berkley Book / published by arrangement with
Walker Publishing Company, Inc.

Printing History
Walker edition published 1998
Berkley trade paperback edition / April 2000

The Penguin Putnam Inc. World Wide Web site address is
http://www.penguinputnam.com

ISBN: 0-425-17291-0

BERKLEY®
Berkley Books are published by The Berkley Publishing Group,
a division of Penguin Putnam Inc.,
375 Hudson Street, New York, New York 10014.
BERKLEY and the "B" design
are trademarks belonging to Penguin Putnam Inc.

Printed in the United States of America

10 9 8 7 6 5 4 3 2 1

Acknowledgments

This novel arose from an earlier project that was submitted for a Master of Arts degree and titled "A Fictional Biography of the French Mathematician Evariste Galois 1811–1832."

I am most grateful to Victoria University and the following people for the support provided at every stage of the project.

Professor John McLaren, who saw merit in a proposal that sought to build bridges between the Humanities and the Sciences, between Literature and Mathematics.

Associate Professor David English and Doctor Michael Baker, who, in their role as supervisors, listened and advised, challenged and encouraged, and steered the work toward a successful end.

Associate Professor Neil Barnett, Head of Computing and Mathematical Sciences, who very generously made available the resources of his Department.

Vicky, Vanessa, and Alexia for supporting me in my struggle with the obstinate, refractory Evariste Galois.

0

I had foreseen it all in precise detail. One step led inevitably to the next, like the proof of a shining theorem, down to the conclusive shot that still echoes through time and space. Facedown in the damp pine needles, I embraced that fatal sphere with my whole body. Dreams, memories, even the mathematics I had cherished and set down in my last will and testament—all receded. I am reduced to a singular point; in an instant I am transformed to i.

$$i = an\ imaginary\ being$$

Here, in this complex space, i am no longer the impetuous youth who wanted to change the world first with a formula and then with a flame. Having learned the meaning of infinite patience, i now rise to the text whenever anyone reads about Evariste Galois, preferring to remain just below the surface, like a goldfish nibbling the fringe of a floating leaf. Ink is more mythical than blood (unless some ancient poet slit his vein and wrote an epic in red): The text is a two-way mirror that allows me to look into the life and times of the reader. Who knows, someday i may rise to a text that will compel me to push through to the other side. Do you want proof that i exist? Where am i? Beneath every word, behind each letter, on the side of a period that will never see the light.

PART ONE

1

I must appear a pathetic figure to that person looking down from that fourth-story window beyond the schoolyard wall. It looks like an artist's studio. Who knows, perhaps I am being sketched with a scrap of charcoal at this very instant—a slight youth with untidy black hair, strong eyebrows, mouth like a sparrow. I have been standing in this corner of the schoolyard since the beginning of morning recess, huddled under an elm, caught in the crisp shadow of its branches. The smell of burning paper fills the yard. Smoke twisting up from a nearby incinerator spreads in a cursive script across the clear winter sky. Arms crossed, fists clenched, fingernails cutting into my palms, I feel sorry for my short, thin shadow which has hardly changed since I came to Louis-le-Grand three years ago. Fifteen last October, I could be mistaken for a twelve-year-old. The boys who started with me have grown noticeably during the past year: Pimples bud from their faces, the down on their cheeks has darkened, their thighs and voices have thickened. I grit my teeth. My recent demotion was due more to lack of physical development than poor performance in a few subjects.

Let them have the present—the future belongs to me.

When their idiotic games turn to stone and their laughter vanishes in the wind, my thoughts will live on, not only in this language, but in those which today still lack alphabets. From the time I learned to read under Mother's prodding eyes, I have been intrigued by the magic of ink and sensed that my name would be preserved in print. Is this why my inner voice is so pronounced? Am I projecting myself into the future by means of this inner voice? A message put in a bottle and thrown into the ocean. If I am destined to be written about, my conscious effort here and now might influence how my life will be represented.

—Galois the girl! Galois the girl!

A burst of warm vapor blasts my ear. Before I am able to retaliate the name-caller is sprinting across the yard, laughing wildly, shoes crackling over small pools laced with ice. I hate them all—the students, the teachers, the Director. This school is no better than a prison. Why did Father insist I study in Paris? I was happy at home in Bourg-la-Reine. Mother could have seen to my education. After all, she taught me to read and write, introduced me to Greek and Latin, and later made a point of reading from the Bible. Yes, she was demanding, harsh at times, especially when it came to the Bible, but there was always Father's company to make up for this. My happiest memories are with him: times when we would sing together, recite his own poems, entertain guests with short plays based on the *Iliad*, Racine, even Shakespeare, who was such a favorite of Father's that he claimed the name was a corruption of the French Jacques-Pierre. We often performed the ghost scene from *Hamlet:* He was the dead King, and I, the Prince. I became so worked up over the scene that I trembled and tears blurred my vision as I listened to Father. The guests would break out in good-natured laughter and applause. Those were bright days, a world away from this gloomy place.

Four boys are playing a game that involves throwing fingers, adding the number each has thrown, and counting clockwise. The player on whom the counting stops is then slapped on the back of the hand by the others. If they counted in the other direction would the same player be slapped? I see at once, accompanied by a sense of certainty, that if the sum is even and the count begins with the same person in both cases, then the direction affects the outcome; if the sum is odd there is no difference.

Mother's voice suddenly comes to me, harsh and high-pitched. I remember how the sinews in her neck would twitch as she read to me from the *Iliad*. My favorite was the story of Ajax. How I felt for the poor tragic hero! I understood his dejection and that desperate last act. Often, when refused something, or when I did not get my own way, I would take my wooden sword and run off to the back of the house, where I pretended to be Ajax. On one occasion, buried in the maple's red leaves, I imagined myself hovering over my prostrate body, looking down sadly on the victim of a cruel fate, deriving a strange pleasure in feeling sorry for myself. There is no time for such games in this prison, no opportunity for make-believe, no place for privacy. I sleep with forty others in the dormitory, wait in a line to wash each morning, eat in the refectory and attend classes from six in the morning until nine at night. Continually in the presence of those I despise, my only respite is the liberating dark when the dormitory lamps are extinguished, and I can follow memory and imagination without interruption.

And now, after a term in the third and final year, this demotion to the second! Confinement in this prison extended by another six months!

Rhetoric! I could have easily passed that useless subject. They call me dunce. I will show them! I played the fool in class to make fools of them. I did poorly in Rhetoric in order to spite the teacher, whose smugness I could not bear. Effective use of language! I refused to follow his rules of grammar and construction. To defy him, I often submitted work written with the rules of my own grammar, constructed sentences that expressed the movement of my own mind, not that of others. I enjoyed these games whose meaning was perfectly clear to me, but which confused him.

Sometimes I would daydream of a private language; magic sounds and symbols that transported me to another world. But the teacher's growl would tear me from such reveries, and he would read my nonsense to the others. The students howled, the teacher grinned. I would bite my lower lip, suppressing my delight, feeling superior to them all because I had set out to reduce them to laughter, to make them look ridiculous. The more they laughed, the stronger my heart pounded in the knowledge of my superiority. Only the foolish and small-minded gaped like that. And then I would imagine the exiled Napoleon, arms crossed, brooding on a rocky beach, waiting for his moment, while the Royalists spent their evenings in frivolous laughter.

Gleaming on the chapel's cross, a crow complains raucously, then flaps to a bough above my head, where it preens its wings. A large feather twirls through the branches and falls at my feet. I admire its shape and point. It would make a fine quill. The ancient Greeks augured

8

the future from birds. What would they have made of this feather?

Over the past year dark feelings have been stirring within me, not only hatred of those around me, but a frustrated desire for something I cannot define, an ambition without a goal, a sense of leaving childhood and moving toward a distant, barely audible calling, which sometimes sounds like nothing more than a faint echo of my own voice, and other times a voice I have never heard before, calling compellingly in a language I do not fully understand. I know I am destined for something, though I do not know exactly what.

Three boys appear from the latrines, glance in the direction of the teachers' quarters, and hurry across the yard. Two of them are in the third year, the other is in the second. This one seems frightened, and he is almost carried along by the others. Another initiation! One of the third-year boys tried to initiate me when I first arrived. He spoke of a secret source of pleasure, a way to overcome sleepless nights, said it was the only way to manhood. I followed him into the stinking latrines. Smiling, swearing the pleasure was beyond words, he unbuttoned his trousers and put his hand inside. I ran out and retched in a corner of the yard. There and then I vowed never to degrade myself through that disgusting practice. Not because the Church condemned it, but because I realized that those who abstained were somehow superior to those who indulged. To abstain meant to overcome instinct with intellect, to live by a higher morality, to raise oneself to the level of the hero. A few days later, the pimply third-year student accosted me in the yard and shouted in my face that I would never grow to be a man. I replied that I would sooner kill myself than follow his example. He gave a green-toothed grin and ran off toward the latrines.

The bell rings chillingly for the next class. Mathematics. I have not studied it before. Mother taught me little more than the basics of arithmetic. I have been in Vernier's class two weeks, doing a course for beginners. Still smarting from the demotion, I cannot motivate myself to work or even to take an interest in the subject. I spent the first few lessons at the back of the room, brooding, sketching Napoleon's profile instead of doing the exercises. Damned demotion! I will show them! The teachers conspired against me. They misrepresented me to Father, who read their reports when I went home for Christmas two months ago.

Called to the study on the afternoon of my arrival, I was struck by how he had aged since my last visit home. His dark hair had turned ashen and there was an unusually somber look about him. Was he working too hard? He was the mayor of Bourg-la-Reine, a position he won during the Hundred Days, and which he continued to hold even after Napoleon's defeat. When the monarchy was restored he took an oath to Louis XVIII without renouncing his strong liberal views and ardent Republican sentiments. Father is neither a hypocrite nor an opportunist: He took that oath in order to keep a monarchist from the position. Apart from his duties as mayor, he also runs the town's boarding school, which he inherited from Grandfather, who obtained it during the Revolution. The school is a profitable business, and I know Father is grooming me for it.

—You have disappointed me, Son, he said in a flat

voice, pinching the flesh under his chin. I refused to have you demoted last August because I believed in your ability. I hoped you would prove me right. Seems I was mistaken.

I did not look up from the inkpot on his desk. Were my poor grades responsible for the change that had come over him?

—But your reports show no progress. Quite the opposite. How do you account for this? "Apart from the last few weeks when he has worked a little, and then only from fear of punishment, this student has generally neglected his studies. The strangeness of his character keeps him from his companions."

—And this: "Though somewhat strange in his manner, the student is very gentle and filled with innocence and good qualities. He never knows a lesson badly—either he hasn't learned it at all, or knows it well."

—What am I to make of this, Son? Is this why I sent you to Paris?

I felt a pang of remorse. Loving Father more than anybody else, I wanted to please him, to obtain good grades, but I could not overcome the hatred I felt for everyone at school.

—Well, there's no avoiding it this time. I cannot intercede again. You will just have to endure another six months in the second year. You might as well get something out of the demotion. Do something different, maybe a course in mathematics.

Placing his hand on my shoulder, he looked at me tenderly. I wanted to apologize, to promise I would do better, but I fought back an impulse to embrace him and cry in his arms. Noticing the emotion rising to my eyes, he moved to the window overlooking the town square, pulled aside the lace curtain, and gazed at the church at the far end.

—We're living in uncertain times, he said. There's no telling what will happen next year. You can't rely on anything but your own intelligence, Evariste. A good education will serve you well for the rest of your life.

I wanted to see him cheerful again, and if a course of mathematics were needed to dispel that worried look, so be it.

The bell-ringer threatens the stragglers and those reluctant to leave their games. Holding the feather in one palm, I balance it against a thin spread of light in the other.

Should I make an effort? Should I stop playing the fool, at least in mathematics, for Father's sake?

I am now alone in the yard, with a few springy starlings pecking at my cobbled shadow. As though signing a resolution, I use the feather's bony point to scratch my name and date on the back of my hand crimson from the cold: Evariste Galois, 14 February 1827.

2

—Geometry, announces Vernier.

In three weeks of arithmetic his voice has never risen above a dull drone, and now he introduces the new topic as though it is the title of an epic poem he is about to recite by heart. For the first time since my demotion, I sit up and take note. Geometry. The word has a certain resonance. Or is it just Vernier's enthusiasm coming through? His words strike a chord within me, stir me, make me quiver with wonder. At times, for minutes on end, as he paces and gesticulates, I forget the shadow of the window's grille falling obliquely on my bare hands, forget the anxiety and frustration that has unsettled me during the past year, forget my demotion. During these moments I neither love nor hate, neither fear nor hope. Drawn from the emotional chaos of recent months, I feel at ease in the order and certainty of geometry.

—Euclid's *Elements*, Vernier continues.

He is about thirty, with black hair fringed across his forehead and spectacles made of circles, lines, and arcs. He wears gray gloves to prevent chalk dust irritating his dermatitis. As he raises the book high above his head, its image is skewed in the lamp's concave reflector.

13

—The Book of Books, gentlemen. The most influential text ever written, more so than the Bible. It has leaped across centuries, nations, languages, religions. Its relevance is timeless; its nationality, universal; its language, logic. Truth, gentlemen! Absolute, transcendental truth. You have done your exercises in arithmetic: You have added, subtracted, multiplied, divided, and extracted roots. Well and good, all very useful. I would be the last to deny the usefulness of arithmetic. It goes hand in hand with money, and, as we know, coins make the world go round. It is vital to examiners, bankers, and generals. It determines pass and fail, measures profit and loss, counts life and death.

—But, gentlemen, despite its prevalence in the affairs of the world, arithmetic has nothing to do with the spirit of mathematics. That spirit finds its first expression in geometry. The spirit, gentlemen! Think about it. A spirit not unlike the Holy Spirit, and just as the Holy Spirit cannot be apprehended merely by attending church regularly on Sundays, dropping a coin on a collection plate, saying one hundred Hail Marys and two hundred Our Fathers, so the spirit of mathematics cannot be grasped by the repetitive exercises of arithmetic. Many are called, gentlemen. Some are chosen to serve in schools, and others at higher institutions such as our Polytechnic, but few, perhaps a handful in each generation, are chosen to become initiates, to partake of the mysteries, to serve the spirit in the inner sanctum.

I am entranced by the brown book whose binding has frayed, its gold lettering faded. And when, looking directly at me, Vernier asks which of us will be among the chosen few, my heart leaps. I want to know more about Euclid.

14

Is absolute truth possible in these confusing times, when countless groups claim to have the truth, and the world seems on the brink of chaos? Royalists, Republicans, Bonapartists, Socialists, Saint-Simonists, Anarchists, the reemerging Jesuits—they are all active among students, all seeking to make converts to their particular truth. There seems no end to it, especially when combinations of some groups produce new truths. Perhaps Euclid, having stood the test of time, might dispel the chaos churning inside me and help make sense of the world. My attention is caught by Vernier's gloved hand—the book's truth is too pure to be held by naked flesh.

—Since 1482 more than a thousand editions have appeared in print, he continues, walking with measured strides between our desks. We know Euclid compiled the work in thirteen books covering the geometry of triangles, circles, and various quadrilaterals; the theory of proportion; number theory; irrationals; solid geometry. As for geometry, which will be our main concern, we know that he based everything on twenty-three definitions and ten axioms, five of which he called common notions, the other five propositions. From all this, we know the mind of Euclid, but what of the man?

—I put it to you, gentlemen: Does the man matter in the dazzling light of this creation? Beyond the fact that Euclid taught in Alexandria around 300 B.C., probably summoned there by Ptolemy, little else is known about him. We do not know where and when he was born. We do not know his nationality. Some maintain he was not Greek at all, but Egyptian. We do not know how he felt about the gods of the day; whether he was kind or cruel; whether he was fond of wine; or whether he had children. The personality does not matter, gentlemen. For most of us it disappears without trace in four generations, let alone forty. What matters is the idea, the ideal, truth. But the truths in this book are not easy to grasp. There is no royal road to geometry. It will require hard work and concentration. Some of you will fall by the wayside early, but those who persevere will see a world more dazzling than Alexander's conquests, one that withstood the might of Imperial Rome and outlived the shadow of the Dark Ages. A world to which our French mathematicians have contributed greatly since the time of Descartes.

—The call has gone out, gentlemen. Who will heed it? Who will serve the spirit? Who will deny themselves for the sake of truth?

My hand shoots up involuntarily. The room explodes with laughter, which once again proves their stupidity. They are insensitive to the spirit of mathematics, unable to grasp the subtlety of Vernier's words. Let them laugh. It confirms that I am smarter than them.

How can Vernier tolerate them? He should threaten them with detention. Why is he smiling faintly, rubbing the lenses of his spectacles, squinting as he holds them up to the light? When the laughter finally subsides, he picks up another book and holds it up to the class.

—Euclid has been excellently interpreted and presented by Adrien-Marie Legendre in his *Elements of Geometry,* a text written for the purpose of teaching the subject in a modern way, and from which I will be drawing heavily. Open your books, gentlemen, and let us commence.

Held firmly in his gloved hand, the chalk scuttles quickly across the blackboard, striking at periods, scratching in underlining, sometimes screeching in its haste. From the back of the room, straining to read the board (my eyesight has always been weak, but it appears to have deteriorated in the past few months), I do my best to keep up with Vernier and copy in my book the definitions, propositions, axioms, and theorems. One idea leads to another, naturally, effortlessly, like the notes that combine to form a pleasing melody. As Vernier erases the restrictive board (the night sky is not wide enough to accommodate the possibilities of geometry), I contemplate the first definition: A point is that which has no part. It seems that a point is and is not. If I represent it on the page, it is no longer a point. If I try to grasp it in thought, it vanishes. I imagine a point moving at a great speed; at that instant it is both a point and a line, a particle and a process. If I grasp the line, I lose sight of the point. If I focus on the point, the line proves an illusion. Astonishing that something so intangible should be the basis of all geometry! In a flash, I see the indivisible point as the seed of creation. Perhaps the universe exploded from the primal point. Perhaps God is the primal point. Perhaps the soul is nothing more than a point.

—What use is geometry? mumbles a student in the front row.

—Use? snaps Vernier.

He takes out a coin and extends it to the student.

—Here! If you cannot see the value of knowledge as an end in itself, I had better pay you for learning.

The student bows without a word.

—Now for a few simple proofs, Vernier glares. Those not completed in class must be done before our next lesson.

The student beside me bites his knuckles over the first

problem, but I see the proof at once, as though a long-dormant sense has suddenly been awakened. My heart beats strongly against the edge of the desk, my hand shakes, I am unable to keep my writing on a straight line. I complete the exercise in a few minutes, most of them in my head, while my neighbor sighs, scrapes the floor, and chews his pen in frustration. The bell sounds. Shuffling above Vernier's instructions, the students bustle from the room.

There is a fire in me. I have never been in love, and what little I know has come from books, but it must be something very much like this, a flesh-consuming fire. I want to know more about geometry. I want to ask Vernier whether I might borrow Euclid and Legendre. But how can I explain my insight? Is it intuition? A kind of sixth sense? A feel for geometry? He would not understand.

At the start of the afternoon recreation hour, I hurry to the library. Locating both books, I sit at a window overlooking the courtyard and the Preparatory School, an annex of Louis-le-Grand where students train to become secondary school teachers. I pick up Euclid first, feel the textured cover with my palm, and then flick through the yellowing pages, inhaling their mustiness. I read all that Vernier covered, and continue through more propositions, theorems, and proofs. I read quickly, as though it is a biography or a work of fiction, comprehending everything at once, my mind moving as though it has finally found its element.

I make my way to Rhetoric class as though in a trance, and stare through the lesson without opening my book. The afternoon has turned gray, and grayness now clings to the dreary walls, embraces the potbelly stove bulging with fire, leans against the blackboard, gathers around the overhead lamps. After another three unbearable lessons I hurry back to the library.

—Geometry?

As though surprised in an illicit activity, I shut the book with a thud, my index finger between the pages. An elderly fellow with a fleshy smile peers over my shoulder.

—They haven't been touched in years, says the librarian.

He leans over me, his puffy hands on the table like two spotted toads.

—It's the language of the future, he whispers. When Greek and Latin die out, geometry will be the language of the world.

What does he want? He is depriving me of valuable reading time. He straightens up and becomes thoughtful, hairy nose wheezing at each breath. I am struck by the thought that, despite the book's eventual decay, the ideas of geometry will remain intact for another two thousand years and that ideas are like parasites, burrowing into suitable minds, feeding on young thought, moving through time in the vehicle of the human skull. I would gladly give my mind for the sake of these ideas, sacrifice myself for a new theorem. Suddenly, as the librarian is mumbling something, as two boys are chuckling at a corner table, as the night muzzles the window, as a church bell's toll is muffled by the thick dark, I know that I am destined to become a mathematician. Ignoring the librarian's chatter about mildew slowly destroying the library, I spring up from the table. He grasps my forearm and offers me the books, even though they are not for loan, saying they will not be missed for a few days. I embrace them like a youth embracing his first love.

3

Compelled to be in the refectory for the evening meal (I would rather spend the hour with my books) I sit uneasily, head bowed, staring at the ceiling's triangular beams warped in the spoon's hump. Teased by some, taunted by others for my sudden seriousness in class, I respond with grim silence. As the student next to me grovels in his bowl, stuffing his face and mashing his words with boiled potatoes, I keep my hands under the table, fingers tightly crossed, determined not to touch a scrap of food, despite hunger churning in my stomach.

I hate them all. Food is for animals like them. My sustenance is the purity of geometry, just as a flower's beauty is sustained by light.

The last bell of the day prods students loitering in the corridor, driving them to their dormitories. For me it is a welcome sound, now more than ever. It signals my liberation, a time when I can finally get away from the others and concentrate on geometry. Two weeks since my introduction to the subject, I am surprised by my ability not only to prove theorems which baffle the others, but to prove them without paper and ink. It is as if I can see the proof in the very theorem, and this seeing is enhanced at night when I am in bed and the darkness becomes a vast blackboard on which I project my thoughts. Two weeks, and the initial enthusiasm has grown to a kind of passion. Half past nine. A teacher inspects the dormitory and extinguishes the lamps. The door's click frees me. Up till now I have looked forward to the period between lights-out and sleep because I could finally pursue my own thoughts and fantasies. I could follow Alexander to India or plan with Napoleon for the third coming. Now, as some snore, others whisper, and a few thrash about on their straw mattresses, I reach under my bed, locate the library books, and place them on my chest. In an instant the darkness is covered in geometry. I recall a problem from Legendre's book. The next instant, the proof is before me: the lettered diagram, followed by lines of Euclidean logic, until the final QED. I recall other problems, diagrams, and detailed proofs, some of which I have only glanced at during the course of the day. I have always been good at remembering names, dates, lists of Greek and Latin words, but they cannot compare with this newly awakened faculty. Excited, I test myself by proposing problems of my own, and in a flash I see their proofs, as though they are physical objects. Chess players visualize the board and perform complicated maneuvers, musicians compose as though hearing an imaginary orchestra. Is my talent for geometry similar?

Limping along, tapping the darkness with a silver-tipped stick, the dormitory's clock strikes once. Whispers have turned to wheezing and the thrashing seed has spent itself in a spurt. And still I cannot sleep. Embracing the books, I drift off for a few minutes, dream vividly, then wake with a start. I feel feverish.

In one dream I was Jason leading the Argonauts to the cave of the Euclidean point. The challenge had gone out: Whoever grasped that elusive entity, that nothingness, would possess the greatest treasure, the very source of the physical world. I struggled through crisscrossing lines which threatened to imprison me in grids and grilles like those on the windows. I walked barefoot over jagged triangles without flinching. I pushed forward through the surrounding chaos. A man appeared and held up his right palm: An open eye was circumscribed by an equilateral triangle. The eye winked, and the man vanished. Farther on, two pythons were twined in a tight braid. Unwinding as I approached, one became a circle, the other coiled itself into a spiral. The circle hissed as I stepped inside to continue my journey. I entered the cave, but instead of finding the point, I stood before a woman glowing in the dark, her breasts visible through a golden gauze-like gown. She caught me with the gravity of her eyes and drew me with the fullness of her smile. I resisted and struggled, urged myself on in the name of the point. She was the great temptress, the whore of Babylon, who wanted to seduce me from my quest. And then her presence became a challenge in itself, a test to determine whether I would be initiated into the secrets of geometry, whether I had the strength of character and the purity of soul for the transcendent point, whether I was worthy of the source. She whispered that she was the source of the world, and that she would show me the secrets of life. My heart quickened, body tingled; my limbs began to loosen. Another minute . . . if I could withstand her for another hundred heartbeats I would vanquish her charm, reduce her sensuality to smoke, and the point would appear. I exhorted myself by chanting: A point is that which has no eyes, a point is that which has no mouth, a point is that which has no body, a point is . . .

I awake with a start. My heart is thumping against the weighty books on my chest, my blood is throbbing. I have an erection, but she could not tempt me further than that—I did not ejaculate.

I feel flushed, and my neck is moist. A shiver trickles down my spine. The words "a baptism of fire" echo in my ears as I doze off again. I hover in that region of no-man's-land, that plane between consciousness and dreaming where moments of lucidity alternate with the ludicrous. Euclid's fifth postulate flashes to mind with startling clarity. And in the next instant I am in an endless field, running frantically between furrows, determined to reach their point of convergence at the horizon.

A bell shatters my dream. The lamps are lit, windows squeal open, and louvered shutters are pushed out to the black morning. Exhausted, feeling feverish, I can hardly lift my head from the pillow. As the others yawn, stretch, and bustle in preparation, I locate the warm books under the blankets and draw them to my chest.

—Up, Galois, barks the monitor.

My throat is dry and my words are a raspy whisper.

—You've caught a chill! he snaps. Too skinny, that's your problem. You wouldn't get the shakes if you were more robust.

He instructs me to rest for the remainder of the morning, and says he will arrange for breakfast to be brought up. He leaves, scratching his head, holding the bell by its clapper. Alone in the still dormitory, I feel a tremor of excitement. Privacy is precious, I must not waste it by dozing off. I prop myself on the pillow, reach under the blankets, and pull out Legendre's text. On the title page an inky fingerprint has been pressed beneath the year of publication. I read from theorem to construction, admiring the elegant language, often anticipating the detailed proofs. I skim over each page, grasping the essentials at a glance, reading the way others read adventure novels.

The darkness has started to gray. Chimneys and rooflines appear. A bird's call trickles from the rooftop onto the cobbled courtyard.

Novels! A waste of time, nothing but diversion, titillation, amusement for the idle. Enough of Homer! From now on it will be Euclid. Any fool can pick up a novel, read it from cover to cover, and understand it as thoroughly as any professor. Two professors might read the same novel and disagree as to its merits. Where is the truth? The permanence? Novelists pander to the literary fashions of the day, writing for money and fame. And then there is the content of their work: arbitrary, gratuitous, whimsical, the chaotic parading as form. Rubbish, all of it! I would not exchange a single geometrical proof for the collected works of a dozen novelists.

Mathematics or nothing. Truth, not fiction. There is no disputing geometry: Euclid's fifth postulate was true in third-century Alexandria, and it will still be true on the North Pole in two thousand years. I am glad the others find geometry difficult. It means that, unlike the novel, geometry is not for everyone. The masses will never be able to enter the holy shrine; it is reserved for the select few in any generation, those who will add to the body of knowledge. The others can have their novels—let them identify with their heroes and heroines! I have outgrown all that. Reading Euclid and Legendre, I feel . . . what do I feel? It is as though I have no feelings when I concentrate on theorems and proofs. I am no longer Evariste Galois, the insignificant schoolboy, but a new person in the purging purity of geometry. No, not a new person, not even the sense of a different I, but a state of being that transcends the individual. A oneness with the eternal truth and order of geometry. Yes, I have suffered the humiliation of repeating the year, but I have found the truth. I will become a famous mathematician, and those who now laugh at me will choke on their laughter.

4

Their sarcastic laughter cannot distract me from my pursuit. If anything it spurs me forward, strengthens my belief that geometry is for the chosen few. I live geometry with a passion verging on obsession, a zeal that drives those imbued with religion. Rhetoric, Latin, Greek, Physics—they are now more unbearable than before. I am constantly at odds with the teachers of those subjects because of their attempts to drag me away from the purest of all languages, my one love, geometry.

Suddenly the world is full of geometrical wonder, problems that absorb me to an extent where everything else loses its significance. There was geometry in those three pigeons circling the school yesterday, sharply defined against a sky swept blue by an icy wind. As the trio changed their positions relative to each other, their beaks became points, forming continually changing triangles. If these instantaneous triangles were drawn, would there be a tendency for a particular triangle to emerge? Does nature prefer the isosceles or the equilateral? Given that countless different triangles were possible in a five-minute period, would any one of them be repeated? Plotting the positions of the beaks on graph paper bluer than the sky, would some order and pattern emerge from the pigeons' playfully chaotic activity?

Returning to the dormitory from the latrines last night, I stopped beneath the elm in the schoolyard and looked up through its bare branches. The moon was a fine arc scratched onto the frozen sky. The stars were pinpricks made by a compass, like perforations in the great master plan that separated heaven and earth, and whose dark underside only was visible to humans. Through my breath dispersing in vapor, I connected a group of stars into a regular pentagon. The origin of geometry might well be up there. A primal star had died in an explosion, and from its death countless others came into being. The night sky was full of geometry: Given three fixed stars, three distinct lines and one triangle could be drawn. With four stars, six distinct lines, four triangles, and one quadrilateral were possible. With five stars, ten lines, ten triangles, five quadrilaterals, one pentagon. As the different figures quickly outnumbered the quantity of stars, it followed that given an infinite number of stars there must be . . . how many geometrical figures? Every conceivable figure had its source up there; figures so perfect they could never be drawn on paper, whose perfection would be spoiled by a line, even though it were thinner than a thought. God was a geometer. He designed the universe with nothing but a compass and an unmarked straightedge, and His blueprint was the night sky, which He unscrolled in order to plan for the future. This had been indisputable fact to ancient civilizations and still was to modern astrologists. The individual was nothing compared to the forms up there. Perhaps the human condition could only be overcome through contemplation and appreciation of the night sky's geometry. Perhaps . . .

— Presentation, says Vernier, rousing me from my reverie.

Normally taciturn with the other teachers, I am more responsive to Vernier, but conceal my appreciation for his interest in me behind a surly expression. Impressed by my understanding of the subject, he has encouraged me to read widely, recommending not only textbooks, but biographies of mathematicians. At the same time he has often reproved me for my reluctance to work methodically and my impatience with detail, which result in leaps he finds difficult to follow.

— How did you arrive at this? he asks.

Now, admonished once again for the careless presentation of my work, I grudgingly explain the missing steps in my reasoning. The whole exercise is a waste of time. The problems are trivial, intended for fools like the boy next to me, who is still struggling with cyclic quadrilaterals, which I mastered in the first few days of the course. Fool! Sitting there picking his pimples, drawing circles, and within each circle sketching a woman with legs spread obtusely apart. A world away from fools like him, I am already thinking about squaring the circle and trisecting an angle with only compass and straightedge, problems which still challenge mathematicians after two thousand years and whose solution promises instant fame.

Having dismissed the class with a sigh of exasperation (the students have become more boisterous as the work has become more difficult), Vernier removes his gloves and slaps them against a desk, sending up a cloud of white dust. He has asked me to stay behind again.

—An original idea is worthless if it's not communicated clearly. It's no more than a vapor and one's head may just as well be empty. Many people have ideas, intuitions, and remarkable insights, but few are able to translate them from the personal to the public domain.

—How many great ideas have never seen the light of day? How many remain in the dark cranium through a lack of expression? Descartes put it well: When one deals with transcendental matters, and nothing is more transcendental than mathematics, one must be transcendentally clear. Your fault, Galois, is that you're too quick for your own good. You fail to show the necessary steps in flying toward your goal, which you somehow see even before you set ink to paper. A proof doesn't lie in the final QED but in the process that leads to it; in the logic that binds the parts into a harmonious whole. Just as a note omitted from a Mozart piece would upset the balance of the composition, so a missing line of logic can make a proof questionable. Not only omissions, your very exposition is at times so terse, your syntax so cryptic, it could pass for a language of your own making.

Vernier's long-winded sermon upsets me. Why doesn't he rebuke the others—the talkers and the troublemakers? Why is he always lecturing me? What does he know about the mathematical mind anyway? He has been at Louis-le-Grand for ten years, and he will probably spend the rest of his life in this prison, teaching the same material to dull plodders. And what is the extent of his mathematical

29

knowledge? He probably knows what the curriculum requires and nothing more. I am on the verge of telling him that there is one law for the ox and another for the eagle when he removes his spectacles and squints feebly. Something in that squint and the pink indentations on the bridge of his broad nose makes me swallow my words, and I remind myself that he is the only teacher who recognizes my talent.

Reading the biographies of mathematicians is a good break from the intense concentration on theory. But more than this, these biographies have become both a source of inspiration and a means of measuring myself against the great minds at a comparable age. I am moved by the life and work of Archimedes. His quadrature of the parabola—the method whereby he calculated the area of a parabola—is astonishing for its beauty and elegance. The Rhetoric teacher is forever prattling about the beauty of poetry: Pindaric odes, Catullan lyrics, Petrarchan sonnets, Hugo's Alexandrines. Yet none of this nor any poetry ever to be written can compare with the beautiful way in which Archimedes showed that the area of a parabolic segment is four-thirds the area of the largest inscribed triangle. As for Archimedes the man, I admire him because he considered his investigations of circles more important than the practical ingenuity which calculated the amount of gold in King Hieron's crown. I agree with him—pure mathematics is the noblest pursuit because it has least to do with the corrupting influences of the world.

But my admiration for Archimedes is not restricted to his work and life. The manner of the old man's death has left an equally deep impression on me. Up to this point in my life, and like most fifteen-year-olds, my image of a hero has been the fighter who gives his life for others. Now I see that there are four kinds of heroes. The first, and least, the Three Hundred Spartans, who combed their long hair as the Persians converged upon them. Second, Socrates, and those who sacrifice their life for a moral or ethical ideal. Third, the martyrs, like the young Saint Sebastian, who died, and maybe still die, for their faith. Fourth, and highest, Archimedes, the man who gave his life for nothing more than a circle. As the Roman sword rose above his head, Archimedes was not thinking of his country's welfare nor strengthened by a sense of moral or ethical righteousness. He was not looking beyond the blade to paradise. At that instant, sitting in a circle drawn on the sandy floor, he vanquished the sword through geometry. And when the sword fell, the old man was embraced at once by the circle he loved.

In contrast to my veneration of Archimedes, I am envious of Pascal. At the age of sixteen he wrote his *Essay on Conic Sections*, which contained what was later called Pascal's Theorem. At nineteen he invented a calculating machine. My attitude vacillates when I consider my compatriot. Sometimes I am goaded to more concerted study, at other times I am gnawed by self-doubt. I will be sixteen in October and what have I done? What have I discovered? I do nothing but dream of great works! But I remind myself that I am still a relative newcomer to geometry, whereas Pascal had been tutored by his father from the age of seven or eight. Who knows, if Mother had at least introduced me to mathematics instead of spending all that time on the Bible I might have made a few discoveries by now. Still, I am making rapid progress. Pascal discovered a minor theorem concerning a hexagon contained by a conic section at sixteen. My sixteenth birthday is seven months away.

5

I arrived home last night on the last carriage from Paris. Second term is finally over. I had worked it out well: The evening meal was over, Father was out, my younger brother Alfred and older sister Nathalie were asleep, and Mother was entertaining a few lady friends. I left my bag with Mother and slipped up to my room without too many questions, just as I wanted. Solitude, that is what I need if my mathematics is to develop.

I remain in bed until the activity in the house subsides. Finally, avoiding the creaking floorboards, I make my way to the kitchen, where I quickly and quietly spread some quince jam on a slice of bread. On my way out for a walk through town to ponder a few advanced problems that Vernier has brought to my attention, I stop beside the partly open door of the study and hear my father's voice.

—Some thoughtlessness. A character I find difficult to understand, but which I see dominated by conceit. His abilities appear to be far beyond the average. Has neglected most of his work in class.

Father is reading from my reportbook. Mother must have taken it from my bag. The smell of tobacco mingles with a hint of perfume.

—Works little in my subject and talks little. His ability, in which one is supposed to believe, but of which I have yet to see proof, will lead him nowhere. There is no trace of anything but strangeness and negligence.

—Isn't there one good comment? Mother asks.

—Only this from Vernier, his mathematics teacher: zeal and progress very distinct.

—Mathematics?

—Seems it's the only subject that interests him.

—What are we going to do with him, Nicholas? I can't talk to him anymore. He has become so aloof, so distant. I knew we shouldn't have sent him to Paris. That infernal place has changed him, made a stranger of him. Between the two of us we could have supervised his education.

—The mayor's son educated at home? You know what people would have said. Besides, a good school is important for the boy's development.

—Development? He's going backward!

Father's footsteps scrape heavily across the room. When they stop, an intermittent squeaking begins. I recognize this at once: He is standing at the window overlooking the town square, spinning the large sphere of the earth.

—Talk to him, Nicholas, Mother pleads. He was so fond of you before he went to Paris. Find out why he has become so sullen.

—Look at him, Father snaps.

Startled, I spring to attention.

—Napoleon should have destroyed them all.

—Nicholas!

—Damned Jesuit!

—Stop it!

—He's a black snake, Adelaide. Don't you see what the Jesuits are up to? They are determined to win back all they lost under Napoleon, and will resort to anything to achieve their goal. They go around with a kind of missionary fervor, spreading rumors and lies, putting the fear of the devil into people, attacking those who espouse freedom and equality.

—He is here to spread the teachings of Christ.

—No, Adelaide! He's here to undermine my position, put a conservative mayor in my place, and take the school from me. He's spreading vicious lies about me, saying that I'm in league with the Freemasons and corrupting the students of my boarding school with atheistic ideas. It's a Jesuit plot, Adelaide. They want to rule France by taking control of education.

—I've spoken to him, Nicholas. He isn't like that at all. He is concerned for the welfare of our youth; he has organized Bible-reading classes for them.

—Are you also turning against me, Adelaide?

—If more young people studied the Bible there would be less confusion and disenchantment. Paris would not be the Babylon of Revelation.

—People I thought loyal have changed, Father says in a voice that is suddenly flat. They do not greet me on the street anymore. Some even turn away when they see me coming. And each day, the priest's grin looks more and more like a sickle.

There is a pause. The sphere squeals in revolving on its axis. I feel a sense of tenderness for Father, a pang of anger toward the priest. But I do not want to get caught up in these affairs. There are more important problems that need to be solved.

—Please, Nicholas, talk to Evariste before he returns to Paris. I tried last night, but he wouldn't even look at me. He appears more preoccupied than the last time he was home. I'm worried about him. If something is bothering him we must find out before . . .

—All right, all right. As if I haven't got enough to worry about! Problems with Evariste! How is a man expected to cope with everything? At times I feel like . . .

—Faith, Mother says, her dress rustling toward the door.

I sneak out by the back and step out into a brilliant spring morning. The scented wind feels mild. Here and there white and pink blossoms push through the pimples of the fruit trees. Swallows are darting about, collecting scraps of winter, adding small domes to houses and buildings. The hills surrounding the town are covered in green down. Tired of admiring itself in yellow puddles, the sun now flashes from the gold tooth in the mouth of an old woman, or from small mirrors in the hands of playful children, or from an adolescent girl's sidelong glance.

In the town square I am absorbed by one of Vernier's problems: the construction of a regular pentagon with only a compass and an unmarked straightedge. A month ago, in the first flush of enthusiasm—and in an attempt to better Pascal at a similar age—I tackled the classical problem of trisecting an angle using only compass and straightedge. But after a week of concentration, and moments of disconcerting light-headedness, I gave up in frustration. Vernier commended me on my endeavor, and pointed out that a construction might not be possible. This grated on me. It was my first encounter with an imperfection in geometry. Could the problem be solved or not? More important, why had no one come up with a theory that could determine whether or not such problems could be solved? To look at a problem and, from its external features and form, say something about its essential nature? *There* was something worth discovering.

In the case of the pentagon, however, Vernier's hint that a construction is possible serves at least to dispel the nagging thought that I may be wasting precious time. Was the week on the trisection problem wasted? If someone in the future should prove it cannot be done, and demonstrate it with a few lines of reasoning, would that necessarily reduce to rubble the efforts of all those who have cudgeled their brains for a construction? Or would such a proof somehow arise from the mountainous rubble of thought, justifying all who have spent time on the problem? But the pentagon problem appears more accessible. I sense that I am not far from a solution. Even now, passing through the market, I can visualize the diagram despite the surrounding noise. If the diagonal corners of a regular pentagon are connected by straight lines, the intersecting points of these lines will form a smaller regular pentagon. If this is repeated, smaller and smaller pentagons will be produced, receding to the center of the circle circumscribing the largest. And if the situation is reversed: Starting from the seed of a point, countless five-petaled flowers will unfold, each a perfect replica of the preceding.

There is something universal, something subtle, in

this self-generating property of the pentagon, but just as the subtlety is on the verge of becoming a thought, a cabbage vendor bellows in my ear and everything disperses, like a sphere of thistledown scattered by a child's thoughtlessness.

I stop and watch two blue-gray pigeons performing what looks like a courtship ritual. The male puffs itself with expectation—cooing, croaking, fanning its tail, bobbing its head—as it dances around the female, which, seemingly uninterested, trots away from these advances, arousing him to wilder displays of passion. At one point she stops as though about to give in to his throbbing anguish, but when he makes his move she hurries away coquettishly and flies onto the fountain's circular basin. Another pigeon appears on the scene: not a common town-square type, but a fancy feather-foot, with a crest on the back of its head. It begins courting the female by throwing out its chest and throbbing riotously. The first male attacks the intruder, pecking and flicking its wings until the feather-foot flies off to the other side of the basin. Puffed with pride, the first male starts cooing around the female, but she ignores his attention and flutters to the feather-foot, from where they both flap away to the church roof. As though its strength and vigor have suddenly ebbed away the rejected male wilts, deflates to half its size, and lies sadly on the basin wall.

Stupid bird! Serves you right! The coquette made a fool of you and flew away. But I rebuke myself for allowing the affair to distract me from the pentagon. Angry, I hurry past the prostrate bird, deliberately startling it to flight.

I try to concentrate on the pentagon, but the market is too distracting. There is too much disorder in human activity. Where geometry is held together by a handful of propositions and axioms, life appears random, unstructured, chaotic. If I were an artist I might arrange the unrelated activities according to the dynamics of harmony, order people in groups according to the laws governing color, and juxtapose events for the sake of contrast. This is the artist's advantage—given elements a, b, c, ∂ . . . he can combine and arrange them in various ways, at times producing a masterpiece. But a mathematician? What can he do with this chaos? What can he make of life? Gazing at a wine merchant extending a palm wide as a collection plate, I am struck by the thought that life and mathematics are mutually exclusive.

From the church's sunlit steps a flower vendor offers me a sprig of pink blossom.

—For luck, she winks.

Stunned, I stare at the smiling gypsy. She must be about twenty, with two black braids falling over her bare shoulders, and strange symbols tattooed on both forearms. She meets my look directly, fully. For an instant I feel as though I am being drawn away from myself, away from geometry, into the gypsy's dark world.

—Maybe you'd like your palm read, she says in a singsong voice.

Clenching my fists, I hurry away, darting a glance at the church's dark entrance open to the morning sun. The gypsy's laughter flutters after me. Confused, striding without purpose, I cannot get her eyes out of my mind.

What has she done to me? What is the matter with me? What sort of mathematician am I, allowing a woman like that to agitate me? Where is the truth of geometry?

How steadfast is my dream of becoming a mathematician, of devoting myself to higher ideas, if the eyes of a gypsy can throw me into confusion? My heart is thumping, blood is whistling in my ears, and my legs feel weak. I should go back and silence her laughter with a Euclidean theorem, dismiss those superstitious symbols on her arms with the logic of mathematics. Others like that student in the latrines would have allowed her to read their palms, been duped by her lies. Not me! I banish her from my thoughts with the image of a perfect pentagon.

When I return at midday Father calls me into the study. I spent many hours in this room before going to Paris. Mother taught me to read and write in here, and often read to me from the classics on the shelves. I liked her melodious voice, especially when she read myths and legends. The gleam of those golden titles on certain sunlit afternoons would always stir my sense of wonder. I imagined that God had created light so that people could read, and through reading, see other worlds. I check the swell of nostalgia: There is no time for that. Besides, these books no longer interest me. If only there were a few books on mathematics on the shelves, just one, who knows what I would have achieved by now?

Father looks preoccupied. The parallel furrows across his brow are deeper, his cheekbones more prominent, and his thin lips sag. Standing slightly hunched, he directs me to a chair and walks slowly to his desk, sits with a grimace, and draws on his pipe. Solemn on the wall behind him, the portrait of Grandfather Galois stares into the distant future.

—It has been ages since our last chat, he begins, turning a silver envelope knife. Remember the plays we put on for visitors?

His feeble smile turns into a frown.

—We've read your reports, Evariste. Your mother and I are very disappointed. We know you are capable of better. Is anything the matter, Son? Some reason why, apart from mathematics, you've done so poorly in the other subjects?

—I'll do better.

Avoiding his eyes, I glance at Grandfather's portrait. A pistol rests on an open book.

—Mathematics is good for mental discipline, he says, feeling the point of the knife. But in the end it's nothing more than amusement, diversion, a refined pastime. Rhetoric! That's what you should be concentrating on. The alphabet, not numbers. Words, not symbols. That's what moves the world. As your mother will tell you, in the beginning was the word, not the number. And it's the word that will give you a place in life.

—Concentrate on the word, Son. Learn its secrets, discover how to use it effectively, and you will have in your possession a force that moves men's hearts and creates history. The Revolution was not brought about by mathematics, nor by the precise geometry of Dr. Guillotin's machine, but by the power of the words *liberty*, *fraternity*, and *equality*.

Father pauses, draws deeply on his pipe, and lets out a smoky aromatic sigh. A fly describes a few crooked circles and stops on the bronze head of Marcus Aurelius, like a stray thought returning to its place of origin.

—Is politics interfering with your studies? he asks, running the blunt blade across his palm.

I reply with a soft no, watching the fly crawling over the emperor's ear, looking for a way in.

—Look, Son, I know there has been a lot of unrest at school. I know about the students who were expelled recently for defying the Director and expressing revolutionary sentiments. Your generation is going through what I experienced at your age. The Revolution was sure to transform society. A new world order was going to be established with the fall of Louis XVI. Ours would be a better, fairer world. As youths, we adored Danton, until Robespierre persuaded us that Danton's passion went against the Revolution. We supported the Reign of Terror until others convinced us that rational Robespierre was a butcher who had to be guillotined. We worshiped Napoleon and approved the changes he made to the constitution that gave him unlimited power. We rejoiced in his victories. We believed that conquest would bring peace. But Napoleon was defeated, and suddenly we were no longer young. Suddenly we were middle-aged, our dreams devastated. France was brought to her knees before foreign powers, and we could only watch helplessly as the monarchy was restored. Such is politics, Evariste. It promises paradise, takes your youth, and in the end fills you with bitter disappointment. And now there's talk of another revolution, this time to overthrow Charles. It seems the cycle is about to start again.

He stands, walks thoughtfully around the desk, and sits in front of me, our knees almost touching. Darting a glance into his eyes, I am surprised by my reflection circumscribed in his dilated pupils.

—Learn from my experience, Son, he says, leaning

42

forward confidentially. Concentrate on your studies. Do well in Rhetoric. Become a lawyer. There are plenty of them on your mother's side of the family. Who knows, one day you might end up a judge like your grandfather Thomas. Don't misunderstand me, Son. I would like you to take charge of the boarding school. My father left it to me, and I want to leave it to you. It has been a good source of income for the family. But things are changing daily, Eva-riste. There's no certainty anymore. My enemies have joined forces with the new priest in town and they're doing their utmost to undermine my position and take the school from me. Don't add to my problems, Son. Help me by help-ing yourself. If you're involved with a political group at school, please break away from it now, before it's too late.

Father has never spoken to me like this before. What is happening to him? Who are these enemies? How have they managed to frighten him so much, to the point where he is renouncing everything that was once so dear to him? I am moved by his words, by the sadness in his eyes. I want to allay his concerns, to tell him I am not involved with any political group, that I am not even interested in politics. And mathematics? Will I curb my enthusiasm for the sub-ject? I stand without replying, eager to leave the study be-fore my emotions are agitated further. How can I con-centrate on geometry if I allow myself to be drawn into the family's problems?

Father places his hands on my shoulders, looks me in the eyes, and embraces me tightly. Looking over his padded shoulder, I contain my emotion by staring at the sunlit sphere of the earth near the window, at the jagged outline of Australia.

43

What can I do to help Father? Renounce mathematics? If only I were in Australia, away from these distractions, concentrating single-mindedly on my mathematics.

—Don't throw away your youth on empty promises, Son, he whispers in my ear. There is no better world.

6

Al jabr w'al muqabala.

Vernier writes that cryptic line on the blackboard washed clean over the break. There is not a ghost of a word or figure from last term, as though it too has been prepared for this new topic. He picks up a measuring stick, balances it on his gloved finger for an instant, then taps for attention. When the talking subsides, he reads the strange words aloud three times, accentuating each syllable by prodding the board with the stick.

— Arabic, gentlemen. It means restoration and reduction, give and take, to have and have not.

Warm sunlight slanting through the windows casts a skewed grid over the words, and reveals chalk dust falling from the letters like dandruff from a scalp scratched in perplexity.

— *Al jabr,* he chants, walking down the aisle. Say it after me. Louder. Open your mouths. Again. Close your eyes. Allow the sounds to enter your body. Good. Allow them to take possession of you. Give yourselves to them wholly, and they in turn will reveal their secret.

As he stops beside me the shadow of his stick falls across my desk.

45

—*Al jabr,* gentlemen. We begin our study of algebra with these three syllables.

His words have fired my imagination. Perhaps there is a word or a particular arrangement of letters and symbols that holds the key to all mathematics. Said correctly, with just the right pitch, in just the right frame of mind, the sound opens the door to a different world, one based on the laws of geometry, not on the bonds of blood.

I did not solve all the problems Vernier set for me during the term break. Things were too distracting at home. Alfred was at me all the time: wanting to play the latest game, asking me about student life in Paris, begging me to talk to Father about joining me at Louis-le-Grand. Mother seems to have become more religious and tried to fill my head with passages from the Bible at every opportunity. And Father became surlier each day. But all this, including the conversation with Father and his plea for me to concentrate on Rhetoric and consider a career in law, recedes before those mysterious syllables.

—Algebra did not exist in Classical Greece. Even by Euclid's time problems were still solved geometrically. The study was firmly established by Diophantus, rightly called the father of algebra, who lived in Alexandria around A.D. 270.

—Little is recorded about Diophantus, gentlemen, except for what had been supposedly inscribed on his tomb, which is where we will begin our study of algebra. The epitaph read: My boyhood lasted one-sixth of my life, my beard grew after one-twelfth more, and after one-seventh more I married. Five years later my son was born, who lived to half my age. I died four years after the death of my son.

Vernier pauses, reads the epitaph again, instructs us to write it, and asks how long Diophantus lived. Silence. He taps the stick against his thigh. One student whispers that he has been dead far longer than he lived. Laughter. I worked it out before Vernier asked the question, but I am not going to answer. I have never been one for answering questions, and I am not going to start now, not even for Vernier.

— Well, gentlemen, any luck?

Squinting through thick lenses, Vernier scans the room, then directs an expectant look at me. I shrug my shoulders and stare into the inkpot.

— Not even a guess?

He leans on the windowsill, his hair glistening in the spring sun. The shadow of his head covers the word *w'al*. Given only the shadow, can one reconstruct its object? But different lengths of straight line all project a point, so given only the point how is one to determine the length of the line? The possibilities are infinite. A line may be the projection of any two-dimensional shape, while a square may be the projection of countless different solids. What about a cube? Or any physical objects, for that matter? What are they projections of? Thoughts? Ideas? The Creator's will?

— Some of you may find the answer by trial and error. If not, be patient. Once you have mastered the essentials of algebra you will solve the problem in a few lines.

He returns to the table and removes his gloves — a sign there is to be no more note-taking. A few students close their books and settle into more comfortable positions. Vernier paces the platform from side to side, his face glowing.

—After Diophantus algebra fell into oblivion for a thousand years, until it was rediscovered in the West through translations of Arabic texts, in particular the works of Al Khowarizmi. The subject made slow but steady progress during the Renaissance, though this was largely a reinterpretation of what the Greeks had known. Matters changed rapidly with Descartes, who combined geometry and algebra. Mathematics made spectacular advances from this unlikely marriage.

Stopping in a cylindrical shaft of light streaming into the room through a small window high in the back wall, he points upward with an inflamed index finger.

—Remember, gentlemen, before Descartes geometry was inextricably bound to the physical world, despite its elevated nature. No matter what Plato had to say about ideal forms, the compass was still needed to represent a circle. Algebra changed all that—it liberated the mind from attachment to things.

Fools! Stirring and shuffling. They do not understand a thing. But Vernier continues, unperturbed by their restlessness, his voice almost lyrical.

—With Descartes's work, the circle parted company with the compass, passing from the domain of the senses to the range of the intellect. Through the sublime language of algebra the circle was translated and restored to its rightful place: the ideal, the realm Plato could only dream of.

Knowing that this historical interlude will not be examined, the boy next to me is studying the text lined on his palm. He has had his first shave during the break: The once dark-downed skin above his upper lip is now pale.

—Geometry has had its day, gentlemen, he says, spreading his arms wide as though to embrace the entire class, at least in the form presented by Euclid and Legendre. It has been a magnificent edifice for two thousand years, just like the Parthenon, which is the very embodiment of geometry. Since the time of Descartes, geometry has been losing ground to algebra, and I venture to predict that in fifty or a hundred years Euclid will no longer be taught.

A murmur of complaint rises from a few students. Why have they spent an entire term on a subject that is not only useless but which might turn out to be obsolete?

—Algebra is the way to the future. The unsolved problems of geometry will yield to the power of x. Algebra has rightly been considered somewhat mystically. Ahmes, the Egyptian, writing more than three thousand years ago, said it is the means of knowing all that exists, of solving the mystery of man, and unlocking the secrets of the universe. In concluding, let me say that if geometry makes us human, algebra makes us divine.

The sound of the bell batters his last words, and before he is able to dismiss us properly the students spring from their seats and scramble out.

—Galois, he calls over the commotion.

Concealing with a grim expression a certain pleasure at being detained, I gather my things and go to his table. He sits with a sigh that makes his shoulders fall.

—Savages, he grimaces, examining the dermatitis between his fingers. Why do I bother? Dreams, Galois, enjoy them while you can, before they turn to chalk dust.

What is he getting at? Why that wistful look at the clear blue sky outside?

—I was also good at mathematics at your age, Galois: I even dreamed of making discoveries and becoming a professor at the Polytechnic. But youth's promise proved a lie. At eighteen I accepted my abilities and reconciled myself to a career in teaching. I was full of high ideals, determined to enthuse my students, and make the subject interesting, relevant, alive. You see, Galois, I was going to be a real teacher, just as Pythagoras had been to his disciples, as Socrates to Plato, Aristotle to Alexander. But year after year of unruly students I realized the futility of my efforts. And since then . . .

Head bowed, I am unsure of what to make of this disclosure.

—Occasionally, I come across a student with a real talent for mathematics, who revives my idealism, and for whose sake I try to summon a little of my remaining enthusiasm. Galois, you are such a student. But what will become of you? Will your talent flower? I hope so, Galois. I've been teaching for ten years now, and I'll probably teach for another thirty. A lifetime of bells, bored students, the same notes turning more yellow and tattered each year.

—Develop your dream, Galois. Avoid politics and promiscuity. Become a mathematician, discover a great theorem, and get a position at the Polytechnic. But please work methodically, lay good foundations, and, above all, express yourself clearly. Unlike geometry, which relies on a diagram, algebra has no objective reference: It's an abstract language that requires great precision.

He removes his glasses, extends them at arm's length, and squints as though he is trying to focus on me. Sensing another long-winded lecture, I pick at a thread on the spine of my book. *Ha-ha* on each lens, and he rubs them with a piece of green felt.

—How was your break?

—I tried the trisection problem again.

—A construction that has eluded some of the greatest minds.

—It might not be possible.

—Perhaps.

—Then I've wasted my time, I say, baiting him.

—Thinking about mathematics is never a waste of time, he says with conviction. Like prayer and meditation, it raises the spirit from wasteful passions, material pursuits, and the present political madness. I tell you, Galois, I would rather devote a lifetime to a problem that proved unsolvable than be drawn into the chaos of life without mathematics.

—I was about your age when I tried to prove Fermat's Last Theorem, an unsolved problem that you will learn about in the coming months. It's considered the Gordian knot of pure mathematics, and a place in history awaits the person who unravels it. Fermat wrote his theorem in the margin of Diophantus's text on equations, and beneath it added that he had a truly marvelous proof, but that the margin wasn't wide enough to accommodate it. That margin has become the most famous in history: a few centimeters of blank space has exhausted a sea of ink, produced mountains of scripts. Sometimes I envisage Fermat peeping from behind his theorem, smiling mischievously in the knowledge that he has perpetrated a hoax that will tease and torment countless minds. But even if that were his intention, I would still rather follow Fermat than be drawn into the madness of the so-called real world.

As with geometry, he has aroused my interest and sense of challenge. I will master algebra as I have geometry. I will devote my life to this sublime language, unlock some of the universe's secrets. I will start by tackling Fermat's Theorem.

Glancing at Vernier, I suddenly feel sorry for him. For the inflamed webbing between his fingers, the chalk dust on his elbows, the drop of dried blood on his chin, the streaks of white in his black sideburns. No! I will not end up like him. Better to beg on the streets and remain true to the spirit of mathematics than teach a class of uninterested students for the sake of a comfortable life.

—Have you read the book I gave you? he asks, securing his glasses around his ears.

I slip out a thin volume pressed between two others and place it on the table. *The Golden Verses of Pythagoras* by Fabre d'Olivet. He gave it to me at the end of last term, with the rather cryptic instruction to read it in private, adding that it was not for everyone, but for the few who truly appreciated the spiritual nature of mathematics.

—What do you think of it?

—I didn't understand it all, but it helped me to see Pythagoras as a prophet, his brotherhood as a monastic order with strict vows, and mathematics as a kind of religion. I would like to belong to such a brotherhood, to devote every minute of the day to mathematics.

—Good, Vernier says, and, crossing his inflamed fingers, leans forward confidentially. This isn't an age for books like this, Galois. Mysticism is under attack from all sides. Napoleon hounded d'Olivet, and now the Church condemns his work. The unenlightened fail to see that mathematics is spiritual in essence. Don't be seduced by this secular age. The proponents of industrial progress would have us believe that knowledge should be useful and lead to material prosperity. If mathematics is your calling, Galois, and I believe it is, make sure you leaven your work with a little spirituality.

I ask if there are any other useful texts in the library. Vernier recommends three by Joseph Louis Lagrange: *Resolution of Algebraic Equations, Theory of Analytic Functions,* and *Lessons on the Calculus of Functions.*

7

I finished Lagrange's books in a few days, all three of them, read them more fluently than Euclid's and Legendre's. At times they excited me so much I had to put them aside in order to subdue a tremor that made reading impossible. I have never read like that before: More than just intense reading, each page was an experience, a remembrance, a reacquaintance with things long known. I grasped the abstract language of algebra intuitively, with a sixth sense, as though it were a scent or a melody or an object of one's passion. Has anyone ever read like that? A reading where the reader and the text interact, where the reader becomes the text? A few students are immersed in translations of Walter Scott's adventure novels; caught up in another world, they read voraciously, identifying with the heroes. But identification is one thing—it happens all the time in one form or another—I am talking about becoming the actual text, the very symbols of algebra.

Having spent the last few day wrestling with Fermat's Last Theorem, I now toss fitfully in bed, unable to sleep: x, y, and z swirling in my head like autumn leaves. When I finally sink into a drowsy state, I hear my own voice calling from a distance.

—I am mathematics. I am mathematics.

The idea that I am disembodied thought strikes me like a bolt. I spring awake in a panic, shaking, terrified that I am going to fragment into a chaos of symbols, numerals, and pronumerals. Heart pounding, I reach up and steady myself on the bedhead.

—I'm Evariste Galois. I was born on 25 October 1811. I whisper this over and over, holding on to the bed, straining to hear a sound in the dark—a wheeze, a groan, the rustle of a mattress, anything that might center my thoughts, bring me back to the here and now, and dispel this fear of disintegrating. The panic gradually abates. Hands on my chest, I number heartbeats until I lose count.

Fever burns my forehead; my left ear aches. Confined to bed for the day, I flick through Lagrange's text on equations, my excitement alternating with torpor, lucidity, with murkiness. The warm afternoon sun quilts the gray blanket with the shadow of the window grille. Doves croon on the ledge. I place the text on my chest and succumb to a languor, a drowsiness that loosens my body and carries me off . . .

I am on the front steps of the church in Bourg-la-Reine. The gypsy beckons me with a smile. In approaching her, I notice Father talking to the priest in the steeple's sharp shadow. I offer the gypsy my hand. Dropping a few poppies on the step, she opens my palm and studies it for a moment. What are the symbols on her forearms? I am unable to make out a thing. She draws me up the steps, toward the nave's dark entrance. I turn to Father: He is now arguing with the priest, who sways a gold watch on the end of a chain. I try to pull away from the gypsy, but she holds me firmly and pulls me into the cool nave where she begins undressing. I want to get away, but notice that her body is covered in mathematical symbols. She opens her arms. I want to get closer, to read them, but I am afraid. What if she is a witch like Circe, trying to seduce me from my calling? An equation is tattooed across her breasts. It looks simple enough, but I cannot solve it. What is happening to me? I reach out to touch the equation; her skin is soft as rose petals.

—I am the solution, she laughs.

The text falling to the floor wakes me. Tested even in my dreams! And if the book did not wake me? Would she have aroused me to the point where I . . . ? If only I could control the course of dreams. Still, I must be on my guard. Mathematics requires purity, chastity, all that the great Pythagoras taught.

I feign sleep at the turn of the door handle. I do not want to confront Laborie, the school's Director. I was informed of his intended visit by the janitor, who acts both as nurse and food bearer. Shoes, several pairs, scrape the floorboards, approaching in stops and starts. Has Laborie brought a few teachers with him? Are they going to interrogate me? Threaten to tell Father of my poor progress? Advise me to curtail my zeal for mathematics not only to avoid outright failure, but for the sake of my health? A web of whispers surrounds the bed.

—Galois? Are you asleep?

Four students are standing above me, all looking very serious. What do they want? I have had little to do with the others since immersing myself in mathematics, and they in turn have reciprocated with indifference. Not only have they stopped teasing and taunting me, they now completely ignore me, which suits me perfectly.

—What is it? I ask, sitting up.

They are political activists and have approached me several times about joining their group. Their aim is to continue the work of the students who were expelled, and to keep the ideals of the Revolution alive. I have made it clear I am not interested.

Two on each side, they lean over me, their faces grim with determination.

—The school's freedom is at stake, says the tallest, spraying his words.

—I don't care.

Reaching down between the two on my right, I pick up the book and place it on my chest. They exchange looks upon reading the title.

—Six, I remark.

—What's that supposed to mean?

—The number of ways four people can look into each other's pupils.

—This is serious, retorts the tallest, tapping the spine of my book.

—More serious than mathematics?

—Robespierre was a student here, snaps another. We must follow his example. The damned conservatives will turn the place into a seminary if we don't defend our rights.

—I'm not interested in Robespierre. There's more heroism and nobility in the death of Archimedes than in all your revolutionary martyrs put together.

—You're too smart for your own good, Galois!

—This is my good, I reply, holding up the book.

—You're nothing but an insect!

—People with brains aren't demoted.

—Idiots! I shout, blood throbbing against my temples. This is where real freedom lies!

—Stop acting so superior, Galois! You're nothing but a silverfish crawling between pages.

I throw the book at the tall student. It brushes his face and crashes against the window. The others restrain him from springing at me, and they leave with a chorus of abuse.

As a few flies drone in drowsy circles, I shake with indignation at having allowed myself to be upset by those I despise. I should have dismissed them by calmly reading my book; instead, I acted like a fool myself. I recall the *Golden Verses of Pythagoras:* Control your emotions with enlightened reason; bear ridicule in silence. His novices had practiced restraint in order to be accepted into the mathematical fraternity. My behavior just now was childish, not in keeping with one aspiring to enter the sacred temple. From now on I will subdue and bridle my heart. I will avoid others even more assiduously. Solitude: That is the golden rule. Silence: That is the source of mathematics. I feel light-headed, unsteady on my feet as I walk to the window. The impact has cracked the book's spine and its covers are bent back like the wings of a dead bird. I brush away the dust, press the book to my chest with crossed arms, and gaze beyond the walls surrounding the school.

Impressed by my understanding of Lagrange, Vernier now allows me to follow my own inclinations, occasionally commenting on my poor presentation or hasty conclusions, and even then tactful in what he says, as though mindful of my reputation for being irascible. I am already solving cubics when he begins the topic of equations. There is little he can teach me about theory and application, but I enjoy his historical introduction to a topic and the anecdotes about the mathematicians responsible for its development. Precisely when the others are most inattentive, knowing that the material will not be tested, I sit up and listen.

Vernier now strains to make himself heard over the noise.

— The Egyptians were able to solve equations with one unknown, but their method was tedious. They considered a linear equation like $2x + 5 = 13$ difficult. Of course, they did not use the decimal system of counting, nor did they express the problem in that form, and that is precisely the reason for its difficulty. Without x, that great liberator, they could not state the answer as an arithmetical combination of the digits 2, 5, and 13.

— Quadratic equations such as $2x^2 + 11x + 5 = 0$ were solved in various ways by the Egyptians, Greeks, Hindus, Arabs, and Chinese. You will see that a formula for the solution of the general quadratic can be obtained by means of the four arithmetical operations and the extraction of a square root. This is known as a solution by radicals. In fact, this solution amounts to reducing the quadratic to two simple linear equations.

— Cubic equations such as $2x^3 + 13x^2 + 16x + 5 = 0$ were known to the Greeks, but a formula for the general solution was not discovered until the sixteenth century. Again this solution involved reducing the cubic to a quadratic and a linear equation.

Scratching the webbing between his thumb and forefinger, he pauses and silences a grinning student with his glare.

—The background to the cubic solution is a story in itself, he says, taking off his jacket. The intense rivalry and intrigue between the people involved would make a fascinating novel. There is little mathematics in our literature: Aspiring writers among you would do well to keep this story in mind.

—The formula for the solution of the general cubic arose from the solution of particular types of cubics. Early in the sixteenth century Scippione del Ferro, a professor of mathematics at the University of Bologna, discovered the solution of cubics of the form $x^3 + ax = b$, which he passed on to his pupil Antonio Florido under a vow of secrecy. At that time in Italy mathematical contests were as popular and lucrative as the chess tournaments of today. Florido, thinking to use the secret for financial gain, contested with the great Niccolo Tartaglia, a self-taught mathematician whose real name was Fontana but was called Tartaglia, which meant stammerer, because he had been slashed across the mouth by a sword as a child. It appears Tartaglia knew, perhaps through Florido's inability to keep his secret, that his opponent would set problems of the sort $x^3 + ax = b$, so he spent weeks seeking the solution, because he in turn was certain that Florido could not possibly solve cubics of the form $x^3 + ax^2 = b$, whose solution he knew. Solving the problem on the evening before the contest, Tartaglia went on to get the better of his opponent and collect a good deal of money.

—Tartaglia refused to publish his solution, no doubt

banking on other contests and more prize money. However, Girolamo Cardano, a professor at the University of Milan, appeared on the scene and implored him for the solution. Tartaglia relented. Pledging Cardano to secrecy, he revealed the solution in a twenty-five-line cryptic poem, which he later followed with a full explanation.

— How did Cardano manage to extract the solution? Some scholars maintain that he threatened to kill Tartaglia, which is quite plausible, for Cardano was a man of violent temper, who not only severed his son's ear in a domestic quarrel, but was rumored to have murdered someone. Well, acknowledging only that he had received a small hint from Tartaglia, Cardano published the solution of the cubic in his famous *Ars Magna*. Seething with anger, Tartaglia challenged Cardano to a mathematical duel in a church in Milan. On the day, however, Cardano failed to show, sending instead his student Lodovico Ferrari. The affair ended in a brawl and Tartaglia claimed he was lucky to escape alive.

— Whose story shall we accept, gentlemen? Vernier asks. It appears history has gone against Cardano, and little wonder, when we consider his personality. It seems he divided his days between mechanics and mathematics, and devoted his nights to astronomy and debauchery. He was imprisoned for the heretical act of publishing Christ's horoscope. It is said that astrology was his downfall: Having calculated his own horoscope, in which he foretold the date of his death, he felt compelled to take his own life when the day arrived in order to preserve his reputation.

Despite the increasing rowdiness, I lean forward attentively. Was Cardano justified in breaking his vow of secrecy, even though it announced to the world the general solution of the cubic? What right did Tartaglia have to withhold a piece of knowledge that would advance mathematics? As he was self-taught, perhaps from a poor background, and possibly unable to obtain a professorship because of his speech impediment, mathematics may have been his only means of livelihood. But even so, there is a question of honor, of noble-mindedness. Mathematics should not be corrupted by avarice. A copyright cannot be placed on theorems and proofs. Mathematicians are not the custodians of higher knowledge, but simply its sounding board. Cardano did well to break his vow. What would have happened if Tartaglia had died, taking his important findings to the grave? Mathematics would have been denied its expression, and scholars set back years.

Face flushed, Vernier struggles to raise his voice above the growing restlessness.

—After the cubic, interest naturally turned to the quartic or bi-quadratic. A certain Colla, or Coi, proposed a problem which was translated to $x^4 + 6x^2 + 36 = 60x$. Cardano tried unsuccessfully to solve this equation and passed it on to Ferrari, who solved it by substitution and reduction to a cubic. In his *Ars Magna,* Cardano credits Ferrari with the solution, though he does not fail to mention that his pupil made the discovery at his request.

—Finally we come to the quintic: the general equation to the power of five. The ablest mathematicians have attempted to find its solution, without success. Euler and Lagrange tried reducing it to a quartic but ended up with an equation of the sixth degree instead. And that is where matters stand at the moment, gentlemen. There is no solution to the general quintic. Some maintain it cannot be solved by radicals. Recently, Ruffini, another Italian, thought he had proof of this, but his argument was shown to be flawed.

—So, gentlemen, as with geometry, the challenge is before you. Honor, position, and immortality await the person able to conquer the quintic. To find its solution or prove that it cannot be solved.

Hardly able to contain my excitement, I want to tell Vernier I have read of the quintic in Lagrange's book, and that I have been looking for a point of entry into the problem. But will this rabble understand me? The two behind me have been whispering about visiting a brothel. Others have been discussing the Republican cause all lesson, planning to take part in a demonstration on Sunday. Would any of them understand that this struggle with the quintic is more heroic than the struggle against oppression? It is easy to die for a political cause; countless died for such causes instinctively, without a second thought. But how many could devote their lives to struggle with an abstraction? Risk having one's mind shattered for what may eventually prove an impossibility? Sacrifice family, happiness, and love for the sake of an equation?

8

In the coach bound for Bourg-la-Reine, which is located about ten kilometers south of Paris, my sense of foreboding grows. How am I going to confront Father? I do not want to disappoint him again. There is already enough concern etched in his face, enough sorrow in those eyes that used to flash and ignite my boyhood with happiness. But my grades have deteriorated still further since my visit home during the summer vacation, when I promised that I would bring home a better report for Christmas. How am I going to tell him that I cannot concentrate on anything but mathematics? I should confide in him, get closer to him, make him feel a little happier. I want things between us to be as they were.

The coach passes between two rows of naked poplars. Here and there, black nests are wedged between branches like empty hearts. Jackdaws screech against the icy-blue sky. A priest with a bovine neck squeezed into a white circle is dozing in one corner, head swaying from side to side. A young woman buttoned in an overcoat, hands hidden in a furry burrow on her lap, sits very stiffly next to the priest, gazing from the window. Lilac-scented perfume fills the coach.

I open my notebook and look over my scribbled attempts at solving the quintic. I steal a glance at her. What is her beauty compared to the truth of mathematics? Her beauty is nothing more than conceit and deceit, meant to seduce the foolish, and then for her own selfish ends. The coach jolts over a ditch, and our shoes touch. A charge goes through me as she turns and apologizes. Equations disintegrate, x's scatter like a flock of jackdaws. In an instant, my eyes ricochet from hers, to the priest's red-stoned ring, to a willow uprooted in a creek, and back to my notebook. I must overcome her if I am to aspire to a higher calling. For the novice monk she is the temptress luring his soul to infernal fires; for me she is the hell of chaos and confusion. I must overcome her proximity, her perfume, her tightly laced boots pointed directly at me. Sitting more upright, I bow to the notes I have been scribbling over the past few months until the driver shouts my stop. The priest's eyelids flutter, his broad face opens in a yawn. The woman's fingers crawl from their hiding place. I am pleased with myself for not having allowed her to distract me for the remainder of the journey. Prominent veins cross the back of her hands. Who knows, just as the solution of an equation lies in a certain grouping of its coefficients, perhaps that configuration of veins . . .

— Evariste! Evariste!

Running across the town square, Alfred collides with an artist carrying a few framed canvasses under his arm and a triangular easel strapped to his back. He hurls a few curses in Alfred's direction and sets off grittily, intent on making the most of the thin afternoon light.

Alfred wraps me in a strong embrace. Two years younger than I, he has grown so much during the past year that he is half a head taller. His bony wrists protrude from the sleeves of his jacket.

—You must help me, he says, placing his arm over my shoulder. They let you go at twelve—I'm already thirteen!

He is almost in tears. I attempt to calm him by pointing out that Louis-le-Grand is like a prison, and that he is much better off here, where he is free to come and go.

There is a cool atmosphere in the house despite the healthy fire cracking in the living room. Mother has just returned from church and stands very stiffly as I kiss one cold cheek, then the other. The smell of candle smoke is tangled in her black hair. At forty-two, she is still youthfully thin, and her movements are quick, at times abrupt. Her jawline, a sharply defined right angle, is accentuated by the way she carries her head. Alfred is sitting in the corner, biting his knuckles. Nathalie hurries in, kisses me, asks about my studies, and, without waiting for a reply, rustles out, saying she will be late for her lesson with the seamstress.

—Where's Father? I ask Alfred.

—Politics! Mother says. Work of the devil! Dividing people in order to fill the jaws of hell. I hope you've got good news for your father this time, Evariste. God knows, the poor man needs something to raise his spirits.

—What's happened?

—The conservatives, Alfred replies, springing to his feet. They're trying to take his position. Jesuit sympathizers! We'll show them!

66

—We? I ask.

—The Republicans, Alfred declares, looking at me in a surprised manner. We had a stone fight last Sunday. Should have seen how those Royalist cowards ran.

—Enough! Mother demands.

—Today it's stones; tomorrow, bullets on the streets of Paris.

—You will never leave Bourg-la-Reine! she retorts.

—Paris isn't far away, he smiles, and leaves the room whistling the "Marseillaise."

—See? Is it any wonder your father's nerves are at breaking point?

She paces the room with short, sharp steps. I am uncomfortable in her presence. I want to be alone, to concentrate on the quintic. A log snaps, spitting a shower of sparks.

—A boy, and already talking of bullets. It's the work of Satan. Armageddon is not far off. I sense chaos and destruction in the air. Paris! It's Babylon, Sodom, Gomorrah all in one.

I have heard this before. Whenever Mother is irritable or angry she invokes Revelation, often quoting long passages, as though the vivid, violent images somehow dispel her anxiety.

—Father might be a while, I say, picking up my bag.

—Show me your report book.

Standing beneath a lamp on the wall, she reads in silence, her lips nibbling each word, her eyebrows rising by degrees, jawline becoming rigid. If I had my own place, if I were allowed to stay in Father's apartment in Paris, I would not have to put up with these time-consuming formalities.

An hour here, an afternoon there, and my youth is slipping away, my energy and talent squandered on matters that are of no interest to me.

—This is totally unacceptable, Evariste, Mother glares, waving the report. It's going to upset your father. No progress whatever! I knew we should not have sent you to Paris.

As she harangues Paris and me, I stare at the clock on the mantelpiece above the fire. It is striking five. Numbers in a circle. Numbers in a line. Time as a circle. Time as a serpent. There is some relationship between time, number, and the circle, but before I am able to grasp it Father enters the room, bringing the evening chill with him. I help him remove his overcoat.

—It will be an icy Christmas, he says, going to the fire. That mistral is keen as a saber, friendly as the smile of our town priest.

A forced chuckle crumbles into a cough. He stands with his back to the fire, toasting his palms.

—Well, what have you brought home for us, Evariste?

Mother gives him the report with a pointed look and leaves. He sits in an armchair, crosses his thin legs, and reads at arm's length. I recall the happy occasions with Father in this room: the songs, the poetry recitals, the short dramatic sketches. Happiness, laughter—they have no place in mathematics. Maybe I have outgrown all that. What are those verses from Corinthians Mother is so fond of quoting? When I was a child I spoke as a child, thought as a child, understood as a child. Since my initiation into mathematics I have become a man, and I am determined to put aside those childish things.

Shaking his head, pinching the skin above his jagged Adam's apple, Father places the report on a side table and points to the chair beside him.

—You promised to do better, Son.

The flames writhe and twist to free themselves from the charred logs.

—You promised to help me in these difficult times.

—I . . . tried, Father.

—And the report? he asks, tapping the table. It's worse than the last one.

—The teachers don't understand me.

—But they say you're not making an effort, Son.

—It's not true.

—Ah, Evariste, he sighs, closing his eyes and rubbing his forehead. I expected some hope from your report. It seems everybody is turning against me. My enemies are closing in on me, Son.

The tone of his voice alarms me. Hunched in the armchair, he seems a shadow of the man he was a year ago. In a flash, I understand Alfred's anger. I want to reach out to Father, to restore the light in his dull eyes, smash his enemies. But I quickly check this impulse. What about my mission? Should I deny my higher calling? Become embroiled in politics?

—Help me, Evariste, he says.

Suddenly, for the first time, I see myself in his features, in the shape of his mouth and chin. No! I must not be drawn into his affair. Sympathy must not divert me from my calling.

—What can I do? I ask in a flat tone.

—Have you forgotten our last talk?

Should I tell him about the progress I have made in mathematics? Why hasn't he commented on Vernier's report? But I recall his attitude to mathematics: a diversion, a topic for conversation over a glass of wine. He will never understand that it is as compelling as religion, politics, the pursuit of profit.

—Have you joined a student group? Is that why your grades are so bad?

—No, Father.

—Alfred is neglecting his studies for politics. How can I consider sending him to Paris when you come home with a report like this? He looks up to you, Evariste. Please, Son, set a good example for the boy.

—I'll do my best.

It has become dark outside. The sounding wind rattles the fig tree, causing a few branches to scratch the windowpane. Our conversation lapses for a moment. Father is thoughtfully pinching his neck. I turn to the fire: If all is number, as Pythagoras said, what is the relationship between fire and number?

Prometheus and Pythagoras: both benefactors of mankind. One elevated mankind to a higher plane by the gift of fire, the other offered the key to divinity. More than any natural thing, fire is most like the mind, especially a mind filled with . . .

—Don't waste another year, Son. Obtain your baccalaureate. Help me with the boarding school. Together we will defeat those trying to undermine the school's reputation. We will make it more liberal, more prosperous. The Jesuits will never stop us!

The idea of running the school alarms me. I do not

want to end up like Vernier: teaching an undisciplined class, straining to impart a few scraps of knowledge. I do not want to return to Bourg-la-Reine. Over the last few months I have been thinking about the Polytechnic. It is one of the world's great centers for the study of mathematics, with some of the finest teachers and researchers. That is where I belong, where I would be able to devote myself to my calling. This dream of going to the Polytechnic has made my confinement at Louis-le-Grand bearable, especially during the last few weeks, when bleak weather and early nights have forced students indoors, into each other's company. Entry to the Polytechnic is by a special examination, which can be taken without restriction on age. Father's desperate wish for me to run the boarding school makes me even more determined to sit the examination as soon as possible.

9

My stay at home was hell, and for once I am relieved to be back at school. Hopes of using the holiday for serious work amounted to nothing. When I wasn't hounded by Alfred, who implored me with tears to intercede in his quest to study in Paris, I was cornered by Mother, who cautioned me against temptation with passages from the Bible, or called into the study by Father, who sought my support against the growing enemy. Only Nathalie made no demands on me; she was preoccupied with some fellow who had come to the house a few times, whom I had managed to avoid meeting. If it had not been so cold I would have gone to Grandfather's cottage in the almond grove just out of town, as I had done during the summer. I could have carried out my investigations into the quintic and indulged in reveries of the Polytechnic.

One afternoon, having been confined indoors for a few days by rain lashing obliquely against the house, I grew so agitated that, the moment there was a lull in the rain, I took my notebook and left without a word.

There were few people outside. Clouds lumbered across the sky. The razor-edged wind slashed the white Royal flag raised in the center of the town square. A ragpicker in an army greatcoat pushed a wheelbarrow piled with whatever he had managed to scavenge from the town's refuse heaps. A small boy ran out from a lane rolling a hoop which rang over the glistening cobbles. Striking a protruding stone, the hoop jumped from the rod guiding it and struck me on the knee. As the boy came running I picked up the hoop, surprised by its warmth.

—Sorry, he puffed, his face red from the cold.

I gave him the hoop, and in an instant it rang across the square. Walking on, I wondered about the difference between the hoop and the circle that absorbed old Archimedes before his death. The hoop was its own end, and even though it may have once been the rim of a small wheel, it was now an object of free play, no longer pushed with a purpose. Absorbing the boy with its form, the hoop was essentially the same as Archimedes' circle, which had also been an object of pure play, pleasing the old sage, restoring him to a state of innocence.

A sudden chill roused me from these thoughts: I had walked across the square and was now in the wet shadow of the church, where I had seen the gypsy last spring. Open, beckoning passersby to take shelter from the cold, the doors were paneled with two rows of rectangles carved with chaotic scenes from the Apocalypse. Finally, a refuge where I could sit alone for hours and concentrate on more important things, away from the family.

The church was empty. Seven spearheads glowed from a candelabra at each end of the altar. I went in and sat at a rear pew. A burst of sunlight beamed through the circular stained-glass window above the altar. I tried concentrating on the quintic, but the vivid colors and forms distracted me.

The circle of light, the circle of life, I repeated several times. Mother brought me here regularly as a child. Sitting quietly beside her, I would close my eyes and inhale the curious blend of perfume and candle smoke. At ten or eleven I became very religious for a short time. I think I preferred the order and harmony inside the church to the senseless commotion in the town square. The precision of the Sunday service, the meaning of every word, the significance of every gesture—all this was far more fascinating than games with sticks and stones. At the time, I would often gaze at the window circling the yellow-haired Christ with crimson roses blooming from his brow, his palms, his overlapping feet. The similarity between Christ's figure and that of the marble dove with outspread wings always impressed me. Both appeared as if they were in full flight. I went through a period of intense admiration of Christ, almost hero-worship, and I would daydream of giving my life in some great act of self-sacrifice. But the period didn't last long. Napoleon soon took over from Christ and I was sent off to Louis-le-Grand.

That day I felt detached, distant from the figure in the circular window. Had Christ heard of Euclid? Could he understand geometry? Perform a miracle by cubing the sphere or squaring the circle or trisecting an angle? Where did Christ and mathematics meet? Were they mutually exclusive? A more significant miracle, one more convincing than turning water to wine, would have been to outline a general solution of the quintic fifteen hundred years before anyone had even conceived of the quintic. I compared Christ and Pythagoras. Both were spiritual, ascetic, reformers, teachers. Both died for their beliefs at the hands of an ignorant society. The Triad was an important symbol for both. Christ's teaching was contained in the Trinity, Pythagoras's in the right-angled triangle. But how was one to grasp the Trinity? Though I had admired the figure of Christ as a boy, I could never comprehend the threefold Father, Son, and Holy Spirit. Now, in a flash, I saw Pythagoras's Theorem in a different light: The simple relationship between the perpendicular sides and the hypotenuse was true for all faiths and everywhere in the universe. Not only this, the Theorem had a miraculous power: Given two sides one could, without measurement, with eyes closed, determine the length of the third side. This could not be done with the Trinity. Given the Father and Son, one could not grasp the Holy Spirit; or given the Father and Holy Spirit, one could not pinpoint the Son; or given the Son and Holy Spirit, one could not specify the Father.

I gazed at Christ's golden halo. Was it a coincidence that the circle had been used as the sign of sanctity and divinity? As the old religions appeared to be losing their relevance, mathematics would become the new religion, with the triangle and circle symbolizing God the geometer.

Shawled in black, an old woman limped in, carrying a basket containing wrinkled pomegranates. She dipped her fingers in the holy water and shuffled to a pew at the front. The old cross was for her: a crutch for flesh and bone. The symbol of the new religion would be the pronumeral x: the great liberator, as Vernier had said. It would empower the mind to overcome its dependence on matter and rise to the highest realms. This holy x would restore the mind to a state of innocence, fill people with the sense of wonder enjoyed in antiquity, before the onset of the Dark Ages, when people were burdened with guilt.

I was startled by a tap on the shoulder. A priest was sitting on the edge of the pew behind me, leaning forward, smiling. Confused, as though caught doing something wrong, I sprang up and would have dashed out if he had not extended a palm in a gesture of reassurance.

— Don't be alarmed, he said.

He was about thirty, sharp-nosed, with ginger hair cropped close to the scalp. I slipped the notebook into my pocket.

— Can I be of some help?

— I have to go, I said, taking a few steps.

— Would you prefer the confessional? A gingery finger pointed to the compartment across the nave.

— Youth can be a difficult time, he smiled.

— I've come here to be alone for a while.

— Then you have done well to come.

He paused, scratched a spot of candle wax from the pew's backrest, and then focused on my notebook, whose top was just visible.

— What have you got there?

I reached for the book as though someone had tried to snatch it from me.

— A diary? he nodded. Do not be embarrassed. I know the temptations of the flesh. I have also felt Satan drawing me toward sin and self-abuse. I struggled, resisted, succumbed, was torn by remorse, and the cycle started again. One night, as I lay in self-loathing, the image of Christ crucified appeared and gave me the strength to overcome

Satan. I entered a seminary shortly after and dedicated my life to God.

I was angry. What gave him the right to assume that I was like others? I wanted to get away from talk of self-abuse, sin, and salvation. I would overcome Satan not with a wooden cross, but through the power of x.

—It's a perilous time for young people, he continued, adjusting the black band around his waist. Do not be misled by the atheists. They come in all sorts of guises: lovers of freedom, Republicans, humanists. When the liberals had their way, they drenched Paris in blood and instituted a Republic. And what happened? Napoleon emerged, crowned himself emperor, and attempted to take the place of God. That incarnation of evil led France into the abyss. A curse on all liberals! When men turn from God they embark on self-destruction. Don't be misled by those who encourage the young to be open-minded and receptive to fashionable ideas. Heresy is only an idea, they say. What harm is it to question Scripture? But ideas are deadlier than cholera. They can ravage the young, whose minds are especially susceptible to the new. Attend church, read the Bible, fortify your mind and spirit against contagious ideas.

His face glowed as though licked by flames, yet his eyes were like icicles. The large vein in his neck swelled, protruded, appeared ready to burst under the constricting collar. I suddenly realized that this was the priest who was undermining Father's position, and in the same instant I saw Father screaming in the grip of infernal fires, calling out to me for help.

—Father wouldn't condemn anyone to hell, I snapped.

The words reverberated in the still nave. Taken aback,

he squeezed his forefinger between collar and neck and moved it from side to side along the sharp edge.

—Your time's over, I continued, my voice quivering. This is the new religion.

I pulled out the notebook, opened it to a page covered in algebra, and raised it triumphantly.

—Mathematics! I shouted.

The word echoed in the nave. Kneeling, the old woman raised her head.

—These are the symbols, this is the new cross!

Shaking, I flicked the pages in his face, pointing to circles, equations, x's. I had intended to defend Father, but a latch had sprung open and my innermost thoughts spilled out. I felt a liberation in this outburst, as though the words severed whatever tenuous thread existed between the Church and me.

—Mathematics is the new savior! I shouted, emboldened by his silence. Your cross is a millstone around people's necks. The x of mathematics will give people wings!

—You're not well, my boy.

—I've never felt better!

—We must talk, he said, hiding his hands in his wide sleeves. Are you a student at the boarding school? Who has infected you with these ideas?

I was about to retort that I was the mayor's son, and that together we would overcome the enemies of the school, but Pythagorean restraint checked this impulse. I shoved the notebook into my pocket and swept passed him. Near the door I brushed the old woman, who stepped aside awkwardly, spilling her pomegranates around the base of a baptismal font.

10

I follow my brisk shadow out of the Louis-le-Grand court-yard, barely able to contain my excitement. A few more months, and I will be out of here for good! I have not bothered with doing any special preparation for the examination to the Polytechnic—my superior knowledge of both algebra and geometry will overcome any challenge.

—Be patient, Vernier advised a few days ago. Do a year of mathematics with Monsieur Louis Richard. He's highly regarded and his advanced class is excellent. Prepare thoroughly for the Polytechnic. Pass with distinction. Why run the risk of failing?

I am still annoyed and disappointed by Vernier's talk of failure. He has often commented on my ability, so why this restraint now? While most of the class are still struggling with quadratic equations, I have been working on the solution to the quintic. No doubt he means well, but when it comes to mathematics he has the mind of a shopkeeper.

To enter the Polytechnic a year early—that would be an achievement, a sign of precocity! More than my desire to escape the confines of Louis-le-Grand, I want to spite the teachers who consider me a pretentious fool. I will show them! Tomorrow I will laugh in their faces!

It is a warm July morning, and I sense that a new life is only hours away. I walk without my usual stoop, a spring in my step, taking in the surroundings. The leafy boulevards are bustling with carts and carriages. In dazzling squares hawkers grab the unsuspecting by the ear. In the poorer suburbs the air is heavy with wine, even at this hour. Everywhere shutters opened wide embrace the sun, welcome it into living rooms glittering with chandeliers, or blackened by coal smoke. On balconies women beat winter from colored rugs, men scrape soot from braziers and flues, mattresses are bent over railings, bristling with straw.

People gather in groups large and small: groups speculating outside the Bourse, groups conversing at circular tables in cafés, groups loyal to this newspaper or that, groups packed in small reading rooms, groups assessing the quality of trout at the fish market, groups in public squares around speakers proclaiming the virtues of Bourbons, Orleanists, Bonapartists, Republicans, Saint-Simonists, Socialists, Utopians, Anarchists. Groups everywhere, all different, undergoing constant change, with members coming and going. Groups dispersing and new ones forming. Where does it all end? A multiplicity of truths. If one were to take the different arrangements of truth within each group, truth would multiply without end.

I must not be sidetracked by all these impressions. I must keep my mind on the Polytechnic, try to anticipate likely questions, prepare mentally. If only it were a written examination. I am not good at expressing myself orally. Looking people in the eye makes me uneasy. A blank sheet—that is different. A rectangle of paper draws ideas the way the circle of the sun draws the world.

80

A noisy crowd has gathered on a stone bridge arching over a canal. The water is sluggish, green, its flow perceptible in the refuse floating on it. People are shouting and pointing to something among a flotilla of books and papers. A head! A man's, mouth gaping at the sun. As it drifts under the bridge, a rat appears from the mouth, clawing its way onto the forehead, where it begins nibbling voraciously in the socket. The crowd's cries become wilder, followed by a volley of stones aimed at the head. A grappling hook flies in the air, but falls short of its mark. Raising its snout, the rat twitches, then darts back into the mouth, causing the head to bob and shake from side to side. One of the soggy books touching the head is open, warped pages contain diagrams of Euclidean geometry. I hurry off before a feeling of revulsion rises any higher.

—Out of the way!

I spring aside as a barrel-chested fellow with a plow on his shoulders trots past, heaving at each step, broad feet slapping the slimy water oozing down the middle of the cobbled street. I am in a suburb whose squalor is highlighted by the searching sun. I have never walked through such misery before, never seen such poverty, so much overcrowding, so many forlorn faces.

If I were to discover a formula for generating prime numbers, would that in any way assuage the young woman I notice smothering her sobs with her palms? And if I were to solve the quintic, would that alleviate the suffering in this place by even a fraction? How can I, or anyone, justify the pursuit of mathematics in light of such conditions? This place reduces everything to insignificance, like multiplication by zero. What is the meaning of transcendent truth to that old woman elbowing a bare table? What is the relevance of imaginary numbers to the people in that basement foundry? Their sweat is the only reality, and it drips into molten metal, fusing with the white-hot soul that will be cast as letters for printing presses. This terrible squalor is Dante's purgatory.

A sense of dark futility begins to overtake me. I feel like Dante being led through the horrors of purgatory. But why was he taken on such a journey? Not to alleviate the suffering of the damned; it was a test of his vision of paradise. And if the horrors had overwhelmed that vision, it would have proved him unworthy of his ideal. If I can withstand this hell and keep my vision intact, the Polytechnic will open its doors and greet me as a mathematician. This thought strengthens me. I feel a little more secure, my sense of insignificance begins to abate. The world will always have suffering, but those called to serve mathematics must rise above the debilitating pity it evokes.

And now mathematics appears through the human condition, transforming everything, perhaps as poetry and painting elevate suffering to art.

A deranged man howls at me from a dark doorway — Pythagoras's clear voice teaches that all is number. A beggar accosts me, his arms amputated and a placard around his neck blaming Napoleon. There is an equation of a parabola in the pink scar stitching each stump. I hold my breath against the sulfurous stench rising from an open sewer circled by children — Euclid's pristine postulates exist only in a vacuum. Gradually, as mathematics imposes itself on the surrounding squalor and chaos, it restores my buoyancy, hope, and sense of meaning in an otherwise meaningless world. And as I leave the suburb, my vision of the Polytechnic is brighter than ever, my faith in mathematics restored.

On a spacious boulevard carriages with fashionable passengers gleam past; pedestrians stroll leisurely, spinning parasols, tipping hats polished black, chatting about Hugo's latest play; peddlers, observing propriety, tone down the virtues of their wares. Dazzled by a building with a classical façade, I stop to admire its clean lines. A perfect example of geometry filling space, mind projecting itself into matter, the Pythagorean ideal.

I am standing before an ancient temple. My novitiate completed, I am going to be accepted by the highest order of the mathematical fraternity. I climb the steps, whose height increases in geometric ratio, to a pair of bronze doors paneled with scenes from the lives of mathematicians. It is cool inside, dim. The floor is tiled with a regular pentagon: Golden lines connect its diagonal corners to form a pentagram, which in turn embraces a smaller inverted pentagon, in which the altar stands: a marble cube the height of a man. Sunlight streams through an opening at the crown of the dome, fuses with the fragrant smoke spiraling from lamps and censers, and illuminates the altar. Faces emerge, heads, busts—statues positioned on tiers around the temple's circular walls. Mathematicians have assembled to witness my initiation. A cowled figure, the fraternity's high priest, appears from a thicket of shadow and smoke, places a compass and straightedge on the altar, and beckons me with a hand that glows in the swirling light. I walk forward, stopping abruptly on a vertex of the pentagram as the priest raises a hand, fingers outstretched, except the fifth, which is bent at the second joint. The light intensifies. The priest climbs onto the altar and unfastens a star-shaped brooch. The hood slips off. A woman! She extends her arms in a line perpendicular to her body. I turn away in confusion. Is this a joke? The faces are grimly serious. A woman officiating in the temple of mathematics! Initiation through . . .

A vendor's cry dispels my reverie. Continuing along the boulevard toward the Polytechnic, I reprimand myself for allowing such a capricious idea to enter my head. Yes, I have read that priestesses often officiated at the ancient oracles, that Pythia was the priestess at Apollo's temple, through whom oracles were delivered. But women have played no role in the mysteries of mathematics. Why did that image come to me? In broad daylight, too. Is there a region of the mind, beyond the reach of will, where absurd ideas are spawned? Ideas that defy one's most cherished beliefs? Pythia and Pythagoras? Surely that is nothing more than a linguistic coincidence?

—Like a lesson from me, schoolboy? says a lilting voice.

A young woman leaning on the sill of a first-floor window winks at me with a blue eye outlined in black. Her hands hang limply from thin wrists.

—I can teach you a lot in an hour, she smiles.

I look around: It is one of those streets the boys at school whisper about.

—Coming? they have asked on numerous occasions. At first they went for the excitement of walking along and asking the prostitutes for their prices. Later, to visit their rooms.

—Come on, Galois, they insisted.

—What have you got down there? Marble spheres?

Smarting at their laughter, my contempt for them was matched by fierce pride in my talent. Let them wallow in filth, I thought with sharp delight. I have my pure mathematics. These encounters always acted as a spur: They drove me to concentrate more intensely, to work with greater zeal, to believe with even more conviction that my efforts would be rewarded with a place in history.

And now, quite by chance, I find myself in this place, followed by leering looks, prodded by sidelong glances. A woman confronts me, her face pale with powder.

—First time, sweetheart? she grins, revealing large, uneven teeth.

—He's mine, shouts the woman from the window.

—She's clapped, whispers the other.

—What's that, you old hag?

They will not seduce me! I must keep my emotions under control, thoughts clear, reasoning sharp. Weakness! That is why men and boys come here. But the sexual instinct must be overcome if we are to rise to a higher level of awareness. It is easy to succumb to these women: It proves that one is merely human. We must strive to be more than human, to withstand instinct by means of an ideal. Up to now that ideal has been religious: the flesh denied for the sake of paradise. Mathematics is the new ideal. The flesh denied for the sake of . . . what? Ultimate truth?

I am being tested yet again. The proximity of these women, their languid gestures, words laced with perfume, hair bright with henna—all this is intended to seduce me from my ideal. I am Ulysses in the vicinity of the sirens. But I will not stop my ears with wax nor allow myself to be tied to a mast. I am going to overcome the sirens with my own inner resources, by concentrating on the solution of the quintic.

Sing your seductions! — I am going to pass through your midst unmoved. I slow down, walk with measured steps — to walk quickly would be like fleeing a feared enemy — my body set rigidly, the quintic clearly before me.

Proud of my triumph over the sirens, walking with a lighter step, I see mathematics everywhere. The curve of a clothesline hanging between two walls can be expressed in terms of the magical x. Water streaming from a tap is a continuous function. (Someday there may be a state of being where such functions are as vital as water.) An old man shuffling in a pair of large army boots, with a round loaf tucked under his arm, makes me lament that man cannot live on circles alone. Four cardplayers seated in a smoky café hold the secret of the behavior of groups intimated by the great Lagrange. Where a poet might transform things to image and metaphor, I transform the world into mathematical concepts, impose order on chaos, relate things to each other and, through the miracle of x, to myself.

In a quieter suburb, narrow streets and lanes wind and twist into each other. Heading in what seems the direction of the Polytechnic, I come to a fork in an uphill street. I go left, and continue climbing until I encounter another fork, this one with three branches. Guessing, I choose the middle and follow it for a short distance. A dead end: a bluestone wall painted with concentric yellow circles. Anxious about being late for the examination, I hurry back to the fork, take the left branch, and find myself in a small square which radiates five streets.

I take a few deep breaths. I must not leave this decision to chance. The square is deserted; distant music mingles with the trickle of a nearby tap. A gray horse nods in plodding past.

Reflected in its moist eyes, this square has become a rhombus and the surrounding buildings tilt precariously toward my enlarged image. Which way? Don't panic. Is that movement in a shop?

A silver bell giggles as I open the door. Inside, clocks of all shapes and sizes, from those in massive wooden cases to others in delicate crystal cylinders. Hands are set at various angles of prayer. Pendulums move at different speeds, from the silent motion of tired grandfathers to quick-ticking smaller pieces racing to the future. Chimes range from brassy gong to nervous tinkle. A man with albino features peers at me over the top of his pince-nez. Robust, with the hands of a stonemason, he stands and walks around the workbench.

—At last!

The man's bass voice fills the small shop. Straightening his back, he performs a few head-rolling exercises, cracking the bones in his neck. A clock on the bench chimes a lively waltz.

—So, you're Henri's son?

Intimidated by his size and tone, I remain silent.

—And you want to become a clockmaker? he bellows. It isn't easy, sonny. Making clocks is both an art and a science. You're wasting my time if you don't have a feel for both. A clock's heart is all mathematics, its body all art. And a well-crafted clock is one that has to be both cruel and kind: It must strike out the succession of moments according to an implacable law, while assuaging time's impact with a cherub's smile, a cuckoo's call, or a pleasing melody. Understand?

I feel trapped. The examination is at eleven. I have lost all track of time, though it cannot possibly be past ten. I want to interrupt the clockmaker and ask him for directions to get out of this labyrinth, but his words are like rolling boulders.

—Consider the variety of clocks, he says, and sweeps his powerful arm in a semicircle. Behind their differences they all have something in common.

He moves closer, his enormous girth between me and the door. Removing his pince-nez and slipping them into the top pocket of an oil-stained coat, he leans forward and places his arm over my shoulders, almost overpowering me not only with the weight of his arm, but his body odor.

—Well, if you're going to be my apprentice, listen and learn. It's like this: The endless variety of human features conceals the existence of the springs of the soul.

He pauses, as if to gather his thoughts, swells his chest to release another storm. A blue cuckoo darts from its retreat, teases me, and springs back, repeating this seven times.

—If you're not religious you might prefer this: The spark that inhabits a white pebble in the depths of the ocean is essentially the same as the sun. Likewise, my assembly of pendulum clocks—they have this in common: The period of a pendulum's swing is equal to twice the ratio of a circle's circumference to its diameter, multiplied by the square root of the pendulum's length divided by the constant of gravity.

With his small finger he writes the formula on the

dusty side of a still grandfather clock coffined in oak. He has mistaken me for someone else. I cannot afford to waste more time.

—What time is it? I ask, maneuvering from under the heavy arm.

—Time! Look around you, sonny.

There must be a hundred clocks, yet no two show the same time. On the back wall a small cabin strikes four, while a woodcutter comes down with his ax on each chime.

—No one clock has the correct time, he grins.

He refuses to give any one prominence, and he cannot bear to have them all showing the same time and chiming in unison. So he has arranged them in such a way that the correct time can be calculated with simple arithmetic. All one need do is take any combination of three clocks, arrange them in size from smallest to largest, subtract . . .

Without a word, I slip from under his arm, swing open the door, and dash out into the sunlit square, the silver bell snickering behind me. Not a person in sight. The music is louder, livelier than before. The louvered shutters of a third-story window open. A man leans out, holding a sheet of paper. As our looks meet, he shakes the paper, scattering a flock of pigeons from the spotted balustrade of an adjacent building.

—What's the time? I shout above whirring wings.

The paper slips from his fingers, spins, flutters, twists above the square. Have I startled him? Is it an accident? Did he intend it? As though by reflex, I follow the paper's erratic movement, intent on catching it, but it eludes me and falls in the water trough under the tap. When I retrieve it, the black ink is already running, the letters are losing

89

their shape, the words are dissolving before my very eyes. I focus on the word *Zero* before it blurs to the blackness before all alphabets.

For an instant I sense that I have experienced all this before. Was it in a recent dream? No. It is more like the feeling of waking from a dream in which I have just been reading a detailed proof to a new, wonderful theorem—and waking to find the text crumbling into meaningless scraps, vanishing before my eyes, and the joy turning to disappointment.

I look up, but the louvers are now shut. Was the sheet discarded? Or is the man racing down to get it?

I cannot wait any longer. Placing the sheet beneath a stone on the edge of the trough, I hurry off in the direction taken by the gray horse.

Do not panic. The music is not far off. People are singing, shouting, laughing. The street curves to the right, and when it straightens again, I confront the commotion of a summer carnival. In an instant I am in the middle of a ring of revelers, together with a drummer, a flute player, and a fiddler. As the dancers skip around the musicians, they also move through the parting crowd. Bewildered, I make a desperate dash to escape, but the ring contracts and pushes me back with a burst of laughter. I try to breach another point, but their arms are tightly interlocked. Men and women, angels and demons, gods and beasts howl with happiness. I rush at the clasped hands of two angels. The link snaps and I stumble into the surrounding throng. I elbow and shove toward the periphery, but for every three steps I am pushed back two.

Lagrange! Think of Lagrange. What did he assert?

The solvability of a polynomial equation is somehow related to the substitutions performed on its roots. Think of order, Evariste, arrangements, patterns within a group of substitutions, the structures of groups within groups.

But all this is swept aside by the chaos around me. I am suffocating, drowning in humanity. Everything I have worked for, my faith in mathematics, my very reason for living, all threatened by a carnival of madness. I shout, shove, shoulder my way through to the other side, where, gasping for breath, I ask a national guardsman for the time and directions to the Polytechnic. He replies, smiling enigmatically. Is he really a guardsman? What if he is dressed like that for the carnival?

Run, Evariste, before this whirlpool of madness catches you again.

11

Their laughter brings me back to the classroom. It is a lesson on religion. I have not heard a word the teacher has said.

— It appears you're with us in body only, he says.

I look around. Forty eyes are focused on me, wide with expectation. I am not going to give them what they want. I have stopped playing the fool, outgrown that perverse feeling of exaltation at being ridiculed by teachers I detest. Last week mathematics gave me the strength and confidence to rise above such things. Now I question everything. You are a failure, jeers that inner voice. You were too smart for your own good.

A week already since my failure to enter the Polytechnic. A week of despair, when I have become even more brooding, insular, uncommunicative; a week of regret, when the thought of Father's disappointment has pursued me like a bloodhound; a week of humiliation, when those I despise, teachers and students alike, have laughed and sneered; a week of nightmares, when the memory of that chaotic day has seeped into my dreams; a week of self-doubt, when even my texts have lost their magic; a week of self-loathing, when I feel ashamed at the thought of my former hopes.

It was still before eleven when I entered the Polytechnic's ornate gates. I had ascertained the time a few minutes before in adjacent buildings: The clock in a funeral parlor agreed to the minute with that in a notary's office. Groups of students in bright military-like uniforms were enjoying the warm sun. Expectation was mixed with trepidation: I would soon wear that bright uniform, and study mathematics at the highest level. The students looked so grown up — they had mustaches and whiskers, while I, with my small build and clean cheeks, was still a boy in comparison. Uncertain of whether to interrupt their heated conversation on the need for a Republic, I stood beside three students, until one turned and asked what I wanted. An ink-stained index finger pointed across the courtyard. I was about to set off when another grabbed me by the elbow and asked what I was. I turned from one to the other as they positioned themselves in a triangle around me. I replied that I intended to be a mathematician. They exchanged bemused looks. Was I a Republican? I nodded, not wanting to antagonize them. The triangle opened and they sent me off with a pat on the shoulder.

Lithographs of mathematicians hung from the walls along the corridor which receded to a small window in the distance. Stopping between facing portraits of Newton and Leibniz, I turned from one to the other, trying to read the lines and creases on their faces, to fathom their eyes, determine whose features expressed more genius. Leibniz, his abundant wig coiling onto his shoulders, looked at me with worldly eyes, while his lips seemed to suppress a smile. Within the external borders of a rectangular frame, he was depicted in an oval frame mounted on a mantelpiece. A cape flowing over his left shoulder spilled from the oval, onto the mantelpiece, to the lower edge of the rectangle. Slightly longer, and it would have spilled into the corridor. On the other side, seated rigidly in an armchair, Newton appeared troubled, uneasy, as though resenting this interruption to his work. Sitting for this portrait was a waste of time, he seemed to be thinking. Posterity would not be enlightened by the length of his nose or the curve of his chin. There was no need for portraits. Let future generations re-create his features as they willed. The face, the body, the man: from dust to dust. The corpus of work—that was all that mattered in the end.

Entering the waiting room, I avoided the appraising looks of the other candidates and sat on a bench with two others. A nail head protruding from a black knot in the floorboard held my attention for some time. Papers and pages rustled as a few eager candidates did their last-minute preparations. I shot furtive looks around the room. Did they have the same aspirations as me? Did any of them have my passion for mathematics? Was the Polytechnic sacred to them, or was it nothing more than a means to secure a place in society? Not one of them looked like a mathematician. I could tell at a glance that they were here not for the pursuit of pure knowledge, but for positions of wealth and power.

— . . . Perhaps you'll share your daydream with us, says the teacher, standing above me, beaming with sarcasm. Too personal? In that case, please read the next ten verses.

Stiff in high starched collars and bow ties, two examiners sat at one end of a long table, a bearded secretary at the other, ready to record proceedings. Their questions were taken straight from a textbook, anyone could have answered them—anyone, that is, who had studied methodically, who had drilled themselves on monotonous exercises, had revised thoroughly. I did not expect this type of examination, even though Vernier warned me. I imagined that the examiners would recognize my talent—if not directly from the light in my eyes, then at least from a few probing questions that would test for insight and ingenuity. Instead I stumbled on one question, hit a brick wall on another, fell into a hole with a third. I became flustered, my words would not come out fluently. One of the examiners straightened his tie, ran his fingers through his ashen hair, and blew away the strands. The secretary's pen scratched harshly.

Why had I allowed myself to be subjected to this humiliating interrogation? What did these tenth-rate mathematicians in front of me know about talent? Why didn't they give me a chance to show my understanding of equations? Where were today's Pythagoreans? Those masters who could look into a person's soul and determine whether or not he was suitable for the highest calling?

The examiners' questions were designed to select mediocrity. They were deliberately subjecting me to a farce. At one question, certain the examiners had exchanged winks, I clenched my fists and did not reply. I was not going to give them the pleasure of making a fool of me.

—The next ten verses, insists the teacher.

—I won't read, I retort, angered by the memory of the smug examiners.

—Our dreaming prophet refuses to read.

95

I know this teacher: His subdued authoritarian tone belies the fact that he has been taken aback by my reply.

—May we ask why?

—The Bible's irrelevant.

The murmuring stops. He turns ponderously and walks back to the front platform with harsh heel-grating steps.

—And how have you reached this conclusion?

—Through mathematics.

—Mathematics? echoes the teacher.

In the corridor again, between the gallery of portraits, I sensed eyes following me, and felt humiliated in their presence. I had dreamed of entering this place, and now I was on my way out like a . . .

Descartes held my attention for a moment. I was too presumptuous, he seemed to say, eyebrows arching distinctly. Doubt everything, including your innermost dreams, reduce yourself to nothing, and through that you will know if you are meant for mathematics. I was ashamed. Maybe I lacked talent and my belief in myself was nothing more than conceit. Descartes—there was a real genius, seated on a solid chair, feet squarely on the floor, quill about to dip into a pot to add to that thick volume on the table.

My disappointment was even more bitter outside, among the students strutting about in the uniform of the Polytechnic. Failure! Another year at Louis-le-Grand! If only I did not have to return! On the street, I thought of running away from Louis-le-Grand, Paris, Bourg-la-Reine, France. I wanted to lose myself, get away from everyone and everything, including mathematics. I could board a ship for Africa, America, Australia. But Father's troubled face came to mind. There was no telling what my disappearance might do to him. No! This failure was bad enough.

A whip flicked, horseshoes scattered, a driver spat abuse at me. Heads touching, a fashionably dressed young couple laughed as they sped past. I winced at their frivolous, senseless laughter. Yesterday I would have countered their stupidity with the serious nature of my vocation; now, my faith shattered, I am crushed by it. Was that the essence of life? They found meaning in each other, saw themselves reflected in each other's pupils, gave each other an identity. Where was my meaning now that I had been rejected by the Polytechnic? What was my identity now that I questioned my love for mathematics?

—Go on, Galois, explain yourself, demands the teacher.

On a busy bridge a cocoa vendor shot a hopeful look from under a broad-brimmed hat. A gleaming urn was strapped on his back, small metal cups dangled from a belt around his waist. Even this vendor shuffling past in misshapen shoes had a firmer hold on life than I. Strapped to the urn, he belonged to the city, carried its reflection on his back, served it day and night. By comparison, I was a blank sheet torn from a book and thrown to the wind. Slipping from my image in the urn, I turned and leaned over the railing, only to see myself in dark-green sludge. All I had to do was climb the waist-high wall and . . . but Father's face held me back.

— Mathematics is the religion of the future, I reply.

I am determined to get the better of my inquisitor, not for the amusement of the others, but in the hope of reviving my feeling for mathematics.

— Ah!

I know what lies behind his protracted exclamation. He is considering his next move: Should he pursue the matter in front of the class, or dismiss it for now and deal with it later, when he can talk to me alone? He is aware of liberal and Republican ideas spreading through the school, the whisper of revolution, the atheistic attitudes of a growing number, but this is the first time that religion has been opposed by mathematics.

What should he do? He has been careful not to give radical students a forum for subversive ideas. But this is different, he must be thinking. He is curious about this loner who has never shown any interest in politics. His views cannot possibly be a threat; they are unlikely to find support. Mathematics is the least popular subject on the curriculum, shunned by liberals and conservatives alike. There is no harm in finding out what lies behind that surly face.

Too dispirited to return to school, I wandered in a daze for some time, until I entered a poorer suburb, where thoughts of my rejection were gradually dispersed by the misery of sallow-faced humanity. A group of boys about my age, saddled with baskets, dressed in tatters, their feet wrapped in rags, were scavenging a mountain of refuse. They were the abandoned, the orphaned, the homeless, the

12

After the confrontation with the teacher, I concentrate again on finding the solution to the quintic, this time with even greater intensity, a single-mindedness verging on obsession. This is not an academic exercise, nor a puzzle to be solved as an intellectual challenge—it has become a struggle for my identity, my very existence. In finding the solution I will also resolve the difficult problems in my life. The solution has been there together with the problem since the beginning of time, waiting for the fearless thinker.

Am I that thinker? Will I overcome the obstacles, claim the prize, raise it to the light like a golden fleece? The solution will not only confirm my talent, and open the doors to the Polytechnic without an examination, but also reconcile me to Father. Yes, Father will embrace me, take heart from my talent, and fight back against his enemies.

Absorbed by the problem, able to work on it entirely in my head, I often fall into a kind of trance, and others have to prod me to answer a question or move off at the sound of the bell. There are times when I feel as though I am swimming in mathematics, when my thinking becomes less definite, more expansive, intuitive. At other times I am mathematics—emotions, memories, self-awareness all vanish. These are brief, fleeting moments, and when they pass, I am left feeling light-headed, disoriented, darkness humming in my ears.

Pondering this oneness with mathematics in the light of Descartes's saying *I think, therefore I am,* I wonder what would happen if these states of heightened consciousness were to last longer, or became permanent. Perhaps if I could prolong them, make them last for even a few minutes, I might find the solution to the quintic. And then I curse the fact that I am sinewed to a frail body, distracted by instincts, swayed by emotions.

If only I were disembodied thought! What divine will or diabolical whim has placed mathematics in a vessel subject to fatigue, hunger, decay, death? The irony is exquisite: Rooted in the furrowed brain, mathematics rises above man, and has absolutely nothing to do with the flesh, emotions, or suffering. If mathematics is the new religion, perhaps I should become an ascetic monk. Place this feeble, recalcitrant body under a strict regimen of diet and discipline. Subdue its demands and appetites, and through this, prepare myself for the service of mathematics.

In the refectory, as the others stuff their faces in the short period allotted, I nibble a few scraps while contemplating the quintic.

—Are you all right, Galois? asks the student next to me, mashing a boiled potato. You haven't been eating much lately.

—Man lives by more than bread alone, I reply, gazing at my inverted image in the clean spoon.

—He's become religious, chuckles another.

— Renouncing food for the salvation of his soul? taunts a third.

— To Saint Evariste! proposes a fourth, raising a glass of water.

Four glasses meet in a single click. Let them laugh! Yes, Saint Evariste! A saint in the new religion, a martyr of mathematics. And suddenly I am in a lecture theater, interrogated by a panel of Jesuits.

— You're a heretic! one of them shouts, arrowing me with an index finger.

— Do you deny it? asks another.

— You've taken Christ from the cross and used the symbol to promote freethinking!

It is night, and I am tied to a post in a courtyard lit by crimson torches. Cowled figures appear, each with an armful of books, their shadows looming on the walls of a cathedral. They throw their load in a ring around my feet, going back and forth until they bury me in books to my neck. I strain to read a few titles or to deduce an author from a few lines of text: Euler's *Introduction to Analysis*, Newton's *Of Analysis*, Diophantus's *Arithmetic*, Cardano's *Ars Magna*, Apollonius's *Conics*, Cauchy's *A Course in Analysis at the Polytechnic*, Lagrange's *Theory of Analytic Functions*. As each armful falls on the pile, a faceless voice asks whether I will renounce my heresy and all the works spawned by godless pride. I remain silent, eyes fixed on the books. And then a figure appears holding a torch, face scourged by the flame.

— For the last time, will you renounce these Satanic texts?

My attention is caught by an open book. Equations! I

strain to it as though it is my salvation. I recognize it from the first line—Lagrange's *Reflections on the Algebraic Solutions of Equations*. I read it aloud, chant it as though it were a prayer, a source of courage to face the end without flinching, without renouncing my faith.

—If a function $f(x_1, x_2, x_3, \ldots, x_n)$ of the roots of the general equation of degree n admits all the permutations of the x_i that another function $g(x_1, x_2, x_3, \ldots, x_n)$ admits (and possibly other permutations that g does not admit), then the function f can be expressed rationally in terms of g and the coefficients of the general equation of degree n.

And as the torch is lowered, I repeat the passage, chant it with greater fervor in the inquisitor's face. The crisp pages of Euclid's *Elements* begin crackling, curling, cuddling the flame. In an instant a conflagration springs up around me. Liberated from skeletal lines, geometrical figures dance as pure forms; seared from attachment to things, numbers swirl in the lightness of being; overcoming the gravity of paper and ink, the spirit of mathematics rises from its crucifixion to x. My flesh peeling away, I am one with this spirit, ascend to paradise on wings of flame.

After a week of asceticism, a sluggish lethargy. I begin to doze in class and, what is most disconcerting, I am unable to work on the quintic with my former concentration. It is Sunday afternoon. The sky has been scoured blue by the harsh sun. I am in the courtyard, sitting sleepily under the leafy elm. Two students approach me, laughing and gesturing excitedly.

—Coming? asks a face covered in ripe pimples.

—You're overdoing it, says another. You need to get

out of that skull of yours for an afternoon. We're going to Montmartre to hear a few speakers. Come on! We know you're a Republican at heart.

— It's the Champs Elysées after that.

— There'll be plenty of girls on a day like this.

I walk away as though they are not there.

— Too superior for our company!

— A picture of tormented genius!

Drawn by my shadow serrated on the steps, I enter the long cool corridor. The old janitor limps from the other end with a few sooty flues on his shoulder.

— Thank God for summer, he says. Ah, to be young again.

He looks around, exposing a few brown teeth.

— Do you . . . ? he grins, gesturing with a black fist.

What does he take me for?

— Don't waste it, he winks and makes a few deft thrusts with his pelvis.

I hurry away, shocked by the fact that a lame old man is capable of such a supple movement. But that black fist, that revolting thrust, recede the moment I enter the library. There is nobody inside. The afternoon light brightens the otherwise dark furniture, revealing the grain's flow, names and dates scratched over the years, knots like concentrations of pain; it shines on volumes preserved in leather and gold, books whose titles and authors have faded; it illuminates the upper corners and cornices, exposing the collusion between spiders and shadows. A bouquet of white roses on the librarian's table dispels the mustiness that usually pervades the room.

Unable to concentrate on the theory of equations, I

browse without real interest along one of the shelves, pull out Pascal's *Pensées* from its pressing neighbors, and sit in a back corner. I have not read more than a paragraph when a drowsiness descends on me, pulling at my eyelashes. I fight it, sit more upright, focus on each word, but the drowsiness becomes heavier. My eyes close, head falls slowly forward, and when my forehead touches the open book, the thought that I must give up this debilitating asceticism brushes lightly past me.

I am awakened by a crushing weight on my back: The librarian is standing over me, his hand on my shoulder. But I see right through him, to a man sitting on a small casket, bowed to a thick book on his knees, profile framed by a hexagonal window, hawkish nose exaggerated by the absence of background. Carrying a shovelful of ash, I approach the pensive figure, who looks up with visible strain, closes his forefinger in the book, and presses it to his chest.

—Don't be fooled, Evariste, he says in a voice weakened by chronic illness. It's the work of the devil—avoid it if you care about your immortal soul.

Grimacing, he stands, opens the casket, and invites me to look inside.

—My calculating machine, he frowns. I regret the day I constructed the cursed thing. But I was young at the time, seventeen or eighteen, flushed with pride and confidence. Beware, Evariste! Youth is the devil's domain. Now I can't help asking myself what good lies in these cogs, spindles, numbered dials. Does the machine make us more tolerant of each other? Does it in any way promote the spirit of the Gospels? Does it bring us closer to God? No, Evariste. It facilitates the proliferation of commodities and the calculation of profits, thereby separating man from nature, man from man, man from God. I fear that in time to come this machine will spawn countless others. They will manipulate a million digits in a millionth of a second, take the drudgery from all kinds of work, make life more comfortable and man master of the earth, push back the limits of knowledge, and through this, bring about a kind of paradise on earth.

—Where is the harm in this, you ask? Surely, you're thinking, if through this machine even one child's sight is restored, then it will have more than justified its existence. We shouldn't be deceived, Evariste. The devil cogitates behind appearances, working through the machine, seducing souls by its apparent magic. Despite its virtuosity, its ability to outdo the mind in certain things, the machine will always lack a soul, and it's precisely this deficiency that drives it to seduce the souls of others. I haven't got a soul, it whispers beneath each calculation, therefore I'll make others lose theirs, and I'll be the god of the soulless. And so it will lead humanity to perdition.

—Is that you, Blaise? I ask.

He nods, head barely moving, stringy hair slipping from his shoulders. He closes the casket and lays the book on it. Careful not to spill any ash, I take a few hesitant steps toward him.

—Why, Blaise? You could have been one of the greatest mathematicians of all time. You would have discovered the calculus before Newton—you were so close in your article "Treatise on the Sines of a Quadrant of a Circle." Why did you renounce your genius?

Pascal unbuttons his vest, unstitches the lining that has been crookedly sewn, and takes out a scrap of parchment, which he slowly unfolds and reads aloud.

— The year of grace 1654. Monday, 23 November. Eve of Saint Chrysogonus, Martyr, and others. From half past ten to half past midnight. Fire. Certainty, certainty. Heartfelt joy. Peace. God of Jesus Christ. The world renounced, and everything except God. I have cut myself off from Him. Let me never be cut off from Him again. Sweet and total renunciation. Everlasting joy as recompense for one day's effort on earth. Amen.

Carefully keeping to the same creases, he quarters the crackling sheet and slips it back into the lining.

— I thought I was serving absolute truth, he says, picking up the book and embracing it with both arms. I lived and breathed mathematics. My mind glowed white-hot. I couldn't imagine an experience more intense than that of mathematical discovery. But I was mistaken, Evariste, led astray by pride and vanity. Those two hours that November night opened my eyes, and I not only saw the truth but experienced it, felt it with my entire being, as though I were enveloped by wings of fire, but a fire that didn't burn, that was pure light. And when the wings released me, what I had considered the truth paled into insignificance. The physical world, my books, Blaise Pascal—all of that dissolved in those two hours, and I was filled with inexhaustible faith, with a truth that satisfied me fully, that felt like overwhelming love. I felt complete, Evariste. How can I put it to you? In those two hours it was as if I had proved Fermat's conjecture, solved all possible equations, found the ultimate prime, followed numbers to the end and returned to zero. But even that cannot convey the sense of completeness and peace emanating from submission to Christ, a submission that promises eternal life through the salvation of the soul.

—I know what you're going through at the moment, Evariste. Take my advice: Renounce mathematics before it arouses in you a perverse passion that will sap your youth and destroy your soul. In the end mathematics is nothing more than diversion, a means of keeping the mind from death and God. I may know the properties of all conics, the beauty of all cycloids, the sublime virtues of tautochrones, and yet they are no help when I suffer, when I sink in my own night of Gethsemane.

—Enough! I cry.

Pascal takes a few steps toward me, but stops when I extend the shovel.

—I'll never renounce mathematics!

He stares at me for a moment, then turns, sits on the casket, opens the book, and reads. Sprinkling ash from the shovel, I enclose the hunched figure in a powdery equilateral triangle. With the shovel on my shoulder I turn to go, but the shovel becomes so heavy I am unable to take another step.

—Here on such an afternoon? asks the librarian.

Springing to my feet, I steady myself on the table as the shelves sway, as though about to bury me in books.

—You ought to be out there, the librarian advises, indicating the courtyard with a thrust of his forefinger.

He picks up Pascal's book, opens it at random, and reads aloud.

—One added to infinity does not increase it at all. In fact the finite is annihilated in the presence of the infinite and becomes pure nothingness. So it is with the human mind before . . .

A headache drives its spike into my temple.

13

I am determined to avoid the family as much as possible this summer vacation. Unlike the winter break, when I was forced to remain indoors and endure their presence, I will use Grandfather's cottage in the almond grove as my retreat. I must solve the general quintic before returning to school. No more excuses! I am over the disappointment of not entering the Polytechnic. I feel well again, my concentration is sharper than ever since that fainting spell a few weeks ago during Greek class. The teacher asked me to read my translation from the *Iliad*. Apart from mathematics, this was the only other subject in which I showed some preparedness to work, and then only because I admired the ancient mathematicians. As I stood and took a breath to commence, the lines of my handwriting became sinusoidal, the windows and blackboard skewed sharply into parallelograms. Suddenly every right-angle, straightedge, plane surface in the classroom became warped, curved, fluid.

When I regained consciousness, I was in the dormitory, and a doctor was listening to my chest through a silver cone.

—Epilepsy? asked Laborie, lips concealed by a mustache that spilled from his nostrils.

111

Shaking his head, the doctor examined inside both my lower eyelashes, felt around my throat and neck, then prodded my ribs with his third finger. Through all this I could barely keep my eyes open.

—A delicate constitution, remarked the doctor. Seems to be suffering from undernourishment.

—But our boys are fed well.

—I'm sure they are.

—He has been thin and sickly since coming here.

—He needs rest, said the doctor, shutting his bag. Make sure he eats, or there's no telling what may become of him.

As their footsteps receded to the door, I decided there and then to stop my asceticism. If I were to serve mathematics, I must strike a compromise between body and mind. Feed the body's bloodhounds so my mind could move in relative freedom.

The lace curtains stir behind Father hunched at his desk, reading my report. I attempt to decipher the lines creasing his face.

—There's room for improvement, he says.

I nod, unable to say a word, yet wanting to talk to him, to feel comfortable in his presence again, to relate to him the way I did before going to Paris. But a chasm of silence seems to have opened between us, and I sense it is widening, not so much from differences of opinion as from our respective inner preoccupations. Even now he lapses into thoughtfulness, twisting the ends of his cravat, tightening its knot.

—And in your final year? He looks up, his question trailing off.

—I plan to study advanced mathematics with Louis Richard.

—Your failure to . . . ?

—I'll enter the Polytechnic next year.

—And the school here? I need your help, Son.

—Mathematics is my life, Father.

—Yes, that's what your report seems to indicate.

Picking up the paper knife, he stands and paces in front of Grandfather's portrait.

—You must be tired, he says. We'll talk later.

As I turn to the door, he calls me back and embraces me with a sad look.

—The Director wrote you were unwell.

—It was nothing, I reply, moved by his concern.

A splinter of light strikes the blade in Father's hand and dazzles me.

—And you, Father? I begin awkwardly. Alfred tells me you're . . .

A flash of anger rekindles the ashen face.

—They'll use anything to destroy me.

He strides to the desk, opens a drawer, takes out a folded sheet, and hands it to me. It contains a few verses of doggerel ridiculing members of the Demante family.

—See what they're circulating!

But he is not addressing me; there is a desperate look in his eyes as though his enemies stand before him.

—And they attribute it to me! Trying to turn your mother's family against me! That Jesuit—he's behind it!

113

Your uncle received the letter anonymously. He was furious. Demanded an explanation or a duel. I assured him I wasn't the author, that some despicable reprobate had used the letterhead of my office and forged my name in order to drive a wedge between the two families. "But, Nicholas, you're known for your satirical rhymed couplets," he shouted, shuffling the sheet in my face. I pointed out that if I had wanted to denigrate him, or anyone else for that matter, I would have done it with more flair and originality than the mischievous hack who wrote that. I have never used iambic tetrameters with feminine rhymes; my couplets are always dactylic hexameters with masculine rhymes. It took another half an hour of prosody to calm him, and even then he left with a crooked grimace.

Father paces the squealing floorboards. I want to help him, but I feel powerless, inadequate in everything except mathematics. He is the only person I really love, and love often demands sacrifices. Should I take up his fight? Hamlet's father! Renounce my interests for his well-being? Mathematics or politics? But I dislike people, groups, crowds. If I throw myself into the chaos of social and political life I will be swept aside, overwhelmed, rendered useless both to Father and myself.

The quintic! That is how I can best help him. Solve the quintic, enter the Polytechnic, bring honor to the Galois name, and, through this, defeat his enemies.

—But not only this, he continues.

The letter rustles in his left hand; in his right, the rotating knife glints whenever it is grazed by the sunlight.

—They're now accusing me of having used public money to reroof our school. People I considered friends are

114

questioning my honesty. I've given them fifteen years of public service, improved the town for everyone, and they turn away from me, believing instead the lies of a serpent-tongued priest.

The breeze parts the curtains and a black butterfly enters the study, stops on the inkpot, and then flies raggedly to Grandfather's portrait, where it disappears in the dark background.

—Gratitude! Fifteen years of unstinting service, and all for nothing . . . for a Jesuit to come along and call me a Freemason, turn my closest friends against me.

As though an inner support suddenly collapses, his shoulders stoop, his head drops, his gaze falls onto the knife's blunt blade.

—I'll help you, Father, I say, my words charged with emotion.

—There's no telling how things are going to develop, Son. Whatever happens, I want you to know I have always acted honestly, guided by a sense of justice and equality.

—I know.

In the space of a few seconds I am firstly alarmed, then surprised, finally almost overcome by sentiment. Father wipes his eyes, walks toward me with open arms, and embraces me affectionately, as he used to do when I was a child, before departing on those trips that took him away for weeks. Over his shoulder, I notice the butterfly shuddering over the star-shaped decoration pinned to Grandfather's lapel.

The next few days pass quietly, with each member of the family absorbed by their own concerns. Even at mealtimes, there is more clatter than conversation, and whatever is said is either strained or superficial. I do my best to avoid Mother, though the pronounced arc of her dark eyebrows intimates that she is determined to talk to me. Nathalie is preoccupied with fashion and her fiancé. As for Alfred, he shies away from me, or meets me with a scowl, hurt not only by the fact that I will not help him get to Paris, but also by what he considers my deliberate silence on political matters, for he is certain I am a member of a secret student group with Republican and revolutionary ideals.

Grandfather's cottage is perfect. Satchel packed with paper, ink, and a few texts, I am about to set out for an afternoon of intense work on the quintic, when Nathalie calls me into the dining room, where she is setting cups and saucers on the table. Her fiancé is due shortly, and she would like us to meet. As there is nobody else in the house, I observe propriety and nod, though inwardly chafing at the imposition.

A sharp knock at the door prods Nathalie from the table. She directs me to the chair beside the clock, examines herself in the mirror, skewers a mischievous curl with a long pin, and skips from the room with a sprightly step. She is happy and in love, I reflect, staring at a blaze of roses set in the fireplace.

Happiness? Love? Will I ever fall in love? Will I ever be happy? When was I last happy? I have not been happy in four years at Louis-le-Grand; will I find happiness at the Polytechnic? It will be a different happiness from Nathalie's, a happiness reserved for the few, arising from the beauty and truth of mathematics. And love? No, I will never fall in love with a woman. What is love, anyway?

Why is it given such prominence in literature, opera, art? It is nothing more than an elaborate game disguising the instinct to procreate or a transformation of that instinct into refined sensuality. Love is for those who are unable to be passionate about ideas, whose life is either a burden or filled with boredom. The few with a higher calling are not deceived by flesh's transience: Their love and happiness spring from eternal ideas.

Cheeks flushed, Nathalie introduces her fiancé and goes to make coffee. A robust fellow, with a yellow vest and dark blue coat, he sits opposite me and crosses his thick thighs. I focus on the knots in his laces. How long will this ordeal last?

—Nathalie tells me you're studying in Paris, he says, preening a triangular muttonchop.

—Mathematics.

—Can you make a living from it?

—I live for it.

—Here's one for you, he grins. What's the sum of the first hundred numbers?

I am in no mood for party tricks. It is obvious he has never opened a textbook, and here he is, trying to be a know-it-all. Ignoring his question, I stare at the room swaying in the clock's silver disk.

—5050, he declares, beaming with delight, tapping the floor with the heel of his fashionable boot.

I am about to retaliate with a question on advanced algebra when Nathalie returns. They try drawing me into their gossip, but I resent their patronizing manner, and become surly and abrupt with my replies. Nathalie casts a few pointed looks in my direction, but they soon take the hint and ignore me. They are both happy and in love. What exactly do they see in each other that makes them happy? Their conversation is nothing but meaningless gossip, and yet they carry on as though it is of the utmost importance. No! I will never fall in love, never waste time courting a woman.

The sky grazed red by the setting sun, I return from the cottage feeling buoyant at having made definite progress toward solving the quintic. As my footsteps crunch the gravel path leading to the house, I notice Mother reading on a bench under an oak tree. Wanting to avoid a sermon sure to dampen my spirits, I turn from the gravel onto the recently scythed grass, and head for the back of the house.

—Evariste!

I walk on, acting as though I have not heard, but when she calls again, this time with a sharp edge to her voice, I turn, feign surprise, and crunch toward her.

—We haven't said two words to each other since you've been back, she says, with a hurt expression.

The Bible is open, facedown on her lap.

—Sit down for a moment.

—I've got work to do, I say, shaking my satchel.

—Sit down, she almost whispers.

Using an oak leaf as a bookmark, she closes the Bible. I sit on the edge and cross my arms. A crow calls from the depths of the tree.

—You're spending a lot of time away from the house.

—I'm on the verge of an important result.

—Where do you go?

—Places I'm able to concentrate.

—That doesn't reflect well on the household.

A peasant shambles past with a number of rabbits dangling from a pole balanced on his shoulder.

—Do you want anything else? I ask abruptly.

—My son, she snaps. I want the kind, caring boy who used to love his mother.

—There's no place for love in my life.

—Please, Evariste. We're going through hard times. We need your help and support. Your father isn't well. He imagines he's being persecuted, sees a priest in every shadow, and accuses me of conspiring with his political opponents to bring about his downfall. Please speak to him, Evariste, he won't listen to anyone else. Tell him not to fight the Church; tell him that our ultimate salvation is through Christ, not false prophets like Napoleon.

—My savior's neither Christ nor Napoleon, I say, springing up. I believe in Descartes.

—Evariste! Come back!

But my footsteps are already chuckling over the gravel.

A week before my return to school, I am in the town square on my way to the cottage. It is a broad, blue morning, and I am not distracted by domestic problems, nor the dismal prospect of school, nor that restlessness which creeps upon me from time to time. Today, walking resolutely through the commotion, I am in one of those expansive, receptive states of mind. Mathematics is in everything around me.

Watching a group of men shaking hands, I see at once how many handshakes are possible. I am certain that the

119

order underlying the experience precedes not just the flesh but the physical world. It is an order that holds equally for the joining of people and the combinations of elements. And if four billion hands were to shake? The order would hold, rising miraculously above the laws of nature, which of course preclude such an event. But this is what gives mathematics its supernatural quality: It is able to grasp this transcendent order and express it in terms of a few symbols and equations.

—Seventeen! cries a toothless old vendor, pouring a scoopful of onions into a woman's waiting bag.

The cry echoes in my ears. The number or the word: Which came first? In the beginning was the Word, and the Word was God. Yes, but God is also the indivisible One, from which it follows that number is the source of creation. Take it from the other end: God is infinite. How, then, can His infinite nature best be grasped? All the alphabets that have ever seen, or will see, the human eye, all of them, if taken to the limit of each language, would still generate only a finite number of words, grammars, syntaxes; therefore, there will always be a substantial part of God beyond the grasp of words. Numbers, on the other hand, are infinite, and so of the very essence of God. When one considers the real numbers—let alone the imaginary, the transcendental, and all those yet to be discovered—when one groups them into naturals, integers, rationals, irrationals, when one sees that each group is infinite, and not only this, but that there are as many multiples of ten as there are natural numbers, and that between the natural numbers two and three there is an infinite number of rationals, and that between two rationals there is an irrational consisting of an infinite number of decimal places, then one must acknowledge that numbers are the essence of God, for where else can they all be contained but in the mind of God? Yes, language and words can say "from one to infinity," but if language were to attempt to name every natural number, if it coined new prefixes for illions, and proposed new words for countless zeros, it would eventually exhaust itself and fall silent behind the great forward rush of numbers.

I walk briskly out of town, turn off the main road, and take a dusty uphill path between vineyards heavy with grapes. Stopping on the crest, I admire the different-colored plots which quilt the plain surrounding the town. What is the least number of colors needed so that two plots with a common boundary do not have the same color? Does it depend on the number of plots? The answer leaps at me: four, irrespective of how many plots. But how do I prove something grasped by intuition?

Here and there smoke rises leisurely from stubble-burning. A river slithers through the countryside. The steeples of Paris are just visible on the hazy horizon. I follow the path into a valley, across a creek trickling over smooth rocks to the gentle slope on the other side, where a stone wall surrounds a cluster of almond trees. I shuffle through the thick shade, smile at the scarecrow's ragged greeting, and stride through to the cottage crouching in the far corner of the enclosure. We used to have family picnics here in my childhood. This place was Grandfather's pride and joy. The grass was always scythed in summer, the walls and cottage were whitewashed, even the scarecrow was given a new outfit each spring. But once Grandfather died the picnics and outings stopped and the place was not given the same care and attention.

Birds scatter past me as I enter. Light and shade pattern the small room as I push back the shutters. Placing my satchel on the stout table, I take out my books and writing equipment and bow to work on the quintic. Unlike the other problems on which I have tested my talent, but which proved beyond me, the quintic is difficult yet accessible. It is a labyrinth: a maze of tortuous routes, dilemmas, paths that lead to absurdity, paradox, dead ends. But within this maze of possibilities I have managed to find a few paths which seem promising. I am sure one of these paths will lead to the solution. Now I follow a path suggested by Lagrange, my pen twitching, scratching, struggling to keep up with my thoughts driven by the force of an irresistible logic.

At one point, distracted by the shadow of my hand on the page, I look out of the window across to the other side of the valley, where the vineyard shimmers under the midday sun. Numbers and nature. Natural numbers. 1, 2, 3 . . . There is nothing else in nature. No negatives, no fractions, no irrationals. Nature provides bread and wine, while numbers provide . . . a means of harnessing nature? They make it predictable, subject it to man's will. Perhaps when Pascal's calculating machine becomes more advanced, when it is able to perform a million calculations in a millionth of a second, then nature might be described by a system of equations, by the Grand Equation, which will predict everything from the death of stars to the fall of a vine leaf. And if I can find the solution to the quintic it would be an important step toward the Grand Equation.

A small finch on the scarecrow's sloping shoulder trills piercingly. The symbols on the page draw me into their timeless logic once again, and I move effortlessly along a promising path, one that appears to lead toward the center and the solution.

It is midafternoon when I look up, and cicadas are crackling around the cottage. In a bare patch between two vineyards a painter has set up an easel, and it appears he is painting the grove. He will probably include the cottage. And when the painting hangs in some museum or dining room and people admire the landscape, a few will point to the cottage, not knowing that Evariste Galois was inside, working on the quintic.

And how does the painter compare with the mathematician? The painter's colors are derived from nature, and being natural things they prevent him from transcending nature. The same with the musician's instruments. And the poet's words? They are once removed from nature when read aloud, perhaps twice removed when read in silence. In contrast, the mathematician's signs and symbols are no longer connected to the physical world, and in this they are almost spiritual entities. In the ethereal x a mathematician possesses angel's wings, with which he can soar above the earth and grasp it from a height denied the painter, the poet, the pianist.

My heart is now beating faster than usual. No longer Evariste Galois, I am impersonal, at one with the eternal mind responsible for mathematics, impelled forward to discover the mystery at the center of the labyrinth. But just as the solution is within reach, I am distracted by the scent of chamomile. A woman is standing in the corner, barefooted, holding a basket with flowers and herbs. The gypsy on the steps of the church! I notice the symbols on her forearms. The golden light slanting in through the windows touches her bare shoulders and arms. A breeze blows her thin dress against her thighs. She is here to distract me from the solution! She glides to the front of the table, her shadow covering me and the page. I see her in the inkpot's black pupil. I dip the pen, shatter her image, and scratch frenziedly.

—I am the body of mathematics, she says.

But suddenly I am at the center, and there is no sign of her, only the solution. It is there, glowing in perfection, beautiful, eternal.

14

There was no gypsy, only the lengthening shadow of an almond tree and the scent of chamomile. When I grasped the fact that I had solved the quintic, I gathered my things in the satchel, closed the shutters, and leaped out into the evening spread with a blazing banner. I ran through the grove, past the spot where the painter had been, to the top of the hill, where I stopped to catch my breath. In the distance Paris was burning, and flocks of jackdaws cried toward it from all directions.

For the next three days I kept the pages with the solution in my breast pocket, next to my heart beating stronger than before. The solution transformed me. I now walked more upright, light-footed, and met without flinching the smug looks of those fashionable young men who pursued wealth, positions in society, marriages that would provide a substantial dowry. They could have it all! I possessed something that neither wealth nor power could ever grant—genius.

Walking through the town square, I would sometimes slip my hand in my pocket and feel the textured pages, and this was enough to vanquish the coquettish smiles of young women strolling past. Other times, the mere rustle of the pages in glancing over my shoulder would be enough to silence the bells tolling above me, or reduce the church's stony solemnity to a breeze. I envied nobody in town: not the handsome fellows arm in arm with their ladies, nor the cavalrymen riding imperiously through the square, nor the ruddy, robust peasants whistling after a day in the fields. I had my passport to the Polytechnic, publication, posterity.

A week after the discovery I approached Father sitting thoughtfully in the oak's thick shade. Despite the sound of my steps, he did not look up until I stood over him, and then with a heaviness in his eyes, barely raising his head.

—I'm leaving the day after tomorrow, I said.

—Are the holidays already over? he asked dully.

There was a long crease along the side of his neck as he turned toward me. He was aging before my very eyes.

—What's today? Sunday? Monday? he asked.

My reply faltered, as though caught on something sharp.

—See the state I'm in, he smiled weakly. Can't even keep track of the days anymore.

He brushed a few crisp leaves from the marble bench and moved aside for me. I sat in his warmth, and felt the pages when I crossed my arms.

—Have you thought about things?

I nodded.

—Friends are questioning my integrity and your mother's siding with the priest. Help me, Son.

His head fell forward, and it seemed he would have collapsed but for his elbows resting on his knees.

—Mathematics is my life, Father.

—Mathematics, he echoed.

126

I had never heard the word said like that, with so much anguish. For the first time it seemed to arise from a dark well, not a circle of light. Mathematics has nothing to do with suffering, I told myself, trying to overcome the unsettling effects of the word as Father said it.

—Look, I said, taking out the pages. I'm going to become a great mathematician. I've discovered the solution of a problem that has eluded mathematicians for hundreds of years.

—They're closing in on me, Evariste.

I gripped his thin wrist.

—No, Father, I'll help you! But only through mathematics. Without it, I'm nothing.

Straightening up, he looked at me sadly, searchingly. Mother appeared on the veranda and flapped a tablecloth. After deftly folding and smoothing it, she stared in our direction for a moment and went back inside.

—Do what you must, he said.

—I'll dedicate my work to you, I exclaimed, turning to face him. Your enemies won't slander you when I enter the Polytechnic. The name Galois will take its place beside Pascal.

I knew from his pensive nod that he had not understood my passion; perhaps he mistook my sentiments for youthful exuberance. I did not think less of him for that: If anything, it would spur me on to prove myself to him.

Clouds have brooded over the town all afternoon, and now the smell of an approaching storm spices the air. There is a faint knock on the door as I pack for tomorrow's return to Paris. Thunder rumbles in the distance. I walk toward

Father's winter overcoat which has been hanging from the door hook all summer. Mother enters with a pile of pressed clothes.

—I'll pack these for you, she says.

—There's no need to . . .

—You'll wrinkle them, she insists, going to my bag on the bed.

I stand at the open window. Stubble-burning adds to the sultriness. Alfred strolls away from the house, eating a fleshy fig oozing milkiness. Nathalie and her fiancé are chatting under the oak. The pages in my pocket shuffle as I lean forward to examine a line of ants crawling along the sill.

—You had a good talk with your father yesterday.

—We discussed a few things.

—He's making things very difficult for everyone, she says, buttoning one of my shirt collars.

—It's the priest's fault, I reply, breaking the ant's line with a flick of my finger.

—Look at me, Evariste.

I turn reluctantly, glancing at her reflection in an oval mirror on the dressing table, then fixing my attention on Father's overcoat.

—The priest may be a little overzealous at times, but he is not to blame for your father's state of mind.

—Are you supporting him?

She steps toward me, pressing one of my starched shirts to her breast.

—Your father has turned from God, she glares. Paris! The new Babylon! The haunt of the Evil One! The source of atheism! I fear the Apocalypse is at hand. The signs are there: crime, debauchery, chaos! Don't go back, Evariste. Stay here and help me lead your father back to God. I know he was never one for the Church, but he never opposed it; he was never an atheist. I don't know what will become of him if he persists with his terrible antagonism toward the priest.

—His struggle is my struggle, I reply, snatching the shirt from her embrace. I'm going to help him, not with your Bible, but with this.

I rustle the pages in her face.

—Evariste!

The lamp's glass beads tinkle as thunder grumbles over the house.

—Mathematics, Mother! That's the new Testament, the true Revelation, the way of redemption!

I feel a jab of compunction at the effects of my words, but I urge myself not to succumb to her eyes, now brimming with sadness. She has taught me the Gospel well. I recall how, as a child, I would listen to her modulated voice reading the parables, the miracles, the Passion. Sometimes I would imagine myself one of the disciples, the one who had not fallen asleep in the olive grove, who had not denied the Master, who was martyred for his faith. I would have been no more than ten or eleven when I tested myself by staying awake all night, imagining the world would be devoured by darkness if I fell asleep. Yes, I remembered the Gospel well. Was I treating her harshly? Was I being cruel? But the spirit of mathematics demanded aloofness, as did the spirit of Christianity. After all, when Christ became aware of his higher mission, he spurned his mother at Cana. When the wine had been consumed and she had asked him to perform what was to be his first miracle, he rebuked her with the words, "Woman, what have you got to do with me?" I had my mission in life too, and the spirit of mathematics said, "If you would follow me, deny maternal sentiment." If many were called and few chosen for heaven, few were called and only a fraction were chosen to glimpse not just the face of God, but His very mind.

—Paris has corrupted you, Evariste, my mother said in a restrained voice. It's as I feared. Just as the stench of that place permeates your clothes, liberal ideas have polluted your mind.

—I'm not interested in liberal ideas! I'm a mathematician. I'm going to enter the Polytechnic.

—Stay here, Evariste. Help me, help your father, help Alfred, whose mind is also being poisoned by politics.

—My future is there.

—And your soul? Have you forgotten that?

—I've found salvation in another cross.

—Another cross!

Boulders roll above us, the curtains billow.

—The cross of mathematics, I reply sharply.

—Evariste! she flares, twisting her wedding ring.

I am deliberately provoking her, almost enjoying the effects of my barbed words.

—It's the religion of the future.

—Don't say such things!

—Mathematics will give me eternal life.

—Stop it!

—The old religions have divided mankind, Mother. What good has come from the god of Moses? It's time to break the old tablets, forget the old commandments, and live according to postulates, theorems, proofs.

She stares at me for a moment, speechless, then turns abruptly and leaves. As she pulls the door after her, Father's overcoat slips from the hook and falls in a heap. I pick it up, consider it for a while, then put it on. Standing before the mirror, I observe that the padded shoulders are too wide, the body too loose and long. I recall measuring my height relative to the buttons and asking whether I would grow to be as tall as he. And now, at almost seventeen, I realize that I will never fill this overcoat. Reaching into the right pocket, I find a piece of paper folded carefully in thirds, then in half.

My initial curiosity checked by a sense of propriety, I place it on the table and deliberate whether to read it. Suddenly a squall sweeps aside the curtains and blows the note to my feet. The note is in Father's handwriting. Addressed to Mother! I look up for an instant. A small effeminate face with arching eyebrows returns my look from the mirror. Mother's name is followed by two short lines saying he must leave at once for Paris on urgent business. Nothing more.

Why such an abrupt end? And why the two diagonal lines through the message? Am I making too much of it? Perhaps something had come up that prevented him from going, and he simply dropped the note in his pocket instead of the fireplace. I replace the overcoat on the hook.

Lightning scourges the church steeple. Rain lashes the town. I lie on the bed and feel the pages in my breast pocket, reassuring myself of my significance in the midst of the storm. But the overcoat hanging crookedly fills me with sadness. Thunder groans, as though God is wounded and dying.

I suddenly feel helpless, as though I were going to be scattered like the leaves of our oak. By reflex, as some reach for a cross or talisman in a moment of crisis, I pull out the solution and spring to the table. I have not looked at it since the afternoon of its discovery, and now, reading the first page intently, I am surprised by the leap of my thoughts. The storm might destroy the town, but not the solution. My anxiety abates with the certainty of each mathematical step, and by the second page I read calmly, though at times barely able to make out my own writing, so swift had been my thoughts on that wonderful afternoon.

A line in the middle of the second page trips me. I read it a second time, a third. It does not seem right! I read it a few more times, extract the thought behind the symbols, the assumption behind the thought. I sit upright, stunned. The conjecture is clearly wrong! The false assumption based on my intuition has flawed the entire work. My solution to the quintic is no solution at all. My genius is at best mediocrity, at worst unfounded conceit. I stare dumbly at the overcoat. A roll of thunder shakes the lamp on the table as I scratch a thick black line through the mistake and, head in hands, gaze at the proof of my failure.

—All is vanity and a striving after wind, a voice whispers from my left.

Pascal is leaning on the windowsill.

—Love's the only truth, a voice sings from his right.

The gypsy is sitting on the edge of the bed.

—Fold the pages, says Pascal. Stitch them in the lining

of your jacket, carry them as a reminder of the fallibility of the human mind.

— Burn them, laughs the gypsy. Youth needs flesh.

— Think of your soul, Pascal implores.

— Be happy, smiles the gypsy.

15

Musty autumn light fills the dormitory, down to the depths of the stove whose sooty mouth has been left open during the vacation. Students are talking excitedly in small groups, unpacking, lying with hands behind heads, thoughtful at the prospect of bells, lessons, discipline. I am tapped on the shoulder while putting away a few shirts in a side cupboard.

— How was your break, Galois?

I ignore the suntanned face whose ingratiating smile is friendly as an undertaker's smile. I am in no mood for conversation — the pages in my breast pocket are still like a marble slab over my heart. Besides, I know what he wants. He approached me in the corridor after that exchange with the teacher of Religion. My ideas impressed him. He asked me to attend a talk that would be given by Blanqui, a leader of an organization whose aim was to destroy not only the Church and the monarchy, but every other social institution. I walked off without a word.

— Have you thought about our chat? he asks, sitting on my bed and cracking his knuckles.

— I take out a pair of boots which have been recently resoled and breathe in the smell of new leather.

— Things are moving quickly.

—Get off my bed.

—The Revolution's not far off, Galois. You'd better join us anarchists while there's still time, or when the new Republic rises from the monarchy's ruins we might say you weren't for it.

—You're in my way.

—Watch out, Galois! he snarls, breath heavy with onions. That superior attitude will get you in trouble!

Finally, after a summer of quiet expectation, I sit with fifteen others in Louis Richard's advanced mathematics class. The room is small, with a makeshift blackboard mounted on an easel, and windows high up in the walls. I have heard a lot about Richard. It is said he is an excellent teacher, passionate about his subject, and that he presents his material with originality, preparing his own notes instead of relying on textbooks. His ability is reflected in the number of students who have gone on to study at the Polytechnic. They say he subscribes to French, German, and Italian mathematical journals, keenly following the latest discoveries in order to make his subject more relevant. More important, I have also heard that he has an eye for talent, and that once he spots it in a student he does his utmost to nurture and develop it.

—Why do I teach mathematics? Richard asks, with a frankness that surprises me. Realizing early that I would never be a creative mathematician, I set my mind to becoming a creator of mathematicians.

He chuckles and scans the room with lively, appraising eyes. Short, stocky, probably in his mid-thirties, with receding sandy hair that accentuates his broad forehead, he could pass for a tradesman. As our looks meet momentarily, my heart kicks against the pages with the mistaken solution. What was that glint in his green eyes? Does it signify anything? Can he tell from the look in my eyes that I have talent?

He proceeds to ask each student their surname and reason for studying mathematics, making notes along the way.

— Bravais, says the student next to me. I want to become an industrial chemist. I want to serve society and ease the burden of the worker. I believe that mathematics is important in understanding chemical behavior.

I feel a tightness in my throat. I want to make a good first impression on Richard, but a rush of blood scatters my thoughts. My voice cracks as I say my name, and I swallow the second syllable. Feet shuffle, chairs creak, glances dart around the room.

— And why are you in this class, Galois?

Chairs creak, glances dart around the room, feet shuffle.

— To solve the quintic, I stammer.

Glances dart around the room, feet shuffle, chairs creak. I know they are waiting for a sarcastic remark from Richard, the sort the Rhetoric teacher often made, to which they responded with stupid, forced laughter. Walking around the table, Richard nods for me to sit down, and, standing beside me, places a hand on my shoulder. My face looks up from the bottom of the inkpot.

— A proper study of this course should begin with the recognition that mathematics, more precisely pure mathematics, aims for nothing other than its own unfolding and advancement. While Bravais is to be commended for his desire to improve the human condition, we must not lose sight of the fact that social and material progress are incidental to genuine mathematical inquiry. I cannot convey the spirit of this inquiry any better than to repeat Galois's answer: to solve the quintic.

After the lesson I wait in an inclined shaft of light as Richard erases the blackboard, reducing to dust the list of topics for study. Order and chaos, I think, as the word *geometry* is swept away, reduced in an instant to minute particles swirling in the light. He turns, claps a few times, and brushes his sleeves with the back of his hands.

—Dust to dust, he smiles. That's the body's fate, but ideas are eternal. If all the equilateral triangles were suddenly obliterated from the world, the equilateral triangle would be restored to its ideal state.

Rubbing his palms, he probes me with a searching look and asks my given name. I tell him, but instead of looking aside or down, as I usually do in these situations, I meet his look, see myself in his pupils, wonder whether he has already glimpsed signs of my talent.

—How much do you know about the quintic, Evariste?

I explain that I have been interested in it for the last six months. There is a fine sprinkling of chalk dust on his polished shoes.

—And what if it cannot be solved? he asks.

Should I? Overcoming a fear of exposing myself, I take the pages from my pocket and unfold them on the table.

—I thought this was the solution.

137

After a moment's consideration, Richard picks them up and reads, nodding and humming, his brow creasing and uncreasing. Suddenly I feel vulnerable at having disclosed my innermost thoughts to a stranger. Will he, the most knowledgeable mathematician I know, see talent in my failed attempt, or will he dismiss it as nonsense? I struggle to subdue a rising apprehension by concentrating on the sunlit blackboard, trying to grasp the faint remnants of letters and symbols. Some letters are still discernible; others, due to superimposition, have coupled to create the characters of a new alphabet; while conjunctions of letters and numbers produce the symbols of a new mathematics. Perhaps that coupling of the letters e and s might be a character in a future alphabet, denoting a sound not yet in existence, or even a word in a language still to evolve. Perhaps that conjunction of the letter x and the number 1 might be a cipher denoting at present an entire page of thought.

As he turns to the second page, the one with the mistake, I wait for his judgment, heart jabbing against my folded arms. His face suddenly becomes less intense and a smile seems to be tugging at the corners of his mouth. He is laughing at my mistake, I think, clenching my fists. I should not have shown it to him! I should have kept it to myself, worked in silence until I found the solution. The smile stretches to a grin. I snatch the pages and dash out, ignoring his call.

Serves you right, I chastise myself, leaning against the chapel wall. Don't ever show your work to another teacher.

It is lunchtime and the courtyard is empty. Three sparrows are quarreling with a crow over a crust. A few stray maple leaves are scurrying about in circles in a corner with steps leading down to a basement. Smoke swirls from the kitchen's chimney. The smell of cooking and coal mingles in the breeze.

Hungry? You don't deserve to eat! Fool! What drove you to show him? Conceit! And your Pythagorean ideals? Your resolve to live according to lofty laws of mathematics? Richard! What is so important about his opinion anyway? He is nothing more than a teacher . . . someone lacking the ability to be a real mathematician. Eyes closed, head resting against the wall, face to the sun, I see colors changing from white to pink to fiery red, and I imagine myself a martyr of the new faith—one who has given his eyes for the new cross.

16

I have been in the library for the past hour, absorbed by Lagrange's book on the solution of polynomial equations. Two other students are in here with me, studying diligently: the conscientious Bravais, who has, no doubt, come to learn something about the quintic; and Lanon, who is considered a precocious poet, with a gift for creating original metaphors. The Rhetoric teacher read one of his poems last term, commented on its striking imagery drawn from city life, and praised him as a future Hugo. Have your moment of glory, I thought at the time.

Poetry is rooted not only in the present, but in a given language, so that it dates quickly, making translation impossible. And even if ours is the most refined language, capable of the clearest, the most rhythmic poetry, it is also constantly changing, so that a poem by Villon does not have the same appeal now that it had three hundred years ago.

Lanon can keep his poetry. His laurel wreath will quickly fade. Mathematics, however, is rooted in eternity. Poetry represents the world as a shimmering reflection in a moving stream, whereas mathematics shows it as a diamond in a showcase. First there was the priest, then the poet, but they were only precursors to the pure mathematician.

A student romps in and, ignoring the librarian's admonishing look, marches straight to me. Breathing heavily, he says that Richard wants to see me in his room at once, and races out before I am able to get anything more from him.

On the front steps of the resident teachers' quarters, I caution myself on the need for restraint. Richard must not get the better of me. When my tentative knock is answered with an expansive, friendly welcome, I enter with misgivings. What is his game? Is this show of cordiality intended to increase the impact of his disciplinary measures? He invites me to sit in an armchair and asks if I would like a cup of rose hip tea, adding that it is good for the digestive system. Not waiting for a reply, he shuffles off in a pair of Persian slippers. My suspicion is slightly allayed by the mathematical material in the room: books, journals, manuscripts, busts, lithographs, artefacts, astronomical instruments. When he returns rattling a tray with cups and a teapot, I feel more at ease, as though suddenly finding myself in familiar territory.

—Why did you rush out like that this morning? he asks, extending a jittery cup.

—You were laughing at my mistake.

And as I look down at my image in the steaming, reddish tea, it occurs to me that my very being is evaporating and dispersing in thought.

—I did nothing of the sort, he smiles. On the contrary, I was impressed by your work; it shows real talent.

The cup and saucer chatter in my hands.

—And my mistake?

—I'm forever receiving letters from people claiming

141

they have proved Fermat's Last Theorem. Most of it is sheer nonsense, and the authors are so ignorant of mathematics they fail to see blatant flaws in their reasoning. In your case, Evariste, I was impressed not only by your attempt at the quintic, but by the fact you discovered your mistake.

He picks up an abacus with Chinese characters and flicks the amber counters.

—Have you heard of Abel, Niels Henrik Abel? he asks, settling back in the armchair. No? He's a young Norwegian mathematician, must be twenty-five or -six now. I met him two years ago, when he visited Paris. A very shy, modest fellow, extremely frail, and he had a hacking cough. Fascinated by him, I subsequently learned that Abel was sixteen when he discovered his aptitude for mathematics. His talent was first recognized by his teacher Holmboë, who suggested he read, among other things, Lagrange's work on equations and Gauss's *Disquisitiones Arithmeticae*. His father died when Abel was eighteen, and the burden of providing for a large family fell on his shoulders. To his credit, he took on the responsibility without complaint, offered tuition to private students, and pursued his own research at every opportunity. During these difficult years he was sustained by the hope that his talent would be recognized, and that he would be offered a teaching position at some university. But nothing of the sort eventuated. As things became more desperate Holmboë was always there to help and encourage him. He arranged subsidies for Abel, and, when they were no longer available, provided financial support from his own pocket.

142

Is this the reason Richard has called me to his room? Has he seen the talent in my flawed attempt at the quintic? Does he want to play the same role in my life as Holmboë has in Abel's?

Richard blows gently on his tea, takes a few sips, and continues in an even tone, as though measuring each word. Abel was about my age when he tackled the quintic. Like me, he also thought he had found the solution, only to discover a few days later that he was mistaken. Yes, he was no doubt crushed by his mistake, but only temporarily, for he quickly resumed his work, intensifying his attack. This time, instead of a solution, his efforts led to a brick wall. Was the wall something of his own making? Did it arise from faulty reasoning? Did the solution lie on the other side? And then, in what must have been a flash of inspiration, he accepted the objective reality of the wall, accepted there was no solution on the other side, and, doing an about-face, set out to prove that the quintic could not be solved by radicals. The new direction allowed his genius to emerge: In a burst of brilliance, he verified his conjecture using a proof by contradiction.

The room sways around me, as though about to collapse.

— The proof is an absolute gem, says Richard, nodding emphatically.

No solution! I have devoted the last six months to finding a solution, invested my hopes on a solution, based the purpose and meaning of my life on the existence of a solution, and now Richard is sitting back in a faded armchair, clicking counters, telling me that my efforts were doomed to failure from the very start.

—I must see it, I say, placing the rattling cup on the table. Where can I find it?

He reaches for a few handwritten sheets under the tray, saying he was so impressed by the proof that he translated it. My heart quickens. I want to run out to a quiet corner and examine the work. I subdue my impatience and ask if I might borrow the proof.

—The work has lost nothing in translation, and that's not to praise myself as a translator, but to point out the universal nature of mathematics.

I wish he would finish and let me go, instead of prattling about languages being a curse on mankind for aspiring to heaven through the Tower of Babel, and that a new Tower would be built, higher and stronger than the first, and that mankind would be united again, this time by the language of mathematics.

I race through the courtyard filled with a smoky, sooty night, stopping abruptly on the dormitory's steps. Silence is required for a thorough study of the proof. Yes, solitude, above all else. But where will I find it in this place, at this time? Another hour and the lights will be out. This document is too important to wait for tomorrow. I am too excited, too curious. I need a quiet corner tonight. One of the rooms set aside for private study might be empty! As I bound up the stairs, two figures swoop on me from above, blocking the light from the open door.

—You're late, says one.

—Where have you been? asks the other.

—What are you Republicans planning?

—Is that your manifesto?

144

—Let's see your subversive material.

One of the prefects attempts to snatch the rolled pages, but I step back and point out that the material belongs to Richard, and that they will have to answer to him if it is torn. They retreat, whisper to each other, then approach me again.

—Show us!

In the doorway I unroll the pages and hold them out under a hissing lamp. Heads almost touching, the prefects examine the text.

—What's all this?

—It's either my salvation or my damnation, I say, my excitement ignited by what I see on the first page.

—How do we know it's not a manifesto written in code?

—That's exactly what it is, I retort, piqued by their stupidity. These cryptic symbols are plans for a revolution.

Shoulders touching, alarmed, they bow closer to the text, straining to make it out.

—See this line, I say, pointing.

They follow my finger moving across the page.

—It says "Down with the King." And this one, "Away with the Church." And this, "Long live the new order."

—They're subversive words, Galois.

—Only to those ignorant of mathematics.

Slipping from their midst, I run inside and try a few study rooms before finding one that is empty. I sit and place the proof facedown on the table. I close my eyes and cross my fingers on the sheets. Is it just a coincidence that both Abel and I have been drawn to the quintic? Or is the quintic an entity independent of the mind? Has it chosen us for its fulfillment? Wasn't that the case with calculus? When the time was right, weren't both Newton and Leibniz summoned, quite independently, to bring the new theory into the public domain?

As I begin reading, my mind is no longer burdened by flesh, no longer conscious of place, at one with the immutable will of mathematics.

I am astounded by the proof's elegance: Its graceful development, clear and concise language, irrefutable conclusion. No poem can compare with the beauty of this proof. There is always an element of randomness in poetry: One word is chosen over another because it springs first to mind, a comma is used instead of a semicolon, the syntax may be arranged according to one's whims. There is nothing arbitrary in these seven pages! Each line, each symbol, is inextricably tied to everything else. The entire proof would fall apart, become meaningless by the change of a single sign. Here is the unambiguous clarity of a diamond, not the vaporous beauty of a cloud, which is seen as a whale by some and a weasel by others.

Not only admiration, the proof also stirs my envy. How can I go beyond Abel's findings? All right, he proved that the general equation of degree five and higher cannot be solved by radicals, but what about particular quintics? Isn't there a limitation in his proof?

My approach to the problem is different from Abel's: It uses far less algebra and more intuition, together with the theory of groups and subgroups from Lagrange, whose full significance I haven't quite fathomed, though I am sure there is something fundamental in the theory that Lagrange himself did not fully appreciate. Perhaps this is the key that will enable me to surpass Abel. Once I have grasped the subtle relationship between groups and equations, I will be able to propose conditions for determining the solvability of *any* equation. My theory will subsume Abel's work, proving his result with far greater economy and in a new spirit, taking algebra to new heights of abstraction.

The door opens and a teacher darts in, bawls that it is time for lights out, then dashes off down the corridor. I take out my mistaken solution and reach up to the overhead lamp. In an instant the pages curl and crumple in a tight-fisted flame. I drop them in the fireplace and watch them become black flakes. How willingly, with what complete surrender, the pages give themselves to flame, not just the paper, but the very text, as though it is being redeemed from ink, restored to light. The last word to be lifted from the page is my signature, and in the next instant there is nothing but an obliterated black crisp. I feel unburdened, as though the pages were a weight on my chest. Purged of that mistake, with Abel's proof prodding me in a new direction, and having at last found a competent supporter in Richard, I feel optimistic, ready to return to mathematics with new confidence, to embrace it with increased passion.

The burning pages have set my thoughts alight: I am too worked up to sleep. Through the small windows recessed into the slanting roof I can just make out a steeple's silhouette. Sickled, stalking windows, intent on a rich harvest of dreams, the moon appears and disappears through the clouds.

— Dabot? Are you asleep? whispers the student on my right.

His straw mattress rustles when he doesn't receive a reply.

—Galois? Are you asleep?

—What do you want? I ask, but instantly regret having answered him.

—We're going to be neighbors for a whole year.

—It's late.

—We should get to know each other.

Emerging from a veil of clouds, the moon leers into the room from just above the steeple's crossed apex.

—Do you like girls, Galois?

I remain silent.

—Ever been with one?

I attempt to summon Abel's proof.

—I was initiated by a village girl during the holidays. We did it in a cornfield, in broad daylight, with workers all around us. She raised her skirt and tucked it in at the waist, then she leaned forward with her legs apart and her hands on her knees, and she urged me to do it quickly, because the others were getting closer. And once I started, Galois, I couldn't stop. And she kept on saying, "Faster, faster, before they come." I kept pushing and pushing, and suddenly everything dissolved in a golden light and I understood the meaning of the word *paradise*.

The rustling that has accompanied the student's whisper stops. After a low, protracted moan, his breathing slows, becomes heavy, as though he has fallen asleep.

Paradise! I stare at the cross on the apex, sharp against the clear night sky. Paradise, not through life or death, not in a wheat field or in a coffin, but right here and now, through my passion for pure mathematics.

17

Richard congratulates me with a wish for more publications. Having waited months for this news, I reach out tentatively for the slim journal in his hand. Filtered through cobwebbed windows the evening light slants into his apartment, gilding books, pictures, instruments, the enigmatic engraving in which I can now make out a hybrid beast lying curled at the foot of the muse, beside an inkpot, a hammer, a pair of pliers. We sit at a small round table in front of the window. Swallows crisscross the courtyard.

— Page 294, he says, as though sharing my excitement.

Golden light illuminates the title page, bringing out the texture of the paper, the ink's gloss, the indentations of the letters. Beneath the title I read: *By M. Evariste Galois, Student at the College of Louis-le-Grand.*

A log cracked in the fireplace, sharp as a pistol shot, as I entered his apartment three months ago with my first paper. Watery-eyed, nose chafed red, he caught another sneeze with a soggy handkerchief. I had visited him a number of times prior to this, and on each occasion his encouragement had fueled my confidence, so that I left burning with zeal. As he read my work, I gripped the chair's wooden armrest, gazing from one artifact to another, glancing furtively at him in an attempt to judge his reaction.

An engraving of a shadowy figure hung between two dark bookcases. I could just make out the name in the dimness: Mersenne. Everything fell into place at once: the pointed cowl on his back, the emaciated face, the beard and close-cropped hair. A large book under his left arm, Brother Marin Mersenne looked sideways with a mild expression. I envisaged the Franciscan monk walking thoughtfully in a cold cloister. At a time when the Inquisition was defending the faith with fire, Brother Mersenne had managed to reconcile number theory and theology. In his profound investigation of prime numbers, did he believe in the spiritual essence of number? Did he believe that number preceded the word? That numbers were the purest expressions of the mind of God?

Holy primes—maybe there was something mystical about them! Why else had they intrigued the best mathematicians from Pythagoras to the present? I had also been studying primes, in relation to equations whose highest power was a prime number. As the most essential of numbers, did primes permit a glimpse into the mind of God? Not the chaotic, irascible god of Moses, but the Creator of cosmic order.

But how had Mersenne managed to reconcile his vigorous intellect with vows of poverty, chastity, humility? Weren't Christianity and mathematics mutually exclusive, as Pascal had said? Or had Mersenne lived his monastic vows through mathematics? Had he made chastity possible through the love of pure number? Had he accepted poverty as the natural condition of a life dedicated to the unprofitable pursuit of primes? Had humility been evoked by the constant reminder of the infinititude of number? Yes, Brother Mersenne had glimpsed the awesome splendor of number, and this had transformed his sense of pride to a pious wonder. He stated that $2^{257} - 1$ was a prime. It was impossible to write such a number in digits: It would exhaust not only all the ink and paper, but all the time and space in the universe. And yet that number existed as an entity, perhaps in a state beyond time and space.

What had prompted Mersenne to declare it a prime? A guess? Intuition? Perhaps a kind of revelation? Religious prophets were always looking into the future, why not a prophet of mathematics? Was that number a prime? Nobody had been able to say. Maybe in two hundred years' time Pascal's calculating machine might evolve to a stage where it could determine the nature of any number. And if it verified Mersenne's statement? It would prove he possessed insight into the ineffable.

—"A Proof of a Theorem on Periodic Continued Fractions," said Richard, reading the title. I'm impressed, Evariste. You've proved your theorem very concisely, at times perhaps a little too concisely. Still, it shows real talent. If it were up to me I would have you admitted to the Polytechnic on this alone.

I felt like telling him that the theorem was nothing more than a recreational exercise, and that it had come to me in a flash after reading Lagrange's paper on a related topic. I wanted to tell him that it was trivial compared to my researches during the last few months. If he thought this paper was the work of talent, what would he make of the memoir I was presently writing?

—It ought to be published, continued Richard. I know people on the editorial board of Gergonne's mathematical journal. Leave it with me.

As I stood to go, my attention was momentarily caught by a strange engraving reflected in the oval mirror above the fireplace. Reading backward, I managed to make out the word *Melencolia* written on a banner held by a demonic beast flying through a rainbow. Compass in hand, an angel or muse sat with head propped on arm, surrounded by instruments for measuring matter, space, and time. The artist had not broken with tradition: He had invested his figure with feminine characteristics, like the ancient muses. But if this were the muse of mathematics, why a woman? What did women have to do with the spirit of mathematics? And why was the figure so morose? Had it glimpsed the vastness of knowledge? Was it trying to come to terms with π? Or was it pondering the possibilities of the sixteen-celled magic square above its head? In an instant I saw that the numbers in all rows, columns, and diagonals added to thirty-four. The artist was no mathematician, though, or he would have known that the muse of mathematics was never subject to melancholy.

—You have a great deal of talent, Richard said, smothering a sneeze. But you can't rely on talent alone. Work hard, systematically, and, above all, control the impatience of youth. Who knows, you may turn out to be another Abel, though I sincerely hope your work fares better in the hands of our Academy of Sciences.

—What happened to his? I asked.

—When he came to Paris he entrusted Cauchy with a memoir on transcendental functions. Busy with his own

152

work, Cauchy passed it on to Hachette, who in turn presented it to the Academy. Two years have elapsed, and the memoir has yet to be judged by the Academy. Not only this, it seems to have vanished altogether. I've just learned that Abel is living in abject poverty, and that his health is deteriorating. He was diagnosed as having consumption during his stay here. I fear his days are numbered.

—Living in poverty? With his genius? I exclaimed, glancing at the angelic figure sitting dejectedly in the engraving.

—Genius doesn't always provide food on the table.

—Can't they find him a position?

—It appears not, he said, prodding the slumbering fire.

—Not even for his work on the quintic?

His emphatic reply stunned me. Abel must have had the same dreams as I at sixteen, yet, despite his genius, those dreams had turned to nothing and he was now facing the prospect of dying in his youth.

—My interest and encouragement aren't all altruistic, he smiled, crushing a glowing ember with the poker. When you become famous, and biographers record your life and work, I would like posterity to think well of me. People might say: He wasn't an intellect, but he loved mathematics, and he was the first to recognize and nurture Galois's talent.

Was this his sense of humor? Or did he mean it?

—Mathematics, he mused. The great virgin Queen of Science. We must serve her as best we can, Evariste. Some by running around in her courtyard; others by waiting in her antechamber; the chosen few, those with genius, by taking their orders directly from her. The Queen of Science! What will those Republicans make of that metaphor? Those anarchists would do away with all references to royalty, change the game of chess, reduce all the pieces to the status of pawns. Their ideas are infiltrating the school. Stay away from them, Evariste, and concentrate on your work.

The letters of my name in the journal gleam in the sunlight. I have written it countless times, in black, blue, brown, in cursive and in block, on paper and parchment, but it has never impressed me like this. Catching a glimpse of myself in the mirror, I experience a slight disorientation, as though seeing myself in a different light.

The printing press has made you a public figure, Evariste Galois. It has imposed an identity on you, one that will eventually subsume the name you learned to write under your mother's guidance. You are no longer a youth: The press has turned you into a man, placed you among the ranks of mathematicians. Not only this, but by banishing all trace of your personality as expressed in handwriting — from your habit of crossing t with a long stroke, to the fact that your lines aren't always parallel — the press invests the text with a kind of mathematical precision, stamps it with the authority of an absolute truth, grants it a quality that seems to transcend time. Admire your printed name! Your former self has been crushed by the press. A new Evariste Galois has arisen through the regenerative power of ink.

In skimming over the material which looks less familiar now that it is in print, I encounter an error on page 300.

—They've made a mistake, I say. Here: The equation should be $x = 3 + 1/y$, not $x = 3x + 1/y$.

—Printers! exclaims Richard. They know nothing about algebra.

Fools! It is a blot on my work, even though anyone with even a basic knowledge of algebra could tell it was a printing error.

—It could have been worse, he comments, sunlight penetrating his thinning hair as he bows over the journal. They might have misspelled your name, or worse still, mislaid your manuscript.

A small etching of Euler is inclined on the mantelpiece: An old man blinded by cataracts, he squints at posterity. He is not resigned to darkness and death; his active mind does not need the sun in order to see absolute truth. Who knows, it may be that the sun is the greatest obstacle to mathematics, in that it imposes the physical world upon the senses, making abstract thought that much more difficult. It is said Euler was more prolific than ever at the end of his life, dictating his ideas to family members, who could barely keep up with his swift mind. This superhuman productivity may not have been due to the pressure of impending death, but to the fact that Euler, by virtue of his impairment, had dwelled in a state of pure mathematics.

Gliding my fingers over my name, feeling the letters' crisp indentations, I ask Richard if I might keep the journal. He says he will obtain another, and advises me to be patient. Entrance to the Polytechnic is not determined on the basis of talent alone. I should put aside my present research for the next two months and start preparing for the examination. He will help me: He knows the type of questions the examiners put to candidates. I should remember that sometimes we need to take a few steps back in order to leap into the future.

18

As the others leave the classroom stuffy with heat and body odor, Richard calls for me to stay behind. The old janitor shuffles in and starts wiping a detailed geometric proof from the blackboard. Richard's brow glistens with perspiration as he gathers notes scattered over the table.

—It's already the middle of June, he says. How are your preparations for the Polytechnic?

Grinning, or maybe grimacing, the janitor twists a cloth—gray water trickles into a bucket. Mindful of Richard's earlier advice and being careful not to offend him, I tell him that I have been working on a theory of equations. The remnants of a lettered triangle are obliterated by the cloth.

—It's three weeks to the examination, he frowns.

He appears more concerned than me. Does he have such little faith in my ability? I cannot conceal my pride in telling him that I have sent some papers to the Academy: papers he read a month ago and praised for their originality.

—Slow down, Evariste. Your priority should be the Polytechnic. You'll have time to publish once you're there.

Time? I have realized only recently that the awareness of time varies according to a body's excitement. There is one time for the flame, another for the rock. Appreciating his concern, I reply that Cauchy—considered the best mathematician in France—has been appointed referee of my work and I expect to hear from him soon.

—I hope you fare better than Abel, he sighs. By the way, have you heard? The poor fellow died two months ago. He wasn't quite twenty-seven.

Abel, dead! It is as though he were a close friend, someone I have known intimately, with whom I have shared my deepest secrets. The janitor is now on a chair, wiping vigorously.

—Consumption and poverty, says Richard, leaning on the table with his fingertips. A real loss to mathematics. And to think, only a few days after his death his fiancée received a letter that said Abel had been offered a professorship of mathematics at the University of Berlin.

Fiancée? I don't know why this surprises me. Perhaps I imagined Abel a kindred spirit in all matters. I see his skeletal body among the remaining lines on the blackboard.

—I spoke to Jacobi recently, and he's making quite a fuss about Abel's misplaced manuscript. He considers it one of the most important mathematical discoveries of the century. He is pressing the Academy to find it and honor Abel with a posthumous prize. Mathematics! It's full of coincidence. I learned from Jacobi that Cauchy was to referee Abel's work.

—Cauchy was the last to see the manuscript?

—More than likely.

—Surely he didn't misplace it.

—Why not? He's so occupied with his own ideas it's quite possible he left it in a carriage, where it was found by the driver, who tossed it out, only to be picked up by a

157

vendor, who used the pages to make paper cones for roasted chestnuts.

I walk past the janitor standing with arms akimbo, nodding to his shadow on the spotless blackboard.

A few weeks into summer and the heat is already oppressive in the dormitory: Sheets shuffle, beds creak, hands swipe and slap at persistent mosquitoes. The moon appears in the window, full of loot, struggling to make its ascent. I cannot sleep at the thought of Abel's death. I feel so close to him. The quintic has brought us together, overcoming the barriers of distance, language, time, death. It has occupied our deepest thoughts, stirred our most cherished hopes, created a bond between us. More than blood brothers, we are soul mates.

— Ever been to a brothel, Galois? whispers the student next to me.

I silence him by plugging my ears with bits of wool I keep under the pillow. Having spent its gold in rising to the top of the window, the moon is now smaller, lighter, a silver coin. Everything has its price. My thoughts wander, drift, slip away . . . I wake to someone prodding me and the sound of my name muffled by the wool in my ears. Standing above me, a prefect grins in the morning gray. My dream comes to me in a flash. A woman with a conflagration of red hair is calling my name, her bare feet protruding between the balcony's balustrades. I begin climbing a spiral staircase, but then remember that I have an appointment with Abel. Suddenly, there is a deadline to meet. I race across a stone bridge, only to be swallowed by a woolly fog.

—Abel! I shout.

The name falls at my feet like a dead blackbird.

I walk on, arms extended forward, the fog so thick I cannot see my hands. A bell tolls above me—slow, muffled, mournful—just as when I was a child, curled in bed with the blankets over my head. A door made of rough planks, with soft golden light shining through the gaps, opens at a touch. I find myself in a low-roofed kitchen with a fire struggling feebly in the hearth. In the far corner an old woman is peeling corn, stripping the green skin and red hair with surprising deftness and strength. She smiles, toothless, then places the cob in a pile on her lap. A small girl is kneeling beside her, braiding the flaxen hair into a single strand. The old woman points with a cob. In a narrow bed, a shadow stirs, moans, raises its head with difficulty.

—Abel? I ask.

A gaunt young man nods. His eyes are circled by an inky hue, his lips tinged purple.

—I meant to come earlier, but . . .

Tearing a strip from a sheet covered in mathematics, he puts it in his mouth.

—Why have you come? he asks, chewing the paper.

—I want to live for mathematics.

As he leans forward, I can smell the vinegar in the moist cloth on his forehead.

—Mathematics, he says, forcing a faint smile. She is no queen! More a coquette who uses men for her own whims. She will steal your youth, undermine your health, deprive you of love and happiness. Turn away from her while there's still time.

—You don't mean that, I say, gripping his thin wrist. You've looked into the depths, seen the truth . . .

159

—And now I'm paying for that vision, he sighs, tearing another shred. Listen.

Winding the braid around her head, the girl begins singing a lullaby. Abel's smile becomes stronger. He leans back into the pillow and closes his eyes. The old woman gnaws on a cob with her blue gums.

—You're disappointed, aren't you? I ask, whispering into his ear. I know how much you've suffered. Don't give up. I'll help you.

My sympathy turns to anger, and tears rise to my eyes, blurring my vision. The singing is now louder. A small snake wriggles out of the hearth and hisses toward me, stopping at my feet in the shape of an integration sign. No, it is the letter $\int$! I jab a pen between its eyes. The snake twists, turns, bites its tail, then contracts to a rigid spiral. Still singing, the braid coiled around her head, the girl steps lightly from the shadow and picks up the snake. Suddenly she is the gypsy! Reaching out with a tattooed hand, she takes me by the wrist.

—The martyr of mathematics, says Abel, chewing.

The old woman chuckles behind the cob. The gypsy's grip tightens. Abel throws aside the blankets: He is naked, skin and bone, legs bent as though broken at the knees.

—No, I shout, pulling away from the gypsy.

The room blurs, becomes fluid, and begins dissolving in my hot tears.

—You're immortal, I shout. Get up! Get up!

And I shake Abel by the shoulders, even though I can no longer see him through my tears. The gypsy prods me in the ribs, calling me by name to go with her.

160

PART TWO

19

Grief. A week of it, unrelenting, blackening, numbing. And now, on my way to the Polytechnic to sit the entrance examination, it is made bitter by the sophistication on this boulevard: the perfume, powder, coiffure, fashion, the striving after wealth. It is all an elaborate attempt to conceal the stench of mortality, to allay the fear of death through diversions, entertainments, games of love and profit. I turn off into a squalid suburb, where the ache is made more bearable by the poverty and misery. Death cannot be concealed by finery here. Just as it gnaws at my heart, so it haunts the sockets of the woman emerging from a basement, settles in the lungs of the hawker whose raucous call for old clothes sounds like a cry of help, rises up from sewers and overwhelms the scent of jasmine adorning windowsills, palls the sky with soot and smoke.

Has it already been a week? I have lost all sense of time—apart from the memory of the church bell's slow, bruising count which still echoes in my skull. The calendar and clock have no place in the depths of grief, just as they have no place in the heights of mathematics. What is the date? The tenth of July. Yes, a week to the day.

The letter at school instructed me to return home at once—nothing more. In the coach I tried to overcome the ominous tone of those few words by concentrating on the present. Jolted in passing over a wooden bridge whose boards rattled and rang, I straightened up and inhaled the smell of fennel. Below, swollen yellow by a recent storm, a river surged past rocks and reeds. Here and there fish flashed upstream. I turned to a fellow sitting opposite: He was scribbling musical notes with a stick of charcoal. When he closed his eyes to catch a few more bars, I examined the score on his lap, unable to make out a thing. Mathematics and music: Both used abstract symbols. Emotion without meaning, music used timed intervals to transcend time; meaning without emotion, mathematics used mind to transcend not just time but matter and space. Dispelling a sense of foreboding, these ideas occupied me for the remainder of the journey home.

My uncle met me in the town square. Looking into his eyes, I feared the worst. We both sat on a bench in the shade of a plane tree, beside a melon vendor. A few sharp wedges grinned deliciously.

—What has happened? I asked, bracing myself.

He twisted his black cravat and avoided my eyes.

—Your father . . . he faltered. He's no longer with us.

I was in free fall—falling through darkness, my stomach in a knot. The thought that I would wake up before the impact flashed through the confusion, but I was shattered on the rock-hard fact. Father was dead. My uncle embraced me with one arm, tried to console me with meaningless words. Two boys bought wedges from the melon vendor and ate greedily, juice trickling onto their shirts. My thoughts were in chaos. I was fragmenting. If only I could cry, let out a howl, but nothing came, only a choking frustration, and the terrible sense of my own disintegration, which had to be arrested before it reduced my mind to rubble. And in that moment of dread, with nothing, nobody to turn to, I heard the clear voice of mathematics: *For an irreducible equation of prime degree to be solvable by radicals it is necessary and sufficient that all its roots be rational functions of any two of these roots.* I repeated my finding over and over again. As though a prayer, or a chant, the words steadied me, my sense of being gravitated around them, thoughts and feelings became less confused. More than my uncle's platitudes about courage through Christ, my discovery gave me the strength to face Father's death.

—How did he die? I asked, staring at the boys, who were laughing and spitting black seeds at each other.

—He was a sensitive man . . .

—How?

—He . . . took his own life.

Again I wanted to cry out, scream that my father would not have done such a thing, but I merely gazed at my uncle's black boots and shook my head, dumb with bewilderment. When? Where? My words sounded hollow, distant, as though uttered by someone else.

—Yesterday, in his Paris apartment.

A stone's throw from Louis-le-Grand! So close together at that fateful moment! If only he had come to see me first, if only I had spoken yesterday, if only . . .

—Pistol? I asked, tempted to reach down and write my initials in the fine dust covering his boots.

—Asphyxiation.

165

I walked home in silence, unable to get the image of Father hanging from a window latch out of my mind. I felt betrayed by what he had done. And as I kept asking why, the pain and incomprehension fused into a seething anger. Where was the courage he had always advocated? Where was the will to fight against insurmountable odds? He had acted cowardly. He had forgotten his ideals, deserted his family, forsaken his own son. I had loved him more than anybody, and now that love had been rejected.

Love? Why did religions and poets extol its virtues? It had no virtues, or it would have kept him from that horrible act. It was all nonsense, a fleeting emotion without substance, in the end nothing more than a waste of time. Love? Never again! I would tear it from my heart . . .

I stop before a woman cleaning fish on the edge of the pavement. She deftly scrapes the scales, slits the gleaming body with a serrated knife, and flicks the entrails into the gutter. Was I unfair on Father last week? Dark forces lead a person to such an act: forces which defy society, reason, love. A young fellow with a cap tilted cockily and twirling a chain around his forefinger bumps into me.

—Watch where you're going, schoolboy, he says.

Flies swarm over the woman's sticky hands.

—Cat got your tongue?

Fish glare, howl mutely.

—Get going, scowls the woman.

Tipping his cap over his eyes, the fellow wishes her a good day and strolls off. Before I am able to thank her, she picks up her basket and walks into a courtyard.

The house was dim, with curtains drawn against the summer sun. Mother came toward me in a mourning dress and embraced me tearfully. She was followed by Nathalie and Alfred. Throughout the house friends and relatives stood stiffly, or sat bleary-eyed, or sighed to each other.

— The devil drove him to it, she said in a broken voice.

I barely understood what was being said: Anger still churned inside me, made me insensible to everything but the fact that I had been betrayed, that my father had left this world without so much as a note of explanation or even a word of good-bye.

— The priest's the only devil, sobbed Alfred. He drove Father to his death. He's responsible for . . .

— Alfred!

Tears trickling from his eyes, Alfred looked around self-consciously and ran from the room. I followed and caught up with him on the gravel path. We sat together under the oak as a finch's clear notes sounded from above.

— We've got to fight Father's enemies, he whimpered. It's up to us to avenge his death.

— We will, I said, trying to comfort him.

— He wasn't himself in the last month, he sniffed. The priest and his allies drove him insane, to the point where he suspected everyone of plotting against him. He wouldn't eat or drink from fear of poison. He would lock himself in the study and peer from the closed shutters.

Alfred broke down and cried uncontrollably for a few minutes. I bit my lower lip, checking the swell of emotion by bringing to mind my recent findings: The essence of an equation could be brought to light through the nature of the group formed from its coefficients.

—She made things unbearable for him. Always harping on the Bible, forever quoting Revelation, nagging him to moderate his views. She wanted Father to bow to the authority of the Church and make peace with the town priest. In the end he didn't want to see her. He accused her of betraying him, of plotting with the priest to bring about his downfall. Now, Evariste, she insists we have a church funeral. And, adding insult to injury, she has no objections to the priest responsible for Father's death conducting the requiem mass. We mustn't allow it, Evariste! We have to oppose her, in memory of Father's Republican ideals. His death will have been for nothing if we allow her to do as she wants.

—We'll oppose her, I said, surprised at my conviction, sensing that some of my anger had shifted toward her.

—He spoke of you often.

—What did he say?

—His words in the last few weeks didn't make a lot of sense, but whenever he mentioned you his face would light up. My son will help me, he would say, as if addressing an enemy. My son will become a famous mathematician, bring glory to the Galois name, defend his poor father against serpent-tongued liars. The Polytechnic will fill him not only with the spirit of knowledge, but with the spirit of the Republic. And he will rise in my defense, the torch of mathematics in one hand, the tricolor in the other.

Alfred's words buzzed in my ears all afternoon. To escape the heat, the smell of vinegar permeating the house, the sweating mourners whose mouths were gaping holes that threatened to swallow me, I left for the almond grove. The town square was now quieter. Vendors dozed in the shade, waiting for the sun's ferocity to pass. A dog struggled past me, paws scratching the hot cobblestones, tongue flopping like a wet rag, almost licking its shadow. As it accorded me an apprehensive glance, I saw myself, the square, the church, the blue sky—all distorted in a sorrowful eye. At the fountain a woman was filling buckets containing flowers: marigolds, carnations, chrysanthemums. I noticed the tattoos on her wet hands. As she leaned to fill another bucket, her loose blouse opened at the top. Straightening up, she flashed a smile. I turned away, looked at the steeple, a crow beaking an apple core, the symbols on the back of her left hand: crosses, crescents, circles, others I had never seen before, which were rendered even more incomprehensible by the fact that they merged with her veins, making it impossible to distinguish ink from vein.

—Marigolds for the mayor, she said in a singsong voice, extending a bunch, water dripping on her bare feet.

A rooster shrieked. Her breasts quivered as she shook a shower of drops from the flowers. Confused, heart pounding, I turned to the tap, washed my face and neck, and ran across the square, disturbing the crow, which cried and flew off with the core. I slowed to a walk in the sharp-edged shadow of the church. The doors were open, the nave was dark, still. A cool breath beckoned. I was about to enter, to sit for a few minutes and collect my thoughts and emotions before continuing to the almond grove, when the priest appeared with a pile of hymn books against his chest and under his chin. In turning to see who stood in the doorway, he lost his grip and the books scattered on the ground. We exchanged looks. He smiled. Alfred's words filled my head as cicadas shrilled in the oaks along the side of the church.

—Ah, you've come again, he said, kneeling to gather the books. Would you give me a hand?

I snapped that he was to blame for my father's death, barely able to hear my own words from the cicadas drilling in my ears. Stunned, he stood and brushed the dust from a book. I wanted to pour out a tirade of abuse, to condemn him for his part in Father's death, but words and emotions clogged my throat, and I ran off through the cicadas' rage.

It appeared as though nobody had visited the grove since I was last there. A section of the surrounding wall had crumbled; nettles were flourishing, strangling the trunks; the grass was waist-high; unpruned branches of adjacent trees tangled into each other; the scarecrow had been stripped to a crooked cross. I opened the shutters and sat facing the window. All around, cicadas chorused their dirge. I recalled childhood picnics: dressing the scarecrow, beating the branches with a long pole, the bitter taste of unripe almonds.

And then I sensed Father's presence in the cottage. After Alfred's words and the encounter with the priest, I now felt a pang of remorse at my initial anger toward him. But why didn't he write? I asked as though he were standing in the corner. Why didn't he send for me? I could have helped him. He need not have been alone. The last few weeks would not have been so terrible. He would have had someone to confide in, someone to support him. Why? If we had been together, he would have . . . He was always thinking of me: he did not want to burden me with his problems, did not want to interrupt my studies. My welfare, that's all he thought about, even on that terrible day. With hindsight, that cruelest of faculties, I now see that he tried to reach out to me, tried to tell me how much he was suffering at the hands of his enemies. But I was self-centered, blind to everything except mathematics. Perhaps I was also to blame for what he did. My obsession made me insensitive to his suffering. If only I had listened to him, if only I had not been so absorbed in . . .

—Chimneys swept! A wheelbarrow clatters toward me, pushed by a bare-armed man. Black from soot, a boy of eight or nine lies curled in the barrow, sleeping on a coil of rope.

The Polytechnic is close. I pass through a dim archway reeking of wine and enter a courtyard where a crowd has gathered around a speaker standing on a barrel: a man in his twenties, flourishing a rolled newspaper, his angular face profiled strongly against a section of sky. I stand in a doorway where two girls are rattling knucklebones on bare floorboards.

—We must show Charles and his lackey ministers that we oppose them; that all their threats will never silence us nor stop our presses; that Republicans won't tolerate another increase in the price of bread and wine!

The crowd erupts in applause and a chorus of "Long live the Republic." The speaker becomes even more impassioned, bolder in the way he sweeps the newspaper above his head.

—And how is the Republic going to be won? By blood, good citizens! My blood, your blood, his blood.

He points to me over the heads of those at the front. A few of the listeners turn.

—When the Revolution starts, our students will be in the front ranks.

Disconcerted by the attention, I retreat into the dim doorway. A knucklebone rattles to my feet. I am about to pick it up when one of the girls scurries on hands and knees, snatches it with a grubby hand, and returns to her playmate.

—Freedom of the press, good citizens! he shouts, unrolling the newspaper and holding it up for them to see. We must oppose Charles in his plans to restrict the liberal papers.

Clapping, cheering, cries of "Long live the liberty of the press" fill the courtyard. Five or six youths appear and stand with arms crossed in the arched entrance. The speaker rolls the newspaper, shoves it into his coat, and raises his ink-blackened palms before continuing.

If only I were as fluent as he! But my thoughts leap with a logic of their own, often too quick to be grasped by words, and I become tongue-tied, sound obscure. I envy his ability to arouse people, to inflame them with ideals for which they would sacrifice themselves, and all this with nothing but common words. Will mathematics ever have that effect on a crowd? And will my theory of equations ever be delivered in a way that inspires people to sacrifice themselves for the sake of a republic of mathematics?

—And finally, good citizens, I must warn you of the greatest threat to our Republic: the Jesuits!

I clench my fists and step from the doorway as a stinking old ragpicker scrapes past, bent double by a bundle on her back, muttering to herself that the Kingdom of God is at hand.

—Don't be deceived by them, good citizens. Their rise during the last ten years has been at the expense of you and me. They're in league with the King. Napoleon broke their power, exposed them for what they are, and now they're filled with hatred and revenge. They're an army, good citizens, determined to dominate France by means of Bible and cross. They'll stop at nothing in order to control the hearts and minds of our children.

As the crowd chants "Down with the Jesuits," the youths retaliate "Down with atheists." A section of the crowd turns on the youths, but they manage to flee, pursued by a dozen men spitting obscenities. A horse harnessed to a cart rears, spilling its load of apples. Screaming and shouting, children rush out and fill their arms. The frenzied vendor runs from child to child, struggling to dispossess them of his apples. Uproarious laughter rises from the courtyard, from doorways, balconies, windows on the third and fourth floors. I hurry away before the chaos overwhelms me, trying to focus my thoughts on the examination.

The church bell's leaden toll struck as I returned from the almond grove. Outside the house a crowd surrounded a gleaming hearse hitched to a pair of white horses.

—He was a good mayor, said a man, tapping me on the back.

—We'd still be pushing our wagons through mud if it weren't for him, added a second.

—They won't get away with it, shouted a third.

Inside, people were rushing about from room to room, some carrying articles of Father's clothing, others chairs and trestles. My uncle was counting money onto the extended palm of a man in a leather vest.

—It's a dusty drive back to Paris, the fellow grinned. Mind if I have a drink before I go?

My uncle pointed to the kitchen, and the fellow shambled off, the seat of his trousers shining.

I did not know what to do, where to go. I felt useless, out of place, and barely responded to people who accorded me a sympathetic nod or a faint smile. The air was thick with the smell of candle wax, vinegar, perfume, perspiration. Mother came down the stairs with a pair of shoes belonging to my father. Seeing me, she slipped a black handkerchief from her sleeve.

—Paris, she sniffed. Satan's haunt. He would still be with us if he had kept his faith and stayed away from that place.

Swallowing back a swell of emotion, I took the shoes from her. He had worn them on civic occasions, and now he would wear them in the coffin as his murderer conducted a requiem mass over him. I scratched a spot of dried mud on the heel.

—Come with me, she said peremptorily.

Sleeves rolled to the elbows, an elderly woman, a relative on my mother's side, stopped her as I was about to enter the study. After exchanging a few whispers, the woman wiped the gleam from her brow with the edge of her apron and shuffled off.

The late-afternoon light brought out the iridescence of the pens on the table, the gleam on the frame around

Grandfather Galois who looked down sadly from the wall, the richness of soot in the fireplace.

—The priest had nothing to do with it, she said in a mellow voice.

—He persecuted him, I retorted.

As though her veil of grief had suddenly blown aside, she stepped toward me, eyes glinting and lips sealed in a severe line.

—I know what Alfred has been saying, but it's not true. It's all the work of those Republican freethinkers. Your father was a moderate man when we married, those atheists corrupted him, turned him against the Church, and now they're planning to use the funeral to serve their political ends.

As she spoke I glanced here and there at my father's possessions, and with each glance my affection for him increased.

—Come home, Son. Help me with the school. It can still provide a good income. I know this isn't the time for such things, but they must be said. I can't succumb to grief: The family's needs must be met. Will you help me?

—Father wanted me to become a mathematician, I replied, feeling a nail inside the heel of the right shoe.

—And my wishes? Don't I deserve a little consideration, if not sympathy? You appear to have idolized him at my expense. He wasn't a hero, Evariste! If he were, he would be with us today, standing in those shoes, seeing to the welfare of his family, reconciled to the Church.

—The Church! I retorted, clapping the heels as though crushing an insect. That priest of yours must be gloating over Father's death.

—The Church is still prepared to give him a Christian burial.

—That's very generous of your Jesuit! First he drives Father to his death, now he offers to bury him.

—Evariste!

—Father should be buried in the almond grove.

—Please! Let's not quarrel.

The door opened abruptly and Mother's relative leaned into the study, supporting her bulk on the handle, the edge of the scarf around her head dark from perspiration.

—We've finished, Adelaide, she heaved. Are they the shoes?

Feeling the nail head in the heel, I wondered how Father had put up with it. She took the shoes from me and tucked them under her fleshy arm.

—The hurt will pass, my boy, she said, patting my cheek with a moist hand.

—We'll discuss this later, Mother whispered.

The burnished floorboards creaked as she followed her relative out. I stared at the fireplace for a moment, then walked to the chair behind the desk and touched the outline of Father's head in the upholstered backrest: It was warm from the sun. I picked up his favorite pipe, tapped the ash onto my palm, stared at it for some time, then wrapped the flakes in a handkerchief. I dipped my finger in the inkpot: It was dry. Closing my eyes, I leaned back and succumbed to a sensation of dissolving in liquid light.

The coffin was placed in the middle of the dining room, mounted on trestles, with five candles at either end. Still as spear points, the flames prodded the intrusive darkness, drove it to the corners of the room. Though the windows had been opened, the curtains were still, the air unbearably heavy. As the clock chimed eleven melodious notes, the mourners, who sat on chairs against the walls, stirred, coughed, rattled cups. The oppressive silence was occasionally relieved by someone whispering a consoling word, or relating an anecdote about Father's good character.

I sat next to my uncle, who advised me several times to go to bed, as tomorrow would be very tiring. Despite my drowsiness, I was determined to pay my last respects by staying up all night. Alfred had been sent to a relative's house, while Nathalie dozed on my mother's shoulder. To ward off sleep and make the dreary faces more bearable, I thought about the memoirs I had submitted to the Academy. It had been a month, and I had heard nothing. What would Cauchy think of my findings? As a professor at the Polytechnic, would Cauchy take me under his wing, nurture my talent? Perhaps when all this was over and I returned to Paris, I would find the letter with the Academy's seal, informing me that my mathematics was so advanced I would be granted entrance to the Polytechnic without sitting for the examination.

A woman left the room, and the candles quivered, strained after her. My thoughts gravitated to the coffin, and once again I questioned my work. What was the use of mathematics? Where was its comfort? Its consolation? That human touch that might help lighten this night? And I was struck by the realization that mathematics had nothing to do with death; that, by its very nature, it denied death, and that the two were in fact mutually exclusive. Had Pascal turned away from mathematics because it did not confront death? Mathematics or Christ? One promised eternity through the mind, the other through the body.

The candles blurred, merged into a single flame, transformed the room. The coffin lid was open. I stepped forward and looked inside: it was full of rods with gears, numbered dials, small wheels and sprockets. The soul of man, I thought, standing calmly. Pascal appeared from the farthest corner of the room.

—Diversion, he said in a weak voice, knocking on the calculating machine with his knuckles. Like all art, mathematics is nothing more than diversion from the fact of our mortality. Yes, I indulged in it, imagined that I was serving truth, even constructed this. But all the time I was really placing screens between myself and the true source of enlightenment: death.

Pascal closed the lid and lay on it, head resting on his hands.

—Diversion, so that man can avoid confronting the human condition, he continued. One man is diverted by the pursuit of power, another by passion for women, a third by the practice of gambling. But there's also diversion in knowledge, when it's motivated by a desire for fame. How many mathematicians would pursue the abstractions of algebra if they experienced the fact that death reduces us all to the lowest common denominator?

My head jerked from my uncle's shoulder. Sitting more upright, I reprimanded myself for the lapse. Pascal's words came back to me. No, mathematics was not a diversion for me. There was too much of the priest in Pascal when he wrote his *Pensées*. His faith was a diversion. He was a sick man, and the salve of a soul assuaged his ailing body. No, I would not disappoint my father. This would be my night of Gethsemane. I would watch over him, confront death, my father's death, the person I loved most, not with Pascalian faith but with the spirit of mathematics.

And for the rest of the night I was caught in a struggle between sleep and vigilance, between deliverance and despair, between coefficients and the coffin . . .

A bell booming above me, I quicken my pace along a riverside street, holding my breath in passing a few boning rooms. I try to muster some enthusiasm for the examination, tell myself yet again that I must fulfill Father's wish, and that once in the Polytechnic I will not only bring honor to the Galois name but avenge his death. Bodies of beef hang from bloody hooks; fat and offal float sluggishly downstream. Struggling backward past me, a dog drags a massive bone with an intact ball-and-socket joint. Father had confidence in me, and today I will have to live up to that confidence. A ragpicker appears from a lane, snatches the bone, and swings it like a club above the dog. Whimpering, it cowers away, while the ragpicker drops the bone in a sack and hobbles off with a smile.

Cursing, a man prods a pair of oxen straining with a marble cube. I am in a bustling square, with numerous speakers on crates and stools. With top hats and parasols, arm in arm, step in step, perfect pairs promenade between the speakers. Vendors bark their wares. Eyebrows arched slyly, young men whistle as they stroll. Barefooted street children scurry after scraps. Two small boys are quarreling over a lace handkerchief. A policeman appears, snatches the handkerchief, inhales the perfume with an approving nod, and scatters the boys with a wave, as though they are sparrows.

I stop in front of a speaker wearing a worker's jacket spotted with blue stains. His jugular swells to bursting as he growls over his listeners, many of whom are wearing a similar jacket.

—Think about it, he warns, threatening them with a blackened forefinger. Our trade has been exploited long enough! Others prosper, grow powerful, make a name for themselves, while we sweat in silence, working for a pittance. Enough!

—Enough! they echo.

—We're their fountain of life. They know it, but they won't acknowledge it. A strike! That's the only way to make our point.

—Strike! Strike!

—Let's stop production until the government agrees to increase the price. I tell you, fellow workers, this city will fall into chaos without ink.

He pulls out a wine bottle from his jacket, uncorks it with his teeth, and turns it upside down: A black stream gleams in spilling onto the cobbles, causing those in front to jump back.

—Ink! Society's lifeblood! If the pen's mightier than the sword, we're mightier than the pen, brothers. If we spilled our supplies onto the street, the government would soon enough bow to our demands. Blood and ink, brothers! There's no more explosive mixture. If we strike, you can be sure the government will relent, to avoid crippling itself, for all governments exercise their power through ink. Not only this, brothers, it would be forced to contend with the wrath of journalists, writers, poets, academics, and its strongest ally, the Church. Let's be strong in our resolve. Let's unite. Let's strike.

—Strike! Strike!

The speaker jumps from the stool and leads the chanting group away. Walking on, I ponder whether ink is also the lifeblood of mathematics. What if mathematicians were suddenly unable to record their findings? Would there be a body of mathematics without ink? But perhaps many mathematicians have already become too dependent on ink, and this dependence has weakened their imagination and ability to think abstractly. If ink were scarcer, they might be compelled to work entirely in their heads, mathematics might be restored to its ideal state, and they might develop a faculty for communicating with each other through thought alone, or perhaps . . . What is that slippery feel under my shoes? Manure? I have stepped into the pool of ink. I glance over my shoulder: Bold footprints are following faithfully.

—I hope they don't start anything, Mother whispered, securing her veil against a hot, blustering wind.

I walked on one side of her, my uncle on the other. Listless from a sleepless night, from the emotional and mental struggle, I felt as though I were being drawn by a force beyond my control. As the cortege passed through the town square, the hearse rattled, its silver fittings and trimmings darted needles of light. The bell tolled wearily. The procession stopped before the church and the pallbearers raised the coffin onto their shoulders. The crowd gathered at the steps parted.

—He was a good man, said an old fellow.

—A real Republican, called another.

—We'll avenge his death, shouted a third.

—Down with the Jesuits! yelled a fourth.

The barbed comments roused me.

—Rabble, Mother hissed. They don't respect a thing.

I was moved by the determined faces of my father's friends and supporters: They appeared ready to fight in order to uphold his memory. The affection and respect convinced me that the priest had been behind his death. A surge of anger dispersed the dullness in my head.

—We'll show them, Alfred whispered on entering the cool nave.

He followed this with a few more comments, but his words were swallowed by an organ's lugubrious groan, which hung in the air while the nave filled with flushed faces. As the priest marched crisply to the altar, a long last note trailed away, and a murmur passed through the congregation. Adjusting his collar, the priest nodded to those in the front pew. I clenched my jaw. Mother raised her veil. The mass was conducted against a background of persistent whispers. Several times the priest stopped, eyed the loudest offenders, and asked for silence and respect. When he concluded, a relative stood up and asked if he might deliver the eulogy. The priest replied that it was inappropriate in the present situation. Instantly, a chorus of "Eulogy! Eulogy!" erupted from the back of the nave.

—You're in the house of God, countered the priest.

Another section began hissing at the eulogists, calling on them to leave the church.

—Hypocrites! shouted a youth from the back.

—I didn't want this, said my mother.

—It had to come, I replied.

She gripped my hand, but I pulled away, feeling her nails. The exchanges between the rival factions were becoming more heated, with people standing and hurling abuse at each other. His calls for piety unheeded, the priest turned to the organist and indicated *fortissimo* with an upward gesture of his pink palm. A massive groan overwhelmed the nave, causing many to stop their ears.

—You won't silence us!

—We did it in '93, and by God we'll do it again!

—Down with the Jesuits!

—What are they doing? cried Mother.

—Revolution! yelled a robust youth.

—The Apocalypse, she sighed, lowering her veil.

—Now! bellowed the youth.

A volley of white stones struck the organ pipes. The old organist leaped from his seat and ran for cover. As a chaotic melody chimed against the dying groan, the priest raised his arms and demanded everyone leave the church. Colored glass shattered: Where there had been a small window depicting the stoning of a martyr, there was now a circle of clear blue sky.

—Desecrators! Demons! the priest shouted from the pulpit.

He grimaced and covered his left temple with both hands: Blood oozed between his fingers. The congregation scrambled between the pews, pushing and screaming as they went. The factions attacked each other, first with abuse, then obscenities, finally with fists. Half a dozen youths, the stone throwers, leaped over the pews and surrounded the coffin. Alfred joined them.

—We'll bury the mayor, shouted the robust one.

The others took up the cry, and raised the coffin onto their shoulders.

—No, Alfred, my mother shrieked.

But the young pallbearers had already pushed their way to the back of the nave, where they were confronted by another group of youths.

—Atheists! burst the leader.

—Out of the way, Alfred demanded.

The pallbearers charged through, but the others stood their ground, and the coffin tilted precariously. Brushing past Mother, who had turned as white as the marble altar, I shoved through the crowd, in time to help secure the coffin from falling. The obstructors were soon pushed aside by opponents at their rear. Finding myself at the head of the pallbearers, I led them out into the dazzling light, where we were greeted by a resounding chorus of "Liberty or Death" . . .

The walls of the Polytechnic are covered in political graffiti. Was it there last year or hadn't I noticed it? Students, vendors, and beggars mill around the entrance to the courtyard. A young woman with a basket of breadsticks strapped to her waist approaches four students.

—Man lives by more than bread alone, winks one of the students.

He pays for a long stick and breaks it into quarters for the others. A few gray pigeons swoop on the crumbs, and as they peck the cobbles a rainbow gleams around their throbbing throats. An old beggar in an army greatcoat pounces on them with startling agility. Catching one by the tip of its wing, he stops its wild beating with a deft twist of its neck.

I try to focus on the examination. I realize the importance of what lies ahead, but it has been rendered less urgent by the grief and chaos of the past week. A scrawny broom sweeps my shadow, together with a clump of dry horse manure.

The instant I stepped outside with the coffin, I was strengthened by the sight of hundreds of people chanting support: a strength derived from a feeling of solidarity, belonging, being a member of a group. Would I ever feel like that in mathematics? It was as though the crowd rushed in and filled the vacuum left by my father's death. Those ardent Republicans evoked a sense of communion, a closeness I had only experienced in Father's presence. Later, praised by them for my brave, spontaneous action, I felt a kinship toward them, even though many were complete strangers. I came away from the burial with a slightly different view of mathematics: I might honor my father's memory, avenge his death, through both thought and action, symbol and sentence, ink and blood.

Climbing the steps, my attention is caught by a painter whitewashing a section of wall, vigorously obliterating a red circle. Is it a numeral, perhaps part of a year? Or a letter, perhaps the second in the word for death?

20

It claims the boulevards, smothers every lane, curls into every dog-forsaken corner; it steals into every empty pocket, cap, and sabot left on a doorstep; it fills every fist, ear, mouth that opens to hawk, yawn, talk; it insinuates every lung, skull, soiled and unsoiled soul; it haunts the breath of a young mathematician hurrying from a Republican meeting. It is everywhere, this February fog, fouled by the smell of burning coal, the putrefaction of refuse turned to sludge, the acrid stench of sewers rising to high heaven; this fog that sucks the afternoon sun like a yolk, invades this city of art and reduces it to formlessness, makes people pale, fearful, ghostly; that undermines all laws, crumbles society to individuals, and individuals to criminals; that absorbs all numbers and turns them into the ring puffed out by a child.

Caught in this miasma, thoughts swirling with Republican ideas, having lost my bearings and all track of time, I feel the fog seeping into me, dissolving me, dividing me by zero. I clutch at recent memories to allay the fear of vanishing.

—Stop tormenting me, Evariste!

As though honed by grim determination, Mother's

voice had a sharper edge. It was a month ago, and I was home for the first time since last summer's tragedy. An icy silence pervaded the house. Back two days, I had said no more than a few cold words to her. I avoided being alone with her, even making eye contact with her at the dinner table. That afternoon she surprised me in the study. She had become thinner since the funeral, her round cheekbones more prominent. She was not still for a moment, as though something urgent had to be done, some impending doom to be confronted.

— I can't manage the school any longer, she said, twisting the corner of a handkerchief.

— Sell it, I replied, deciphering the ghost of Father's name on a sheet of blotting paper. The Jesuits will give you a good price for it.

— Evariste!

— I've got my studies to think about.

— Studies or politics?

— Both!

— Please, Evariste, stay away from politics. It destroyed your father.

— They'll pay for his death.

— Don't talk like that! Let's forget the funeral. Let's try to be a family again.

She stopped pacing and leaned forward over the desk. The gold cross around her neck swayed. I looked down, first at Father's pipes, then at her distorted reflection in the paper knife.

— Sometimes I have such terrible visions, Evariste. I see Paris being engulfed by an inferno.

— Republics arise from infernos.

—Heaven forbid!

—Yes, the heaven of your Church forbids the Republic—that's why the Jesuits must be opposed.

Her knuckles were white from supporting her weight. For a moment her features relaxed: Her jawline became less rigid. The cross glowed against her black velvet dress.

—Paris has filled you with so much hatred.

—Hatred and anger, I said, meeting her look until she turned away. To love the future one must hate the present. I'll nurture this hatred until it . . .

A phantom stumbles out of the fog and accosts me with a wild look.

—Are you one of us, brother? he asks, each word a burst of vapor reeking of wine.

—Yes, I falter, squirming in his embrace.

—Long live the Republic!

Issuing from a gaping hole, a sewer, the source of the fog, his words waft over my face, make my stomach turn. His embrace tightens and he kisses me on the cheek with dribbling lips. I break his grip and run off.

—It'll be paradise on earth, brother! Paradise . . .

Words are swallowed, muffled, silenced by the fog. Wiping saliva from my cheek, I continue running, slipping here and there on sludge, until a black elm appears from the whiteness, like a raft to a drowning man. I hold on to the trunk with both hands, fingernails clawing the soft bark, head sagging between extended arms. My lungs are bursting, burning.

❖　❖　❖

188

In Richard's room I stared at the engraving of the muse of mathematics, whose wistful gaze was focused on infinity. Was the muse represented as a woman because Urania, the classical muse of astronomy, was female, and her domain was closest to mathematics? Her melancholy was not that of the poet hurt by unrequited love, wallowing in a swamp of emotion, powerless before a cruel world — this was a brooding pensiveness, a yearning for the ideal, a desire to know everything. In the magic square above her head I now saw that the four-celled subgroups in each corner also added to thirty-four. She was melancholic because she knew this square was a subgroup of an infinite square consisting of all the digits from one to infinity: She had seen it in a flash, but how was she to convey this transcendent vision? There was not enough space or time to channel it to lesser minds.

—You should have taken my advice, Evariste, said Richard. You weren't ready for that examination. I could have arranged for a deferred sitting. Instead, you've gone and ruined everything.

I looked down from the engraving.

Different examiners had been appointed this time. After a few preliminary questions, the older of the two, whose name was Binet or Dinet — a cavalcade went past as he introduced himself — squinted through his pince-nez and asked if I was related to the mayor of Bourg-la-Reine. I was taken aback. I nodded. His fleshy ears suddenly annoyed me. He was a Jesuit sympathizer. I imagined standing before the Grand Inquisitor. The pointed tone of his questions unsettled me. The secretary's pen scratched the proceedings. At the thought of Father I hesitated on a question on advanced trigonometry. The examiner advised me to use the blackboard. Was that a smile or sneer on his face? I did not need his condescending tone. I could see the construction of the question, knew exactly what was required, but a feeling of anger and resentment prevented me from replying. The room swayed from side to side in the pendulum clock's silver disk. I picked up the eraser and chalk.

—The solution, sir, prompted the examiner.

I had worked myself up to such a state that my body became rigid, and I clutched the eraser. I hated this fellow, hated the way he scratched the back of his head, hated his gloating grin. I knew my silence meant failure, but I did not care. Should I throw the eraser in his face? This examination would go down in history. The old man who failed Evariste Galois would fare badly at the hands of biographers. If this inquisitor had asked proper questions, I would have answered them, entered the Polytechnic, produced a substantial amount of work, lived to seventy, but as it was . . . I tossed the eraser on his table and walked out without a word.

—The examiner was an old fool.

—You're the one who acted foolishly, said Richard.

—I don't need the Polytechnic.

—What are you going to do now?

I turned away to the engraving. A little cherub sat on a wheel between the muse and trapezoidal block of stone.

—I suggest you salvage something from the disaster by sitting the baccalaureate examinations in December. If you do well, you'll be accepted into the Preparatory, where you can study to become a teacher of mathematics.

Teach mathematics? Never! The Preparatory? That second-rate institution? Six years in one prison, and Richard wanted me to go next door, to a school that was nothing more than an extension of this place. Now that I had been denied entry to the Polytechnic, I would not spend another two years in a place where freedom was crushed, where students cowered, where the curriculum was under the control of Jesuits.

—Never! I said, going to the window overlooking the courtyard. They'll pay for their plot against me!

—What plot? Who'll pay?

—The Jesuits! The Royalists! They conspired against my father, and they're conspiring against me. That old examiner is one of them. He knew my background. He was determined to fail me from the outset to keep another Republican from entering the Polytechnic. I hate them all: Jesuits, Royalists, conservatives. They're all enemies of freedom.

—Sit down, Evariste, Richard demanded.

My rancor grew at the sight of the Preparatory on the other side of the high wall. Twilight had unfurled its banner. Two years in that place? I would rather . . .

—I warned you, Evariste, he said, flicking the counters of an abacus, but you wouldn't listen. And now you come out with this nonsense. You flatter yourself too much to think there's a plot against you. Conceit and inflated pride, you had better curb those tendencies if you want to get on in the world. You have mathematical talent, I won't deny that, perhaps genius. It's too early to say. Don't squander it on the turmoil of politics. Get this resentment out of your mind, uproot it from your heart. Concentrate on entering the Preparatory. You can still become a mathematician, perhaps a great one, and, who knows, one day you may be granted a professorship at the Polytechnic.

— Yes, when it's too late, like Abel.

— Don't be your own enemy.

— Revolution, I said, gazing at the sphere on the flagpole in the Preparatory. Mathematics will never flourish as long as the conservatives are in power. I refuse to be a mathematician in a prison, and Paris will continue to be a prison until King Charles and the Church are overthrown.

— Enough, Galois! I know you've just lost your father, but that's no excuse for your own shortcomings. Think seriously about what I've said. We'll talk again when you're feeling less resentful.

— Revolution needs *greater* resentment, I said, striding out.

I walk on, rubbing my hands black from the elm's damp bark, the word *resentment* hissing in my ears. Resentment, hatred, anger: How can I feel anything else after what I have been through?

Not only Father's death and my failure to enter the Polytechnic, but I have also been rankled by the Academy's silence. Eight months since I submitted my work, and still not a word! As far as I know the two memoirs are still with Cauchy, who was supposed to have submitted a report on them to the Academy last month but which he deferred until the next sitting. A week after that sitting and still there was nothing. When I visited Cauchy, he advised me to rework my papers, combine them into a single memoir, and submit them for the Academy's annual Grand Prize. Was this his way of dismissing me, in the same way he had dismissed Abel? My suspicions were confirmed the other day when I learned that Cauchy is a staunch Royalist, and devout Catholic, which explained the silver crucifix on his desk. I sensed that it was more than just a paperweight. I could not hope for fair treatment, let alone support, from such a person.

And his advice? Should I submit my work for the Grand Prize anyway? If for no other reason than to spite Cauchy and his kind. Mathematics? Can I contain my hatred and anger in order to concentrate on work? The recent events have exiled me not only from the Polytechnic but also from my inner world of mathematics, from that retreat in which I had found an order and harmony otherwise lacking in my surroundings, a communion with eternal ideas, a sense of belonging that gave me strength and confidence. But having seen death, I now feel somewhat distant from that world, as though it has receded, become illusory. Suddenly, as though the fog has seeped into my soul, I am chilled by the thought that I might never experience that world again.

21

1830: a good number, the sum of the squares of twenty-three, twenty-five, and twenty-six. It is only the beginning of April, but how am I going to see out the remainder of the year?

Not quite two months since coming to the Preparatory school from Louis-le-Grand and the conditions are already unbearable: Discipline is more strictly enforced, informants are rife among the fifty or so students, the curriculum smells of Jesuit influence.

The wind thrashes at each slap of the lily-white Royal flag in the courtyard, rages at each scratch from the elm's bare branches, becomes furious at each gash from the school's spiked walls and gates.

—Traitor! I shout against a blustering squall.

—You're a joke, smiles Corbeau, the leader of the Royalist group at school. He winks at a few of his companions among the students gathered around us.

—And you're Director Guigniault's informant!

—Let's go, Corbeau chuckles, turning to his friends. The girls are waiting for us.

—You're too serious, Galois, says another from his

194

group. Forget your parabolas, come and see some real curves in motion.

— Filthy Royalists!

Benard and Flaugergues hold me by each arm. Fellow Republicans, they have also come here from Louis-le-Grand, though I have had more to do with them in the past two months than in five years in the other place.

— Take him away before he gets hurt, sneers Corbeau.

— Animals! I shout, trying to break free.

— Crawl back into your books, little worm.

— Your days are numbered! Together with your King! The Revolution will sweep you from the face of the earth.

— Yes, prophet Galois.

— Whatever you say, Emperor.

— Take our heads, but leave our bodies.

— We need them for the girls.

The wind scatters their laughter. Tearing loose, I lunge at Corbeau, who, just managing to keep his footing, turns and fists me flush on the mouth. I taste blood. My eyes water. Corbeau and his crew swagger away. My friends come to my assistance, but I walk off without a word. In a sheltered corner of the courtyard, I lie on a bench, head back to stop the bleeding from a cut inside my upper lip. I wipe away my blurred vision. Scrubbed of soot and smoke by the wind, the sky is clear, with a few wispy clouds here and there, like white-feathered pens poised to fill a blue sheet with . . . mathematics?

Feeling my lips throbbing, swelling, I suddenly miss mathematics, that world without blood and pain. Lately my work has been interrupted by political activities. Not long ago I summarized some earlier findings in an article titled "An Analysis of a Memoir on the Algebraic Solution of Equations," which I sent to Férussac's *Bulletin*. This was followed by a paper that combined two earlier memoirs, which I submitted to the Academy for the annual Grand Prize. But these were not creative works: I did not experience that heightened state of being which had accompanied the original ideas. Will I ever experience that again?

I close my eyes. The stone bench is cold, even through my overcoat. The sun's touch stings my lip. I embrace myself to keep the wind from flapping my overcoat.

Mathematics? I did not question its reality and relevance a year ago. I believed in its absolute authority, its precedence over the physical world. Now, with everything that has happened, I am uncertain. Ethereal thoughts, transcendent ideas, soaring flights of mind—were they nothing but an escape into fantasy? A timid mind fleeing the world of flesh and fact? What is the relevance of mathematics to the Revolution and the future Republic? No! Those thoughts and ideas are real, they are relevant. Imaginary numbers were considered useless at the time of their discovery, and now they have a place in the physical world. Perhaps the form of my mathematics has its counterpart in the spirit of Revolution: the ubiquitous spirit acting through politics, literature, music, art. Romanticism—the talk of the salons. What is it if not another word for Revolution? The allied spirit of Romanticism and Revolution will break the monarchy and the Church, just as it is breaking the lifeless forms of Classicism in the arts.

Is my work the first to express this new spirit through

mathematics? How else can I explain my impatience with the pompous exposition of algebra under the old regime, my urge to smash through the superfluous accretions of classical algebra? Richard and Vernier have remarked that I have always expressed myself tersely, in the way poets do; I tend to avoid pedestrian exposition in favor of associative leaps of the imagination. And my application of the theory of groups to equations? Maybe that, better than anything, expresses the spirit of Revolution.

And the Republic? Perhaps mathematics will provide a model for it. After all, wasn't Plato's ideal Republic, his Utopia, based on mathematics? Yes! Maybe this is now my mission in life: to bring mathematics into the open, make it public, use it to impose order on chaos, justice on injustice, the eternal on the fleeting. Yes! I will not rest until the spirit of Revolution fulfills itself in the form of a Republic, where true equality will exist — an equality as absolute as that conferred by $=$.

A shadow settles on my face. The sudden movement in sitting up sharpens the pain in my mouth and fills my eyes with tears again. A student is standing a few steps away, arms folded, smiling faintly.

— What do you want? I ask, hanging my head, feeling with my tongue for blood.

— Did he hurt you?

His concern surprises me. We are in a few classes together, but we have never spoken. He is chubby, pale, with black curly hair and a bad case of acne. His shoes are well-polished, collar starched, fingernails neatly cut, unlike my own, which are bitten almost to the quick.

—I've wanted to talk to you for some time, he says, but the opportunity hasn't arisen. My name is Auguste Chevalier.

He sits beside me and explains in a lively voice that he shares my idealism, and that I have impressed him with my mathematical ability. He does not possess talent—he manages to pass through hard work—but he has long been fascinated by mathematics and believes it is the key to a new society.

—And that proof last week! he smiles, dark eyes gleaming. What a memory!

—Memory? I proved it there and then.

—Without paper and ink?

—In my head.

—You've got a real gift, Evariste.

—I should join a circus, make a living by amazing people with my mental dexterity.

—No, I'm serious. You could become a great mathematician.

—There are more pressing problems to be solved.

—The Republic?

—Revolution first.

—Will you sacrifice your gift for that?

—What's the use of talent if it can't flourish? If it's thwarted at every step by conservative forces?

—Don't abandon mathematics, Evariste. The Republic will need scientists, in particular mathematicians, more than any other professionals. Think about it for a moment: How would France be affected if she were suddenly to lose her Royal family, her ministers of state, her hierarchy of judges, prefects, priests, her wealthy gentry who live solely on income from property? What would this loss do to the status of France? Very little, because these people produce nothing to better the material quality of life. But if France were to lose her leading scientists, and by that I mean also her artisans, architects, engineers, doctors, merchants—if she were to lose them in one swoop, her standing as a civilized nation would fall at once.

My suspicion is allayed not only by his words, sharp with conviction, but by his purposeful gestures, his steady gaze. I sense a kindred spirit, someone with whom I could share my ideas, who might help make this place a little more bearable.

—Your ideas are well-developed, I remark, feeling my front teeth, relieved they're firmly in place.

—They're the ideas of Saint-Simon.

—Are you a member of that society?

—Yes. My brother Michel is editor of the *Globe*, the society's journal.

—What are your views on revolution?

—For Saint-Simon the only legacy of revolution is long-lasting hatred and division.

—There will never be a true Republic without the cleansing fire of a revolution.

—Reason, not passion, was Saint-Simon's guiding principle. He taught that lasting change can only be brought about through education.

—Is that why you're becoming a teacher?

—Yes, to educate the poor, give them a voice, improve their material lot.

—Then we both believe in equality.

—In his last book, *The New Christianity*, Saint-Simon

says that the spiritual and economic direction of society should come from men of science, not priests and politicians. This book has a mystical, prophetic quality about it. He openly declares his belief in God, and insists that a true Republic will only arise when the moral and material conditions of the poorest classes are improved.

— Our ends are the same, I muse. It's a question of means: education or revolution?

— Saint-Simon died five years ago, but his ideas have been taken up by the likes of Rodrigues, Enfantin, Bazard. Why don't you come to one of our meetings? There's no compulsion to become a member. Who knows, you might discover that mathematics is the noblest means to a Republic.

22

—Concentrate on this, says Chevalier, pointing to my article in Férussac's journal.

Despite opposing views concerning the means to a Republic, our friendship has grown since our first meeting several weeks ago. At times I envy his accommodating nature, his restraint in confronting those with different views, his calm temperament. If my emotions were not so easily agitated I would have been in the Polytechnic now, working exclusively on mathematics. Chevalier's ideals are anchored in reality; his politics, based on clear principles; his aims, definite.

Encouraged by him, I have tried to subdue my political passions and pursue my research, but my concentration has lapsed in the face of increasing unrest in Paris. How can I focus on mathematics when the city is on the brink of chaos? The smell of gunpowder mingles with spring's fragrances. Smoke from foundries and ammunition factories blurs the burgeoning sun. Signs of revolution are everywhere. King Charles is becoming more intractable in dealing with the opposition; the Church is reasserting its influence in schools and colleges; strikes are proliferating. The unrest has infiltrated the school, despite the spiked walls, the strong gates, and Guigniault's warning and threats. As one of the leaders of the Republican group at school, I ignore the ban on political gatherings and dismiss with contempt the extensive network of spies that reports to the Director. I am continually urging the other Republicans to be more outspoken, more active in their support.

—There's nothing to fear, I told a group at a secret meeting not long ago. The Revolution is at the gates. Our two-faced Director will be compelled to declare his loyalties. There's no place for neutrality in times like these. Our brothers at the Polytechnic need our support. We must match their courage.

But the majority were not stirred. On the contrary, they were apprehensive, afraid of being expelled. A few even spoke against revolution, saying it would collapse society and precipitate chaos. After that meeting, many distanced themselves from me, accusing me of being a dangerous fanatic who would undermine the cause. But I continued unperturbed, meeting regularly with a small group of committed radicals.

Sitting on the bench where we first met, I squint at the fresh print glistening in the spring sun, at the author's name, bold in black. Unlike my first publication, which excited me for days, the sight of the present article leaves me unmoved. Have I been exiled from mathematics? Is the only way of returning through the future Republic? Yes! Not only will a Republic restore me to my rightful place, it will vindicate Father, prove that his death was not in vain.

—There's no time for mathematics, I say, looking up

from the glare of the page. The Republic needs one's heart and mind.

—Mathematics needs you, Evariste.

—Tell that to those old owls in the Academy! They're blind, the lot of them! I've been there five times and they still can't find my paper.

—Which paper?

—The memoir I submitted for the Grand Prize. Fourier was supposed to read it and pass it on to the committee, to the likes of Legendre, Poisson, Lacroix, Poinsot. But he died and my memoir wasn't submitted. I made inquiries, but there was no trace of it among his papers, nor at the Academy. It seems to have vanished from under the very noses of our most distinguished academics. The only good thing to come out of all this stupidity, or maybe willful negligence, is that this year's Grand Prize was awarded to Abel posthumously for a memoir the Academy lost some years ago, but which somehow surfaced, and then only after a great deal of controversy and pressure from diplomatic quarters. Who knows, perhaps my memoir is buried somewhere, awaiting the same fate.

—It's a slight setback, Evariste. Don't be discouraged. If I had your talent, I would make the Academy take notice.

—Talent! Without the right temperament it's nothing but torment!

Urged by Chevalier to strike while the iron's hot and submit more work to Férussac's journal, I have managed to summon a little enthusiasm during the past week to work on two papers: "Notes on the Solution of Equations" and "On the Theory of Numbers." But, as with the first article,

I wrote these dispassionately, more to please Chevalier than for the sake of seeing them in print. Just as I would once resist anything that interfered with mathematics, so now I resist anything that obstructs my road to the Republic.

Sunday afternoon, the middle of June, and the gardens are colored with summer's crayons, complemented by rich shadows.

Having sidestepped Chevalier's invitation a number of times, I finally succumbed to his disappointed look and agreed to go with him to a meeting of the Saint-Simonists. The hall was full of enthusiastic young men and women, mainly from the bourgeoisie. Throughout the meeting strong perfume wafted my way as the woman next to me fanned herself vigorously.

—Well, what do you think? Chevalier asks excitedly.

—Your society will split in two, I reply.

—What makes you think that?

—Bazard's advocating a Republic with a strong central government, while Enfantin's proposing a mystical paradise. The two are incompatible.

—That's the essence of Saint-Simon.

Chevalier takes me by the arm and pulls me across the street, avoiding a convoy of wagons creaking and grinding under a load of newly hewn cobblestones that spice the air with a phosphorous smell.

—A union of science and religion, body and soul: That's our aim. Saint-Simon saw poetry in machines, and God's spirit in the engine.

—Your ideas may have lived comfortably together in

204

the person of Saint-Simon, but they now inhabit two distinct skulls, and I see nothing but division.

— You're wrong, he protests. Membership has doubled in the past six months, subscriptions to the *Globe* are increasing weekly, we're drawing some of the most promising and talented young men in France.

— Then I had better join. I laugh.

— It's no joke, he says, smarting.

I apologize and we walk in silence for a while.

— What did Bazard mean by the words *rehabilitation of matter?*

— In an earlier talk Bazard explained that industry has for too long used human beings as its cheap and dispensable driving force. It's now time to use natural resources instead of manual power. Through mathematics and science, matter can be transformed into machines that will harness nature and make it serve human needs. Once nature is tamed, human beings will never again be exploited or subjected to degrading labor.

— And Enfantin? What did he mean by the *rehabilitation of the flesh?*

We are now in a square churning with humanity, overflowing with the words of speakers. Students, merchants, seminarians, professionals, tradesmen, farmers: They are all proclaiming their views, all straining to shout above each other. As we make our way through the cacophony, Chevalier points out that in developing Saint-Simon's more mystical ideas, Enfantin urged people to overcome those Christian precepts that denigrate the body and make sexual relations shameful. Economic liberation is not enough: People must also have sexual freedom if they are to realize their potential. For Enfantin—and this is where he alienates the conservative element—people should do away with the present idea of marriage, with all its trappings of ownership and property, and live in a communal arrangement, where men and women share not only their belongings but their bodies. Flesh rehabilitated is a body free of sin and guilt, restored to the glorious form worshiped by the ancient Greeks, the sublime state before the Fall.

—Enfantin's mad, I say. Passion should be used to bring about a revolution, not squandered on debauchery. How can anyone love the Republic if they succumb to the lust he's advocating?

Women are gathered around a speaker with bare arms and red disheveled hair, standing on an upturned tub. In a shrill voice she complains about the inflated price of potatoes and exhorts her listeners to follow the example of their sisters in Chatillon, who banded in force and compelled the merchants to sell below the fixed price.

—And if they don't lower the price?

She takes off her sabots and cracks them against each other. The others follow her example, causing a deafening racket.

—Do you accept Enfantin's views, Auguste?

—I don't know, he replies, cheeks glowing. I haven't had . . . relations with women.

—It's shameful! I would rather remain celibate than wallow in what Enfantin advocates. The Republic will arise from purity, self-denial, self-sacrifice if necessary, not from promiscuity and self-indulgence covered in a veil of mysticism. We must overcome the flesh, not succumb to it.

With the entire afternoon to ourselves, Chevalier and I wander through the square for some time, discussing our views on a Republic, stopping here and there to listen to some of the more animated speakers, avoiding hawkers and beggars. From the back of a cart, standing on a barrel with rusted hoops, a bearded man is raging with all the fury of an Old Testament prophet. We stand beside his gray mule harnessed to the cart.

—They're taxing us to death, he bellows, punching his left palm with a fist the size of a cannonball. Talk! That's all they do! Damned Chamber of Deputies! In the meantime we're being crushed to death. Seventy petitions! Sixty thousand signatures and still no action! Foreigners impose crippling tariffs on our goods, and all they do is talk. In some areas production costs are twice the value of the wine itself, and all they do is talk. And now, on top of everything, we've had such an icy winter. The harvest will be good for nothing but raisins and sultanas. I tell you, we're facing ruin, and what do we get from the King, from Martignac, from the deputies? Talk!

—We've had enough. We'll fight the tax collectors. We'll tear up the vines and plant pumpkins and potatoes. Just think for a moment, good people. What would life be without wine? You, sir, with that crutch, your misery would be unbearable without your daily drop. And you, madam, a sip of red restores the roses on your cheeks. And you, young man—he points to Chevalier—that glass before the evening promenade empowers your heart, and suddenly you're bold as Napoleon, daring as Casanova. The ancients were right: *In vino veritas*. Not only truth, but hopes and dreams.

207

—And let the Church not forget our plight, unless it wants to offer the Eucharist with pumpkin. Remember, citizens, without wine we're doomed to misery, squalor, poverty, crushing injustices. Wine, more than any revolution, is the great liberator. Wine gives us a better future. Wine, more than the words of the priest, fosters communion with God. I urge you, good citizens, to support us in our protest against the taxes on wine. Help us show Martignac and his deputies that the people won't be denied their consolation, their comfort, their hope. I assure you, good men and women, poor students, retired soldiers, I assure you, if we tear out our vines, wine would become so expensive that only the upper classes could afford it.

The crowd erupts in wild clapping, shouting, whistling. Those near the cart reach up to shake the fellow's hand. The mule begins heaving and grunting.

—Listen to that, says one of the listeners. Even the mule's against the government.

As if excited by the show of support, the fellow jumps from the barrel and picks up the reins.

—Follow me, good citizens! To the Hôtel de Ville! Let's pour this barrel of red at the deputies' feet as a sign of what's to come if they don't act.

Chanting "Wine not words," the crowd follows the cart.

—Wine! I hate it.

—If it were up to me, Chevalier nods, I would increase the tax tenfold. There's already too much drunkenness on the streets. The Republic must be founded on solid facts, not vaporous dreams. Besides, there will be no need for

208

wine in a society where science has vouchsafed the happiness of its citizens.

We stop before a fellow addressing a small group of grinning listeners. Despite the afternoon heat, he is wearing a greatcoat shining with grease, covered in pictures, pages, and newspaper cuttings about Napoleon. Sweat sparkles on his rippled forehead, his blue eyes dart about like wrens. He is reciting a poem, written in Alexandrine couplets, eulogizing Napoleon and the Empire, unperturbed by those standing under his nose, reading the articles pinned to his coat. Chevalier sweeps his hand over the fellow's face.

— Blind, he whispers.

— Poets! I scoff. The old Bonapartist will re-create the past under the strong intoxication of nostalgia. Plato was right: Poets should be banned from the Republic.

In the middle of the square, a man is pacing a plank mounted on trestles. He is wearing a red cap and wide belt with carpentry tools dangling from it. As he shouts and swings his arms, the tools rattle, the beam creaks, the trestles strain.

— And, I ask you, brothers, will they give their lives for the Republic? Our lawyers? Doctors? Journalists? Politicians? No! And the poor? They're no better: They'll go and follow whoever promises better living conditions. It's us, brothers! We're the ones who'll die for the Republic. Us carpenters, masons, cobblers, tailors, clockmakers. Priests have been visiting our workshops, pushing the Royalist cause in the name of Christ. Wolves dressed as lambs, brothers! Don't trust them! Don't let them seduce your apprentices with a loaf of bread. I've got nothing against

209

Christ; after all, he was one of us. But I urge you to be on your guard against the Jesuits.

He signals to a boy of twelve or thirteen, who struggles to lift a large wooden cross onto the plank. Holding it upright with one hand, waving the other, the speaker spits out his invectives, spraying those at the front.

—I pulled this out of a schoolyard this morning. A plague of them is springing up all over the place. We've got to uproot them, brothers! Don't let them Jesuits get the better of us. Wood for houses, for tables, for beds—not for the likes of this!

Lowering the cross, resting it against the plank, he calls out to the boy, who springs to action and hands him a bucket and brush. He slaps pitch onto the top section of the cross and sticks on some dry straw, then focuses a magnifying glass on it. In an instant flame bursts from the pitch. Grinning, he raises the cross onto the plank and turns it upside down, making the flame more fierce. Dropping the burning cross onto the cobbles, he signals to his assistant again, who this time hands him a poplar sapling.

—Not crosses, brothers! Not trees of death! This is what we ought to be planting. Trees of light! Trees of life! Trees of liberty! Paris is choking with the stench of oppression. Trees, brothers, as a sign of revolt, a symbol of the future. Follow me, brothers. To the schoolyard where I uprooted that, to plant this.

This is greeted with cries of approval. Jumping from the plank, he raises the sapling high in the air, as though it is a flag, and marches forward, followed by the boisterous crowd. The assistant and a few other boys disassemble the plank and trestles, load them onto their shoulders, and trot after the others.

—The Revolution is not far off, I say.

And as we walk past, I poke at the burning cross with my foot: The head is still flourishing with red hair, the white skin has blistered. The air is strong with paint and pitch.

—When people turn from reason destruction follows, Chevalier frowns, stepping over the cross.

—You Saint-Simonists are too cautious.

—We're realists.

—And what am I, Auguste?

—Shoes! Shoes!

An old fellow with a battered top hat approaches us, hawking an assortment of shoes, boots, sabots, and slippers swaying from a pole balanced on his shoulder. Stopping in front of us, he dances on the flame, extinguishing it. He then picks up the cross, breaks off the arms with a powerful stomp, hoists the two pieces on one shoulder, the pole on the other, and sets off.

—Shoes! Shoes!

Full-moon light squeezes through the dormitory's lou-vered windows. The city's bells strike their twelve-note melody. Unsettled by the confusion of ideas in the square, I stare at apocalyptic images appearing and disappearing in the pressed-metal ceiling.

Who am I? Where are the absolutes by which I can chart a course for myself? As the afternoon flared to a blazing sunset, I was shaken by a feeling of my own insignificance. When we returned to school, I had become so taciturn I left Chevalier in the courtyard and hurried to the library, not to read but to be alone behind the covers of Lagrange's book on algebra. A mosquito whispers over my head.

Where is my center of gravity? Where do I now belong? This time last year I felt at home in mathematics, certain of my talent, driven by the belief that my work on equations would reward me with a place in history.

Now? Instead of the great temple of mathematics I seem to be adrift in blood's turbulence. Will I ever enter that temple again? Experience its order, equanimity, transcendence? I swipe at the mosquito and tighten my fist. Silence. There is a spot of stickiness in my palm. Yes. Pythagoras was burned defending that temple, Archimedes was butchered for it, poor Abel was buried for its sake. If I am to be of some worth, and not a straw in the wind, I must also defend the temple, especially now that it is most under attack from conservative forces. Once the Revolution has been won, the Republic instituted, Father's death avenged, then, purged of anger and hatred, I will wash my hands and enter that temple again.

Can you hear my thoughts, future biographer? I know you are here, in the dark. I can almost feel your presence, like this strip of moonlight on my forehead. You are the thinness of a thought away, listening, taking everything in, as though a confessor behind an opaque screen. Past, present, future: Maybe that is an old way of looking at things, a remnant of the idea of a flat earth. Who knows? A new consciousness may arise where those tenses will be obsolete, a state that will accommodate such grammar as "I died yesterday." After all, time is not a series of discrete points;

it is a wave function, continuous everywhere, each instant related to all others by the ultimate equation. Through this new consciousness I may even learn the meaning of infinite patience.

The ingredients are all here: a life caught between the forces of history and the fate of the individual, between the demands of tradition and the freedom of creativity, between the insights of genius and the passions of adolescence. Not only my life, but the very substance and form of my work expresses the rebellious spirit of the times. Come closer, biographer. Grasp my fitful thoughts, my turbulent emotions; save me from disintegrating in the dark, draw me to the future with the gravity of ink.

23

Thermidor: gift of heat. Thermidor: the eleventh month in the calendar of the Revolution. Thermidor: from 20 July to 18 August. It is the morning of 26 July, and there is not a cloud to threaten the sovereign sun. The heat has been relentless during the past three days. The cobbles in the school courtyard shimmer, the white flag hangs lifeless. Preparing for their lessons, the students move lethargically, yawning so wide their jaws crack and tears squeeze from their eyes. Just before eight o'clock, on my way to Physics, I am roused from thoughts of Thermidor by a commotion in the corridor: The word *Ordinances* buzzes like a belligerent bee, stinging ears, making bodies jump to life.

—Ordinances!

—Four Ordinances!

—King Charles has imposed four Ordinances!

Ignoring the insistent bell summoning them to class, the students gather in groups and discuss the measures taken by Charles. The stinging news could not have come at a better time. Squinting (lately I have been struggling to read the blackboard from the back of the room), I bow close to the *Moniteur*, the official government newspaper, as a few others look over my shoulder.

—He has dissolved the Chamber, called for new elections, revoked the Charter of 1815, and imposed conditions on the freedom of the press.

My words barely contain my emotion. I pass the paper to another student. The fresh ink has stained my palms.

—This means Revolution, I announce. The students must be organized at once. We've got to be on the streets when the first shots are fired, together with our brothers the Polytechnicians, the law students, the medical students.

Excited by the prospect of Revolution, I am surprised by the look of the other students: They appear circumspect, apprehensive, as though uncertain of what the Ordinances will bring.

—Paris has seen enough bloodshed, one of them comments.

—You're too cautious, Molins, I snap. The Republic won't be realized through debate and negotiation. Daring! That's what will win the day. A daring fueled by a blind hatred of injustice.

—Anarchy, sneers Molins, that's what your bloody revolution will bring about. And suppose Charles is driven out, who's to say someone more despotic won't take his place?

—Are you against the cause? I retort, turning on him savagely. Are you saying we should allow the Ordinances? Allow the Jesuits to control education?

—I'm saying we shouldn't rush into things. I'm against Charles, but I don't want another Napoleon either. My father died at Waterloo because of him.

—And the Jesuits killed my father!

215

—I say we wait, says another, stepping between us. Let's see what the liberal deputies do, and the journalists, they're the ones directly affected by the Ordinances.

—Cowards! I shout, snatching the newspaper from Molins. You tremble at Giugniault's shadow!

Dashing out, I am momentarily blinded by the sun: Its circle flashes at each blink. The cobbles are already hot. At the entrance the groundskeeper stands stolidly in the arched gateway.

—Where to? he asks, gnawing on a knuckle.

—I've got an appointment at the Hôtel de Ville.

—Where's your pass?

—It's urgent.

—You'd better run off to your lesson.

I check an impulse to throw the newspaper at the fellow's head and dash out. Expelled, I will not be able to lead the students onto the streets, into the Revolution. I turn back to the corridor, which is swarming with speculation.

The unrest caused by the newspaper continues in class. I attempt to persuade the moderates to boycott the afternoon lessons in protest at the Ordinances, but they will not be drawn in. It is almost the end of the school year, they reply. They have to prepare for examinations. Have I forgotten that the country is in the grip of an economic crisis? Competition for teaching positions is fierce: Those with the highest grades stand the best chance.

—This is no time for petty self-interests, I say to the student next to me.

He takes no notice. He is too busy scribbling the solution to a projectile motion problem before the teacher sweeps the blackboard clean for the next solution.

—Do you hear? I nudge him with my elbow.

He continues to write frantically while staring wide-eyed at the blackboard. I dismiss him from my thoughts and envisage myself in the front lines, a pistol in one hand and the tricolor in the other, leading a group of students. Gazing at the projectile's parabolic path and the solution of the quadratic equation that determines its maximum range, my thoughts flit from the quintic to . . . A temple of mathematics! The very thing the Revolution is fighting against! Temples and Classicism have had their day! It is time for a new mathematics. One that will arise from the furnace of revolution, not the tranquillity of academic retreats. A mathematics engendered on the streets, among the turmoil of humanity, from the chaos of groups clashing, being destroyed, forming new groups. A mathematics grasped in the roar of a cannon as it projects its lethal sphere, or in the flash of a bayonet as it finds its mark, or in the warmth of blood oozing from a wound. What new geometries await the fearless mind? Perhaps triangles whose angles sum to more than 180 degrees. What new arithmetic is to be found in chaos? Perhaps division by zero made legitimate. What new algebras lie behind the phenomena of groups? Perhaps symbols that will replace x, y, and z and give rise to something more dynamic than functions: hyper-functions capable of explaining the universe and predicting the future.

The classroom is empty: I heard neither the bell nor the students as they left. At the blackboard I erase the solution to a problem on a falling body and write in large capitals: LONG LIVE THE REPUBLIC.

❀ ❀ ❀

217

In the stifling heat, just before the end of the last lesson for the day, a prefect enters the Chemistry class and instructs the students to assemble in the dining room for an important announcement by the school's Director.

—Well, Auguste, I say, walking in the corridor. Are you Saint-Simonists going to oppose the Ordinances?

—Don't squander your talent, Evariste.

—My talent is for the Revolution.

Sweating students gather in the dining room made even more oppressive by the smell from the kitchen. All the windows are open, but there is not a breath to stir the curtains. The red-faced chef appears at the back door, appraises the gathering with a few slow nods, and quickly disappears as Guigniault and six teachers enter the room and climb onto the squeaking platform.

—They look worried, I whisper to Chevalier.

The teachers sit on chairs arranged in a semicircle, while Guigniault stands at the front, the toes of his shoes just over the edge of the platform. He is about sixty, short, slow-moving, with bags under his eyes and a nose like a strawberry. In contrast to his movements, he has a habit of deftly licking his lips with the tip of his tongue. Rumor has it he is fond of brandy, and that its taste is always on his lips.

—We'll finally see his true colors, I nudge Chevalier.

—I won't keep you long, Guigniault begins, smoothing back the few remaining strands of hair. Your teachers have informed me that today's lessons were marred by inattention, in some cases by outright disobedience.

He pauses, wipes his palms with a white handkerchief, and arrests a murmur by raising his voice.

—The Ordinances are of no concern to you; their

218

rightness or wrongness will be determined by others. While you're students of this school, I insist you keep your politics to yourselves. It's reported that someone wrote a slogan on the blackboard. That sort of thing will not be tolerated! Anyone who disrupts classes, who engages in writing slogans, who attempts to coerce others toward politics, will be dealt with most severely. For your protection and to avoid disruption to the school, I've decided to keep the front gates closed until further notice.

A few students turn to each other in disbelief. The subdued murmur in the room encourages me to speak out.

—Are we students or prisoners? I protest.

The teachers spring from their chairs and gather around the Director.

—Students in my care, replies Guigniault in a soft tone.

And before I can say another word he turns and walks out, followed by the teachers.

In the dormitory students are standing at the windows, straining to see through the still night, staring in the direction of the Tuileries, the Palais Royal, the Louvre, the Hôtel de Ville—the places where the Revolution is likely to start. But instead of the shot that will spark the city from sleep, the stifling silence is broken by the odd moth thumping blindly against a windowpane, or a clap ending a mosquito's frenzy. I stand with Chevalier, Benard, and Flaugergues at a window overlooking the courtyard. A dog nearby barks, rattling a heavy chain.

—They say Guigniault's against the Ordinances, says Chevalier.

—Who says? asks Flaugergues.

—He told Roden in private this evening.

—Roden! He's a spy! I retort. That's Guigniault's way of trying to keep us quiet. Would he have locked us in if he were really against the Ordinances? Don't believe them! They'll use any ploy to get their way.

—The flag came down well before sunset, says Chevalier. Doesn't that say something about his views?

—And did he hoist the tricolor in its place? I counter. No! That says even more about his views. He's a cunning old fox, all right. He has taken down the flag so that it won't provoke us. Not only that, he's keeping his options open: If the Revolution succeeds, he'll say he took down the Royal flag as an act of protest; if it fails, he'll say he took it down to protect it from the radical elements who threatened to burn it.

—You surprise me, Evariste, says Chevalier. I didn't think you were capable of such cynicism.

—It's subtlety, Auguste. The subtlety that has fathomed the solubility of equations can fathom the motivations of men.

I wake with a start: The louvered shutters have been left open and the dormitory is filled with gunmetal gray. It was well after two when I lay down, and then fully dressed, down to my shoes, just in case. But nothing has happened: The heart of the city is quiet. A bird, perhaps the first, twitters uncertainly, as though trying to find the right pitch in order to greet the sun's ascent.

—Any signs? I call to a student yawning at the window.

—Nothing, not even a breath.

—Fanatics! complains another several beds away. The bell hasn't sounded yet. Sleep's precious.

—Shove your head in the pillow, I say.

—And I was having such a lovely dream, sighs the student, putting his hands under his head. I can still see her bare feet tickling the water. We were on a grassy riverbank, under a willow tree. I slipped my hand into her tight bodice and was about to . . . when a crow called from a tree, and that crow was you, Galois. Fanatic! You've denied me man's greatest pleasure. All your revolutions, all your Republics, all your ideals won't bring back that lost opportunity on the riverbank.

—Degenerate! Paris is poised on the brink of a revolution, men are preparing to die for the Republic, and you dare to talk like that!

—Only fools die for ideals, laughs the student, lying now on his side, his head propped on one arm. I'll let you in on a secret, Galois, but before I do, tell me straight: Have you ever been with a woman?

—There are more important things in life!

—What? Dying for ideals?

—Yes!

—Listen, he whispers. I'd rather mount a woman and ride to paradise than be on horseback facing a cannon.

A prefect shatters the dormitory with a bell.

—Get up! Get dressed! Get out!

Speculation about happenings in the city center grows during the morning. The radicals interpret the silence as the calm before the storm; the Royalists, as a sign that the lib-

221

eral deputies have been intimidated by the King's decisive actions, and that they're afraid to oppose his Ordinances. At midday, with the sun more ferocious than yesterday, my group hurries to the shade of the cypresses along the back wall. Appearing from the dining room's side door, the chef looks around, then hobbles toward us.

—It's hell in that kitchen, he says, wiping his face with a moist red cloth he keeps under his apron string.

—What's happening out there? I ask, seizing him by his hairy forearm.

—The people were out in force protesting against the Ordinances. Ragged street children were chanting: "Long live the Republic." And you should've seen those students from the Polytechnic: strutting about, tapping their canes, waving their hats, shouting "Long live the Republic."

Envy and rage well up in me: I should be out there with them, leading my group, stirring the people to revolt.

—And the newspapers? asks Benard.

The chef looks around, then quickly pulls out a copy of the *Temps* from under his apron.

—Not a word on where you got it, understand?

We gather over it, heads touching, as the chef continues.

—I'm coming here along the Rue Richelieu when I notice a gathering outside the offices of the *Temps*. There's also a detachment of mounted troops, there to confiscate the presses for defiance of the Ordinances. Well, you should've seen the way the editor handled it. His name's Baude, I think. Sent a shiver down my spine. He stands on the step of the printing house, opens a copy of the Code, and reads aloud the law relating to robbery, trespassing, and housebreaking, then dares the troops to push him aside. The crowd roars its support; the troops look at each other, not knowing what to do. I couldn't stay to see the outcome, but Baude's bravery was enough for me. The King's got a real fight on his hands this time. Papers are rustling about like autumn leaves all over the city, in the poor suburbs and the rich, in reading rooms and alehouses, in cafés and canteens, in fashionable restaurants and at the fish market. Journalists are rushing from factory to workshop with piles under their arms, giving away free copies. I tell you, the flame's been lit. Stoked by the newspapers, it will turn into an inferno.

The chef's words have ignited me. I must get out of this prison. I turn to the courtyard: The bare flagpole has gathered its shadow to its base; the front gates are closed; the groundskeeper is sitting in the archway, mending a pair of boots, his arm shoulder-deep in leather.

—I'd better get back, says the chef apprehensively. I'm going out again this afternoon. Meet me here at seven and I'll tell you the latest.

—We've got to stir up the students, I exhort the others. Guigniault's a coward, he doesn't want a revolt in the school. He'll open the gates if we have the numbers. We must get out before the Revolution starts.

Despite my efforts, my impassioned arguments in the name of liberty, my assurance that the Revolution is imminent, even the evidence of the *Temps*—by evening I have not managed to win the numbers needed to challenge the Director's authority. Sunset blazes over the city as we go to our meeting with the chef. Hearts of shopkeepers, the lot of them! Gritting my teeth, I am infuriated by the rejections, the indifference, the outright fear shown by the majority. More cautious than this morning, the chef slinks between cypresses and wall, his limp more pronounced. He leans on the tree trunk and, gasping for air, slaps a wet cloth on the fleshy folds around the back of his neck. We press around him.

— Not so close, boys, he sighs. Let me catch my breath. This heat's unbearable. This leg's killing me, too. Haven't done so much walking since the Russian campaign.

— What's happening out there? I ask.

— The police guarding the Palais Royal were pelted with stones. A barricade went up near the Théâtre Français, followed by two more across the Rue St. Honore. I saw elegant ladies leaning over balconies, waving to confused young recruits, imploring them not to hurt the people. And then, boys, I witnessed a sight that brought tears to these eyes. A young worker, a carpenter by the look of him, ran out on the Quai de l'Ecole waving the tricolor. The crowd along the riverwalls was stunned. We all stood there, speechless, tears in our eyes, as the young man ran past with the flag fluttering and the sole of his left shoe flapping at each step.

— The Revolution's not far off, says Benard.

— It has started, I exclaim. And here we are, still talking, no better than those liberal deputies!

— What can we do? asks Flaugergues, pointing to the locked gate.

— Charras wants you to . . .

Charras. He was a former student of the Polytechnic, expelled six months ago for singing the "Marseillaise" at a school banquet.

—Where did you see him? I ask the chef. What did he say?

The chef looks alarmed by my tone, pulling away from my tight grip on his forearm.

—Tell me! I demand.

—On my way back I was approached by three youths in civilian clothes who said they were students of the Polytechnic. They'd somehow learned that I was a chef here and loyal to the cause, and before I knew it they took me to the Rue des Fosses-du-Temple. A small apartment was packed with students scrambling out of their uniforms and into civilian clothes. A young man pushed through and introduced himself as Charras. He told me to pass on a message to the students in the Preparatory loyal to the cause.

—What message? I prod him.

—He wants you to do whatever's necessary to incite the students here. He said the students of the Polytechnic have boycotted their classes, and that representatives have gone to Laffitte, Casimir Perier, and Lafayette, declaring they are ready to support them not just in word, but in deed.

He looks around from his cover behind a tree trunk, then reaches under his apron, which he wears back to front, and produces a parcel wrapped in newspaper and tied with pink ribbon.

—More newspapers! exclaims Benard, snatching them.

—I don't think so, says the chef. Charras told me to guard it well. Said you'd know what to do with it.

Benard tears away the wrapping—the tricolor.

225

—A blessed day, remarks the chef.

Removing his cap stained with sweat, he bows and kisses the flag. One by one, the others lay their hands on it and close their eyes. Last, I clutch a section of red and make a silent oath to escape from this prison, swearing I will be as active in the Revolution as Charras, vowing to avenge Father's death by fighting for the Republic.

24

At supper the members of my group distributed themselves among the tables, determined to win sympathizers. But when the clatter of cutlery subsided, we did not have the numbers needed to force the Director's hand. Sneering, the Royalists pointed to the relative calm outside as proof of the King's strong position. Even though most students were against the Ordinances, they were nevertheless fearful of a revolution and argued for judicial opposition to the King's measures. Chevalier, the only Saint-Simonist at the school, advocated restraint on the grounds that chaos is against scientific principles.

— Don't do anything rash, Evariste, he whispered, as a few Royalists at our table chuckled provocatively.

I sprang to my feet. Moths fluttered furiously around the overhead lamps. Necks twisted, faces strained, hands clutched knives and forks. The chef appeared and leaned against the back wall. I wanted to rail against the apathetic, exhort the fearful, blast the Royalists. I wanted to move them with words, the way the speakers in the squares moved entire crowds. But once again when emotions got the better of me, words betrayed me: They clotted together, became a constriction in my throat, choked me. A murmur rose from the tables. The chef shook his head. Treacherous words!

—Enough talk! I gasped. It's time for action! The Revolution needs . . .

—You're boring, Galois, shouted a student from a back table.

I snatched a fork and threw it at him—it struck the wall.

—And mad, yelled another, leaping to his feet.

I turned savagely to attack him, but Chevalier and Benard ushered me out. The night was hot, heavy with the smell of smoke. Here and there musket shots were muffled by the pall stifling the city. Horses and carriages rumbled past the school. Light from a three-quarter moon sheened the courtyard, glinted on the spikes along the top of the wall.

—I say we hoist the flag, said Benard.

—Save it for the streets, replied Flaugergues.

—There will be no revolution tonight, added Chevalier.

I stood a few steps from them, under a wall lamp guarded by two gaping griffins. Impelled by blind rage, I leaped down the stairs and ran to the front gate. The large padlock was still warm from the sun. I hammered it against a metal plate. A door in the entrance opened and a shadow spilled onto the curved wall. A shot cracked in the distance.

—Who's there? asked the groundskeeper.

—Open the gate, I screamed, rattling the padlock.

—You again!

—For the Republic's sake! Open the gate!

Broad feet flat on the doorstep, a vest over his bare

chest, he raised both arms and leaned on the low lintel, revealing armpits like nests.

— Get back to the dormitory, son.

— They're fighting for your sake, I pleaded, walking into his shadow. They need help. The Revolution's ready to explode!

— Revolution! he grunted, spitting the word into the dark. I've seen one in my lifetime, and that's more than enough! Listen to me, son, don't be taken in by them smooth-talking professionals. You think they really care about us working folk? Not a bit! They stir us up for their own advantage! I fell for their lies once, never again! If, heaven forbid, a revolution does break out, you won't find them professionals on the streets or at the barricades. Never! It's us working folk who will stain the stones, you can be sure of that. Them cunning rogues stoke the fire with their hot breath, while the poor workers . . .

He snorted and spat into a patch of light.

— Want my advice, son? Look after your own skin and stay away from politics. The Director's given me orders not to open the gates for anyone, and that's how it's going to be. Now go back to the dormitory, read a good adventure story, and get revolution out of your head.

The janitor extinguishes the dormitory lamps and, on instructions from the Director, locks the door, though not before apologizing. Groups of students leave their beds and gather again at the windows. The sky is clearer than last night: Constellations crowd upon the city; bright above cypresses the moon silvers anxious faces. A succession of shots crackle. Tense with expectation, I lean farther forward into the window's alcove for a better look. Silence. Not too far away a few sleepy streetlamps are suddenly blacked out.

—They're breaking the lamps, remarks Chevalier. What demons will be let loose on Paris tonight?

Between the cypresses, I can see a fire flourishing on a nearby crossroad.

Gradually the dormitory becomes quieter, the sporadic shooting outside stops, most of the students have gone to bed. Chevalier and I are still at the window, caught in a prism of light cast by the moon, now almost at its zenith.

—Look up there, Evariste. Look at the order of the stars . . . That's what men should strive for. Newton and Kepler explained the universe in terms of equations, which dealt a deadly blow to the god of Moses. Laplace is my hero, not Napoleon. He banished God from his celestial mechanics and sought to grasp not Europe, but the universe by means of equations.

—The age of the priest, poet, politician is over: The new millennium will be the age of the mathematician. Don't be seduced by what's happening out there, Evariste. The word has had its day: The human condition hasn't been improved by verse, religion, or legislation. It's now time for number to rule the world. You could become a great mathematician, your work on equations may do more to improve people's lives than a hundred revolutions, your theories may turn out to have applications in physics and medicine.

—This is no time for dreams, I say, twisting the window's latch. Laplace's ordered universe is breaking apart. Look out there, not up there. Where's the mathematician who will plunge into chaos and pluck out the new equations? Equations that will subdue chaos and create the Republic? I can't sit back in classical equanimity, Auguste. I've got to throw myself into that chaos. If I survive I might be the founder of a new mathematics; if not, at least I would have been true to my father's memory and given my life in the name of freedom.

—Come on, Evariste, he smiles, placing a hand on my shoulder. Let's go to bed. Your revolution won't start tonight.

—I'm not tired, I reply.

The fire on the crossroad has collapsed to a heap of winking embers, the shadows that flitted around it have disappeared. Three leaden tolls strike against my temples. Not a shot since one. Twisting the latch, I open the window, climb into the alcove, and lean over the sill. A faint breeze whispers in the cypresses, scented with smoke and tinder from the countryside. I look for a way down: nothing, not even a drainpipe. If the shooting had escalated, if the signs had indicated a revolution were imminent, I would have tied sheets and blankets and risked a drop of two or three meters. But the lull alleviates my anxiety. Chevalier is right, at least for the time being. But what if the day's unrest has been contained and crushed by the troops? What if there is nothing more tomorrow? I swipe at a mosquito. No! It is the calm before the storm. The night smells of gunpowder. Tomorrow, Paris will explode. I settle into the alcove, arms wrapped around my legs, chin on knees. As my heart throbs against my thin thighs, I watch, listen, strain for a sign, a sound, the spark that will explode this oppressive night.

✳   ✳   ✳

A volley of shots startles me from sleep. Gray light squeezes through cracks in the dark. Birds chatter in the cypresses. More shots from various quarters. I climb onto the sill for a better view. Thick ropes of smoke twist straight up. Horses are clopping in all directions. The Revolution! The key rattles in the door, the bell blasts, the janitor bawls that all students must assemble in the courtyard at half past five for an address by the Director. He is about to leave when he notices my bed.

—Where's Galois? he demands of the student in the next bed, ringing the bell over him.

Looking around desperately, the janitor sees me on the sill.

—Stop! he shrieks, mouth wide as the bell.

Shocked from sleep, the students freeze at the sight of me standing on the edge of the sill. I seize the moment.

—Cowards! I shout. Hear the shots! The Revolution has begun. People are dying for your sake! Our brothers on the streets need us! We must get him to open the gate, with force if necessary.

The janitor approaches the window stealthily, like a cat stalking a sparrow.

—That's far enough, Henri! I threaten, stepping back, my heels off the sill.

—Evariste! cries Chevalier.

—Don't do it, boy, says the janitor.

—Cowards! The lot of you! If my words can't stir you to oppose tyranny, perhaps my death will.

Holding the top of the window frame, I lean slightly backward. Some of the students wince, others look away. The janitor reaches out with the bell.

—Evariste! Chevalier implores.

—I'm on the edge of a downward asymptote, Auguste! Another step, and . . . negative infinity. Who knows, death might be the singular point in an otherwise continuous function of time. One instant consciousness is free-falling into negative infinity, the next, or maybe the same instant, it soars toward positive infinity. Is death like that, Auguste? An instant when consciousness becomes transcendent, a point where contradictions are reconciled, a state where division by zero has meaning?

I pause, surprised by my fluency. If I were as composed last night I would not have made a fool of myself in the dining room.

—Don't get any closer, Henri. If I can't die on the streets fighting for the Republic, I'll die in an act of protest against you, Henri, and the Director, who keeps us here like common criminals. Maybe you cowards need a martyr.

—Get on with it, shouts the student whose lewd dream I interrupted. Jump or stop posturing. You're keeping us from breakfast.

Posturing!

The act backfires: Instead of inciting the students with theatrics, the word posturing angers me, and the situation becomes deadly serious. Suddenly I have something to prove to those I despise. It is a matter of honor. I have been challenged to a duel.

—Long live the Republic! I shout and turn to the courtyard.

The janitor pounces, catches me by the waist, and lifts me from the alcove. I slump over his shoulder without resistance. Sitting on my bed, I listen passively as the janitor upbraids me until he is short of breath.

—Thanks, Henri, I say softly, smiling. You needn't worry, I won't try it again.

As we wash ourselves at a circular trough, Chevalier leans toward me.

—Were you really going to jump, Evariste? he whispers above the slapping and splashing.

The water cools my burning face and ears. Has the night-long vigil resulted in a temperature? Is this the onset of another fever?

—I gambled on Henri catching me.

—And if he hadn't?

—The Revolution would have had its first martyr.

The bags under Guigniault's eyes are fuller than usual as he waits for the students to assemble. Henri stands beside him on the steps to the dining room, whispering in his ear. Outside the unrest is growing: Shots, probably snipers, crackle from all parts of the city; carriages, probably with merchants, bankers, deputies, editors, rattle past at a gallop; wagons, probably loaded with rocks and wood for the barricades, rumble heavily; children, probably those who live on the streets, sing "Long live the Republic" to the tune of a nursery rhyme; strong voices, probably men sidetracked from their way to work, shout "Liberty," stressing the syllables in time with their marching boots.

—Today's the day, I say to Benard, feeling a hot flush turn to a chill.

—Hear the turmoil out there, begins the Director, licking his lips. It's with great regret I've taken measures to keep you under lock and key. I love liberty as much as anybody here, but there are times when liberty must be curtailed for the sake of the future. I've been a teacher for almost forty years, and I know well the passions, the ideals, the spontaneity of youth. But I also know that there are people who would exploit youth's exuberance for their own ends. I ask you to bear these measures until Saturday, another three days, when I am sure we will see a political solution to the unfortunate business out there. In the meantime, I ask you all to give me your word of honor that you will not attempt to escape, that you will desist from any activity that might endanger other students and the school.

The students exchange looks, some nodding, others uncertain, a few scowling. A shot rings against the school wall.

—He's lying, I whisper to those around me.

—Is there anyone who cannot give their word of honor?

I raise my hand.

—Thank you for your honesty, Galois.

—Will you be honest with us, sir, and declare yourself: Are you for the Charter or against it?

The Director buries both hands in his pockets and bounces on his toes.

—My concern is to preserve the independence of our fine school. As some of you know, I could have retired last August, and led a quiet life, with time to read the many books I've had to put aside because of my duties. Yet I didn't, because I don't want the school to become a pawn in a political game. Education, the nurturing of character and intelligence, must remain independent of politics and religion. The last year has not been easy. I have resisted the Church in its push to exert more influence in schools, and withstood the Socialists, who would do away with a balanced curriculum. And now, I have to steer the school through these troubled times. I am determined to go neither left nor right, but to follow the middle way: the road of reason, the golden mean. And if some of you see me as sitting on the fence, if you accuse me of being weak and indecisive, if you denounce me as an opportunist, I will endure that for the school's sake.

A few students applaud. The janitor, who has been trying to remove something from his left eye, looks around sheepishly and also claps. Raising his arms, hands brightened by sun just peering over the rooftops, the Director thanks the students for their support and implores all for restraint until Saturday.

—Monsieur Guigniault. Another minute, if you please.

Benard attempts to pull me away.

—Haven't you had enough attention for one day? someone hisses.

—You're becoming boring, sneers another.

—What is it, Galois? Guigniault asks, licking a smile.

—I insist you open the gates, sir! For those of us compelled by conscience to help the people.

—And my conscience will not sanction the death of any student.

—When the Revolution has been won and history records how the law students, the medical students, the students of the Polytechnic all fought bravely for liberty, you will be blamed for the absence of students from the

Preparatory. This school will be without honor in the Republic.

We stare at each other for a moment, neither flinching, until the Director brushes back the light gleaming on his scalp, turns abruptly, and enters the dining room.

By midday the clamor of revolt scrambles over the wall and fills the shimmering courtyard. Crazed by the fierce sun, cicadas rage. Too agitated to concentrate on school-work, an agitation exacerbated by flushes and chills, I am in the yard alone, pacing the thick cypress shade, desperate to escape. From time to time, as though in need of a respite from the encroaching chaos, my thoughts turn momentarily to mathematics — flitting from the key for unlocking the secrets of equations, to the belief that the Revolution will eliminate the injustice responsible for Abel's death, to the hope that one day I will have time and peace of mind to develop my findings.

The padlock rattles: The groundskeeper opens the gate. I dart and hide behind a trunk. A boxed cart full of firewood enters the archway. This is my chance. The cart rumbles across the yard on its way to the kitchen. The driver's eyes are covered by a broad-brimmed hat. Flies blacken a gash on the horse's twitching flank. The axles are clogged with golden grease. I wait, squatting behind the tree trunk, my body trembling now with a flush of excitement, now with a chill of misgiving. When the cart returns, clattering louder now that it is empty, I run behind it and climb inside.

—All done? asks the groundskeeper.

—Don't know how I'll get home, drawls the driver. Them barricades are everywhere.

The archway is cool. I lie flat, my cheek pricked by bits of bark, heart beating against the boards.

—Good luck, says the groundskeeper, rattling the lock.

The horse plods a few steps.

—Stop! The janitor's voice stuns me.

—What's the matter? asks the groundskeeper.

Standing on the axle, the janitor leans over the side-board, his face beaming. I stand and brush the dust from my clothes. Suddenly I am in the executioner's cart, on my way to the guillotine, too tired to be afraid, even when the blade appears, dripping with sunlight. I climb the steps calmly, admiring its clean trapezoidal shape.

25

—Made a few notes this time, announces the chef, shuffling a scrap of paper from his apron. There's too much happening out there. Listen. No sign of it easing up. I'm no scholar, but I figured if I didn't write down what I saw soon after seeing it, I might forget it, or tell it different from what really happened. Paper and ink, my father used to say, they keep men honest.

—Is it a revolution?

The chef stops me with a reproving glance from the corner of his eye, then takes out a red cap, smooths out a few creases, and puts it on. His manner annoys me: He may be a good Republican, but this air of self-importance, his conceit in being the sole authority on events outside, has become more noticeable with each meeting. This is no time for haughtiness: The facts must be told plainly, honestly. Alone in the dormitory, I stood at the window all afternoon, straining to make sense of the calamitous events shaking the city, while bracing myself against a rising fever.

—I set out at sunrise with a sea of others for the center of Paris, he says. Groups are gathering at the Porte St. Martin and the Porte St. Denis. A wagonload of paving stones is used to barricade the entrance to the Faubourg

239

St. Denis. Printers are collecting in the Passage Dauphine, where a book warehouse has been turned into an arsenal. The crowd sweeps me along and we storm into the Théâtre du Vaudeville. We take two large wicker baskets full of costumes, arms, imperial uniforms. On the stage we scramble and dress for the greatest drama of our time. In the Rue de la Montagne–Sainte Genevieve we greet a group of students with: "Long live the Polytechnic," and they reply: "Long live Liberty." One of them raises his hat, rips out the white cockade, stamps on it, and shouts: "Down with the King." People tear off the royal arms from the court's workshops and smash them to pieces, or throw them into bonfires. The streetlamps that survived the night are smashed and oil spills onto the pavements. When I ask a fellow why he smashed a lamp, he replies that he wants to grease his boots, to march proudly into battle.

—The troops appear at the Place de Grève and open fire with cannons. The alarm bells from the church of St. Severin are answered by a thundering toll from Notre Dame. Trees from the boulevards are axed and used as barricades to prevent the passage of troops, cannons, cavalry. The fighting intensifies in the midday heat. Doors open to shelter armed revolutionaries, while the poor soldiers roast. Women take pity on the exhausted troops; they stop making lint and gunpowder to bring wine and water to bewildered recruits. By midafternoon the insurrection is raging all over the city, and everywhere the people seem to have the upper hand over troops unsuited to warfare in narrow lanes, against snipers, confronted by barricades. A Swiss detachment marches to help the troops stationed at the Hôtel de Ville. The sight of those hated red uniforms arouses even greater fury from the people, and they pour from every street and alley into the Place de Grève. A barricade is quickly set up. The Swiss press on, and for a short while it seems like they might get the better of us. But a young man, no older than you, runs out waving a tricolor on the end of a lance, shouting, "I'll show you how to die." He charges at the Swiss and is shot a lance's length from the enemy. His self-sacrifice incenses the people. The barricade stands firm against the Swiss, while a flood of humanity pours in from the rear, routing them after a furious engagement.

The chef wipes the saliva sticking to the corners of his mouth, and pauses just long enough to judge the reception of his narrative. The others stare, wide-eyed, waiting for him to continue. A knot tightens in my stomach. I should be out there. The Revolution will be over at this rate. I am envious of the young man with the lance.

—How can my poor words and this scrap of paper convey what I've seen? How can I describe the scene at Sainte-Pélagie prison, where the debtors smashed the gates and joined the guards to prevent hardened criminals from escaping and exploiting the turmoil? How can I convey the bravery of a workman who calmly approached a captain of a company entering the Place de la Bourse and struck him on the head with an iron bar? What's more, how can I convey the magnanimity of the captain who, blood oozing over his face, used his sword to knock down a soldier's musket as he was about to shoot the workman? What more can I tell you, boys? To do justice to all I saw today I'd need to be Hugo or Delacroix, but I'm just a chef with a scrap of paper.

He wipes his face, now redder than the sunset, and

tells us he will meet us again tomorrow. He no longer slinks against the wall but marches boldly across the courtyard. At the bare flagpole he stops for a moment, looks up, adjusts his cap, and continues to the kitchen. We watch him in silence, dazed by what he has related. A shiver passes through me. My shirt is moist with perspiration. I must get out. A cannon thunders in the distance. Tonight is my last chance to fight in the Revolution, to contribute to the Republic, to become blood brothers with the young man with the lance. Tomorrow everything will be over: Victory will have been won, the dead carted away, the cobbles washed clean.

—The flag's under my mattress, says Benard. We'll hoist it after supper.

I hurry away, not knowing where I am going, walking simply to subdue my anxiety, to make this confinement more bearable. In the crimson clouds over the city I see the fallen youth with the lance. A moment later Father arises from the body of the youth. Smiling, he beckons me with tenderness and love, as when I was a child. Suddenly, moved by the vision, I feel a need to belong, to be loved again, to give myself without reservation to someone or something. Father provided that need, but he is now dead. Vernier and Richard were sympathetic. Mathematics gave me meaning, but now, thoughts and emotions in turmoil, I doubt whether I will ever regain the composure needed for work again. The Polytechnic was to be my spiritual home, but I have been refused entry. And now there is only the chaos out there. That is where I belong. To throw myself into it, the way the ancient philosopher Empedocles threw himself into a live volcano. To experience chaos, to be overwhelmed by it, to forget I am Evariste Galois. To be energy, pure thought: energy to subdue the chaos, thought to impose a new order on it, to realize the Republic. That is where I will find my home, where I will be reunited with Father, and finally work again.

I ignore the supper bell. How could they eat at a time like this? I spend the hour pacing under the cypresses. Dusk is now quickly turning to ash. Cicadas screech. The scent of jasmine mingles with gunpowder. The knot in my stomach tightens again: No cannon has fired in an hour, the crackle of shot is subsiding. This is my last chance. I grab the jasmine spilling over the wall, twist it into a thick strand, and tug: It gives way, showering me in white stars. A few shots sound from the direction of the Hôtel de Ville. I try again, twisting a thicker strand.

—What are you doing? asks Benard.

—Help me get out.

—Calm down, Evariste. You're drenched.

Tears stinging my eyes, I hold him by both shoulders and implore for assistance. My words crumble into incoherent sobs. Bigger and stronger than me, Benard squats, puts his head between my legs, and straightens up. Shaking, holding on to the jasmine, I slowly stand on his shoulders and reach up for the overhanging ledge. Benard pushes me up by the soles of my shoes until I grip the spikes along the top of the wall. Smothered in fragrant jasmine, I scramble to raise myself onto the ledge.

—What's going on?

Benard bolts at the janitor's voice.

—Get down, he shouts.

Hanging from the spikes, I thrash against the hand

holding my ankle. Running footsteps. I am caught by the other ankle. I kick and scream against those pulling me down until my grip gives way and I fall into a tangle of arms.

—You again! hisses the janitor.

Gasping for breath, heart pounding, I twist and turn and screech as their grip tightens. Suddenly the lamp on the ground is snuffed out, my strength gives way, and I dissolve in hot damp darkness.

—Get this into you.

Sunlight streams through the window grilles. The janitor is sitting on the edge of the bed, blowing on a spoonful of pumpkin soup.

—First I save your life, now this, he says, extending the spoon.

I am in the school infirmary. The Revolution! I want to speak, to ask what has happened, but the words will not come out. The janitor pushes me back with one hand as I make a feeble attempt to sit up. My head sinks into the pillow, into darkness.

I am on the street with students from the Polytechnic, wearing their uniform and cap. They are marching resolutely, singing the "Marseillaise" to the accompaniment of drummers and fiddlers. And it occurs to me that, like music, mathematics is capable of ordering the surrounding chaos. I glance at a street sign: Rue de Babylone. Mother is standing in a doorway, but I march past her without a word. We break into a barracks, force the soldiers out, and distribute the arms among the followers. The commotion becomes more frenzied. I am now in front of the Louvre. A small barefooted boy climbs nimbly up the spout and hoists the tricolor. The locks are broken and the crowd pours into the corridors. I am swept into a long room with busts of ancient philosophers. Pushed from their pedestals, marble heads crack and crumble. Hands black from gunpowder, a fellow raises Euclid and waits for the moment to shatter him. The parallel lines of the tiled floor converge to a point beneath a window open to the sun. Dropping my musket, I run and save Euclid. The head is heavy, cold, and becomes heavier as I struggle with it on one shoulder through the devastation. Should I leave it and follow the crowd to the Tuileries, where a corpse is to be placed on the King's throne? The students urge me on, but I cannot move my hands. In the confusion somebody whispers my name, and a warm breath caresses my face.

—Evariste.

Chevalier is leaning over me with a gentle look. Twilight fills the room, staining the walls, dying the sheets, tingeing my friend's hair.

—I've brought you something to eat.

I listen intently: Birds are twittering, nothing else. I take my hands from under my head. They are numb.

—What day is it? I ask, mouth and lips dried by fever.

—Thursday.

—The Revolution?

Chevalier helps me sit upright and arranges the pillow behind me.

—The Revolution? I repeat, opening and closing my hands tingling with pins and needles.

—It's over, he says. The troops have fled. Paris belongs to the people. Benard raised the flag and nobody has dared touch it, including the Director.

Closing my eyes, I try to grasp the conflicting emotions evoked by Chevalier's words. Hate vacillates with hope. It is the Director's fault: He is responsible for my confinement and debilitating fever. He will pay for it when the scores are settled. At the same time, I look forward to the future — living in the freedom of a Republic, continuing my work, maybe entering the Polytechnic.

26

—I'm leaving tomorrow.

    —Be reasonable, Evariste, said Mother, twisting the chain of a gold crucifix hanging from her neck.

    The grief of a year ago had given way to a stern resolve. Her hair was pulled back and tied in a tight knot. She looked at me defiantly, then turned to the window for a moment. Sunlight falling on the side of her face revealed fine gray strands I had not noticed before.

    —The doctor said you must rest.

    We were in the study, where I had spent most of my time since coming home for the summer vacation. Weakened by fever, lacking energy to leave the house, I used the study as a retreat, avoiding the others by pretending to be working on mathematics. Upon my arrival home, I tried to subdue my inner turmoil by reworking the manuscript I sent Cauchy, the one that was never submitted for the prize, but I could not concentrate, let alone raise my thoughts to the heightened state which had produced those original ideas. Sometimes I sat there for hours on end, brooding behind Father's desk, feeling his presence in the contours of the chair, the armrests worn by his elbows, the impression made by his head—hours when I scratched absentmindedly on a sheet, covering it with symbols, sketches of battles, profiles of faces. The Revolution had not given birth to a Republic. The fighting subsided on the Thursday, the school gates were opened on Saturday. Still shaking with fever, I went out and saw the destruction, the suffering endured by the people, especially the artisans, who, more than any other group, had made victory possible.

And what did they get for the blood they shed? Betrayal! Their victory usurped by conservative forces! So-called liberal politicians and journalists, the ones who had stoked the fire of Revolution, they were the very ones now afraid of a Republic, afraid it would bring about anarchy and the collapse of society, afraid it would take their property, wealth, positions. Instead of placing their faith in the future and the Republic, those cowards turned to the past; instead of smashing the throne, those self-serving parasites begged Louis Philippe to take the place of Charles. One king for another! Bourbons, Orleanists—they were all the same! A constitutional monarchy in place of a monarchy! Another regent instead of a Republic! The whole thing reeked of betrayal. Collusion between royalty and religion!

—I'm feeling stronger, I said.

—There's a whole month before school starts.

I picked in Father's pipe and crushed a crust of ash between my fingers. Mother's perfume overpowered the smell of tobacco. A splinter of afternoon light darted from her crucifix.

—We've been betrayed, I said, sketching a flock of crows over obliterated names, numbers, symbols. We've got to fight, for Father's sake and all those who died on the streets.

—Fight! Fight! That's all I hear from you! There's been enough bloodshed. Thank God you weren't out on the streets.

—God and the good Director looked after me.

—Please, Evariste, spare a thought for me. My life has been a nightmare since your father's death. Concentrate on your studies. Another year, that's all, and you will be a teacher, qualified to take over the boarding school. I'll manage for another year, but give me some hope, Evariste.

—Sell it.

—Sell it? What about your education? Who's going to pay for that?

—I'm going out, I raised my voice, jabbing the pen in its holder.

—Why can't we talk to each other anymore, Evariste? Why won't you look me in the eyes?

—There's nothing to say. I'm leaving tomorrow.

—And where will you stay?

—In our apartment.

—That cursed place! We can't afford to keep it vacant. I'm selling it at the first opportunity.

—Until then I'll stay there.

—Paris will destroy you, Evariste. Just as it destroyed your father.

—Your Church killed Father! Its alliance with the King killed the people on the streets. If I'm going to be destroyed it will be fighting for liberty and a better life for all.

Twisting the crucifix with her fingertips, she became thoughtful and a shadow settled over her face—but it lasted only a moment, for she brushed back a few strands of hair and approached me with a pointed look. Father's armchair creaked as I sprang up. She tried to keep me from leaving, but I sidestepped her and my blurred reflection slipped from the crucifix's flat surface.

It was sultry outside. A whale of a cloud swallowed the sun. The air was heavy with an approaching thunderstorm. From the depths of the oak tree a finch trilled sharply, as though daring the storm to unleash its fury. I hurried to the cemetery to pay my respects to Father before leaving. Thunder rumbled in the distance, muffled by thick clouds. Avoiding the town square, I followed a dusty path that wound to the hillside cemetery. It was surrounded by a stone wall which Father, as mayor, had repaired not long ago. A thorny bush bright with red berries flourished over the wall near the entrance. I collected a handful and ate the sweet fruit while rustling through knee-high grass bristling with golden barbs. At the grave, I leaned on the granite headstone and passed a finger over the chiseled name and dates. I recalled the vow I had made to Father shortly before his death: to become a mathematician, change the world through mathematics, bring honor to the Galois name. I had been naïve to think I could change the world through mathematics.

Father was right: The word was more powerful than the number. Revolutions were stoked by words, not numbers. Republics were built on the solid foundations of words, not the abstraction of symbols. Maybe I should have taken his advice and studied law or embarked on a career in journalism. After all, it was the lawyers and journalists who inflamed the people to revolt. And when the people had overcome the King, it was lawyers and journalists who stepped in and dictated the course of history. I passed my palm over the headstone's curved top and wiped away a few white, crusty bird droppings, uncovering a small cross chiseled into the granite. Betrayal! The people had been betrayed by the politicians they trusted, Father had been betrayed by Mother. Lightning flashed above the brown fields, like the veins in a clenched fist. Thunder rolled. A breeze scurried through the dry grass. A cuckoo counted nearby.

—I didn't contribute to the Revolution, I said aloud, placing my palm on the headstone. Father, I promise to fight for the Republic. Mathematics won't change the world; words and action will. The great Revolution is yet to be fought—the Revolution that will redeem your death and justify my life.

A few large drops splattered the granite slab. On the path again I picked spiked grass-heads clinging to my trousers. Too agitated to face the household, I hurried to Grandfather's cottage.

As I picked a handful of almonds, warm drops shot through the leaves, struck my face, thumped into the dust. Lightning twitched, thunder shook the ground. I opened the shutters and watched as clouds crumbled and a torrent of rain fell vertically. I sat and began cracking almonds with a rock, recalling with bitterness my excitement at what I thought had been the solution to the quintic. Would I ever again experience that feeling of elation? And my work on a general theory of equations? I was certain of its importance: It was a new, powerful tool for probing the core of any equation. There was no possibility of mistaking its worth. Why hadn't anybody else, even the astute Cauchy, seen the significance of my findings? Was it the way I expressed my ideas?

251

A figure flitted across the window. The next instant the door swung open and a woman appeared. She was drenched: Her black hair was matted, dripping on the step, her floral dress clung to her body, accentuating her breasts and thighs. She was carrying a basket full of small flowers. Her glistening forearms were tattooed with strange symbols. I leaped up, clutching the rock.

—I thought it was empty, she said, stepping inside, her bare feet squashing water from her sandals. Mind if I stay until it passes? I was gathering herbs when the storm broke.

She bowed her head, tossed her long hair over her face, gathered it in a tail, and twisted it several times until water trickled on the stone floor. She then wound it in a bun and skewered it with wicker from the basket.

—That's better, she smiled.

A drop trembled on the tip of each ear. The stories students whispered in the dark flashed through my mind. A fine, steamy vapor rose from her dress. I concentrated on the symbols: concentric circles, diagonal crosses, characters I had never seen before. The rain brought out the fragrance of the herbs.

—Are you from town? she asked, placing the basket on the table.

—I'm studying in Paris.

—A student! she beamed, brushing her eyebrows like a crow's outspread wings. Must be a fine life in Paris, all those beautiful women.

—Those things don't interest me, I said, looking from her dark eyes to the rock in my hand.

Lightning cracked the sky, shaking the cottage. Rain fell in sheets, obscuring the view from the window.

—We might be here for some time, she smiled, adjusting her dress. Not interested in women! I bet you've got a few sweethearts in Paris.

—There are more important things than . . .

Her breasts shook as she laughed.

—What's so funny?

She reached out and took an almond from a few that I had shelled. Splitting it in two with her front teeth, she offered me half. I stepped back.

—Nothing's more important than love, she winked.

I had never believed those stories in the dark, always dismissed them as fantasies, wishful thinking on the part of bragging students, and yet here I was, caught in such a story. She asked my name, pressing her thighs against the table. No sooner did I tell her than I regretted it.

—You've never been with a woman, have you?

—No! And I never will!

—Are you studying to become a priest? Planning to join a monastery? You've got that serious look about you. Or maybe you prefer the company of men.

—I'm a mathematician.

—What? she asked, chewing the almond open-mouthed.

—You wouldn't understand.

—You should have a sweetheart.

—I've got my ideals.

—Don't be fooled by them, Evariste. Love's the only truth.

—Love! Any fool can experience it. The truth lies in mathematics.

Lightning flickered across the sky like a snake's tongue. Her laughter grew with the thunder.

—Words! Can you live them, Evariste? Can you feel them? Do they bring you happiness? No! There's only flesh, Evariste. Only youth. Don't turn away from true happiness.

Crossing her arms, she pulled off her steamy blouse. A rush of confusion overwhelmed me. The rock clattered on the floor. Her sandals squished as she walked around the table.

—Don't be shy, Evariste.

Her nipples were surrounded by pimply disks. I fixed my attention on her arms, to a pair of crescent moons back to back, just touching, forming what seemed like an x, the symbol of liberation from earthly things. I picked up the heavy blouse and threw it to her. She turned and slipped into it. I stood with arms crossed, heart pounding, proud of my victory. The rain abated as suddenly as it had started. The sun pushed through a shaggy cloud and sparkled the drops on the trees. A rainbow appeared, vivid against the pall of clouds, waiting to be described by an equation, perhaps one with imaginary numbers. She had retreated to a corner. I closed the shutters and left.

27

The small fourth-floor apartment has not been opened in months. Furniture is covered in yellowing sheets. Dampness blisters the walls, and the ceiling slants oppressively low. After struggling with the latch, I open the windows and lie on the bed. The journey to Paris was hot, and crowded. I stare at a brown patch of plaster in the ceiling, wondering whether Father gazed at it on the day he died. In the last few weeks his features have become indistinct, as though fading from my memory. I try to project his face onto the patch, but Mother's profile appears instead.

At first she refused to give me the key, but I flared up and threatened to sleep on the streets. She threw it on the table, adding that she did not want me back until I learned the meaning of respect. Alfred entered the study and insisted on joining me.

—You're not going anywhere! she shouted, venting her spleen on him. There's been too much violence. The place is still dangerous.

—There's no other way to the future, he retorted, his face spotted with pimples.

Alfred turned to me for support, but I avoided his

pleading look and tested the key's weight on my palm. I had no time for their arguments; besides, I did not want Alfred in Paris, though I could not tell him in so many words.

—Violence! That's all you know when you don't get things your way. You're all selfish! God won't endure it, though! His wrath will thunder over Paris. It's all written in Revelation.

—It won't be God's wrath, said Alfred. The thunder will be the final Revolution. Isn't that so, Evariste? It'll shake Paris, crush our enemies, and finally clear the air of the oppression that's choking us. We won't be betrayed next time, will we, Evariste?

She had gradually twisted the chain into a single tight strand that cut into her neck, now, releasing the cross, it spun and flashed in the sunlight. She went to the table, picked up her Bible, and flicked the thin pages.

—Armageddon! That's the final Revolution, she declared. It's all in here: "And the seventh angel poured out its vial into the air, and there came a great voice out of the temple of Heaven, from the throne, saying, It is done. And there were voices and thunders and lightnings, and there was a great earthquake, such as was not seen since men were upon the earth."

I replied by quoting a stanza that Father often recited when entertaining visitors with his verse:

Revelation, with seals and rings,
Is intended for women and children.
Revolutions, far more fiery things,
Are driven by furnace-minded men.

—Just like your father! No thought for your soul.

—We believe in the spirit of the Revolution, said Alfred.

He glanced at me, but I met his boyish enthusiasm with deliberate coolness.

—Revolutions are the work of Satan, Mother countered, flicking the pages. You're being seduced by the beast. "And I beheld another beast coming out of the earth, and he had two horns like a lamb and he spoke as a dragon and he displayed all the power of the beast before him. And he performed great wonders and deceived them that lived on the earth by means of those miracles." That's your revolution: the second beast! It promises paradise but casts people into hell.

—Mothers! Alfred sighed. No sense of history, no sense of the future, nothing but the welfare of the nest. If you felt the future as we do, you'd scatter your sons with sweeping gestures: Scatter us so that we may grow and bear fruit and return a hundredfold all that you gave us.

—I'm going, I said, walking between them.

—Please, Evariste, she implored, holding up the Bible. Don't bring more suffering into the house. Lord knows, we've had enough in the past year.

—You're blind, woman! Blind! Your Church is the cause of our suffering.

—I'm coming with you, Evariste, Alfred beamed.

—I need to be alone. My work's at a delicate stage.

—What work? he asked.

—Mathematics.

—How can you concentrate on that in times like these?

—What better time for testing one's beliefs?

No, Father won't be drawn to the patch of plaster. I put my hands under my head and attempt to place myself in his frame of mind on that fateful day. Nobody noticed anything unusual about him that morning. Perhaps he wound his watch before leaving his study, perhaps he tied a knot in his handkerchief, as was his habit when he needed a reminder that something important had to be done. He may have been a little more thoughtful, his step not so crisp on the cobbles, his voice somewhat flatter, but all that was nothing new. He even went to the tobacconist and bought a month's supply. He left the house quietly, just before noon, while Mother was visiting her parents, telling Nathalie that he was going to Paris on business. He kissed her on the forehead, but there was nothing in that to intimate his intentions.

What exactly were his intentions when he boarded the coach? Maybe there was nothing but a black seed at the back of his mind. Maybe he set out with business clearly in mind. He may have been quite affable, discussed the price of wine with a fellow passenger. Maybe he looked out of the coach's window and noticed how the colonnade of poplars shimmered with bright-green leaves, filled his lungs with the fragrance of forest and field, and exhaled in a protracted sigh. And as he entered Paris the black seed grew, silently, without his awareness, still not quite a thought, still far from being a volition.

He must have walked the streets as he had done countless times. Perhaps he bought a newspaper from a ragged boy, and looked forward to reading it over a cup of coffee. Perhaps he saw his reflection in the silver urn strapped to a vendor's back and decided he would have a haircut before leaving Paris. In walking beside the walls of the College Louis-le-Grand, maybe he stopped for a moment, thought about visiting his son—who, at that very instant, may have been gazing from a window—but decided not to distract him with an impromptu visit. And on the way to the apartment, colliding with color, commotion, characters of all sorts, perhaps he was still unaware of the black seed germinating inside his skull. Or maybe by this stage the intention crossed his mind once or twice, but it was fleeting, absurd, something that desperate people did, people who had lost their hold on life, whose existence had become meaningless.

Entering the courtyard, maybe he felt calm and composed, said good day to the officious concierge who just then was replenishing a lamp with oil. Perhaps he counted steps as each polished shoe scraped the winding staircase, and smelled cabbage soup, which aroused his appetite and he thought of a restaurant for lunch. With each scraping step, the seed grew, and by the time he reached the fourth floor perhaps it became a conscious thought, just that, not yet a volition, not something he would carry out. The room was hot and stuffy. He opened the windows and lay down. And as he lay perhaps he looked up at the patch of plaster and saw the face of the town priest. But even then, as he got up and untied the curtain cord, it was not an act of volition. It was the seed: It had become a black cloud that existed outside him, a cloud that drifted inexorably toward him, that made him climb onto the window ledge, fasten one end of the cord on the top section of the window bolt, and loop the other around his neck. And maybe, even at that instant, as he stood on the sill, perhaps he thought he wouldn't really do it. But the cloud suddenly overwhelmed him and he . . .

Terrified by the cloud closing in, I remove the cord from my neck, throw it aside, jump from the sill, rush from the apartment, brush past the gaping concierge in the courtyard, run onto the street, weave through the crowd, pursue my shadow, glance over my shoulder at my pursuing shadow, and stop in the middle of a busy square, where I bow over a fountain, gasping, dazzled by my shattered reflection. Catching my breath, I splash my face with water, and feel the panic abating. I calm myself on familiar sights: Tricolor ribbons hang from the branches of trees, masons are replacing cobbles that were torn out for barricades or to be thrown onto the troops from buildings, sweepers are clearing the stinking rubbish choking the entrance to narrow streets. Everywhere workmen are repairing streetlamps, glazing windows, restoring shopfronts, hanging up signs, changing the names of streets and buildings.

What if the panic strikes again? What if the cloud overwhelms me when I return to the apartment? Is that black seed in me too, or is it all just my mind playing tricks? I enter a reading room, hoping to subdue the questions. Holding the newspaper by its wooden spine, I rustle a few pages, reading with little interest until my attention is caught by an article on the recent death of the Duc de Bourbon, Prince de Condé. He was found a few weeks ago, hanging from the bolt of a window. At first the verdict was suicide: After all, he was a Bourbon, and the recent fall of the Bourbon king would have weighed heavily on him. But subsequent investigations have questioned suicide and suggested murder.

Those who discovered the Duc's body reported that his face was pale, not blackish, as it should have been if he had died from hanging. His tongue did not protrude from his mouth, his eyes were closed, not open and bloodshot, the tips of his toes touched the floor. The knots in the scarf around his neck could not have been tied by him, because his valets swore that he was unable to tie his own shoelaces. What's more, those who first entered the room found two candles which had been extinguished, not left to burn out. It was ludicrous to suggest that the Duc blew out the candles and, feeble as he was, walked across the cluttered room, climbed the chair, and tied the scarf to the bolt — all in pitch dark.

The black cloud is dispersing, my heart is racing. Father might not have committed suicide! Too agitated to remain seated, I leave the reading room. On the street the idea begins to grow. There was no investigation into Father's death, no details. Why? Was he a victim of a conspiracy? He came to Paris on business. He was stalked by assassins hired by his political enemies, who killed him and made it look like suicide. Maybe the Prefect of Police was involved. That would explain the lack of details. Yes! That is what happened. Returning to the apartment, I am convinced that is how Father met his end. As I stand at the window, gazing at twilight's ash settling over the city, I no longer feel the irrational dread, only a burning anger at those who murdered Father.

28

—Have you thought about joining us? asks Chevalier.

We are on the east side of the Louvre, in a procession filing past the common burial place of thirty people who died in the fighting. I drop a coin in a large copper bowl for the orphans of those killed.

—The Saint-Simonists are the voice of reason, he urges.

—Reason? I need a society that proclaims anger, that will avenge Father's death. Anger, Auguste. I'll go mad if I don't vent it soon.

—And your mathematics?

We continue in silence for a while. Staying in Father's apartment for the past few weeks, I have neglected mathematics for politics. New groups and societies have sprung up since the Revolution, all promising a better future. Desperate to find a group whose beliefs would accommodate my anger, I have been doing the rounds of forums, meetings, speeches in public squares.

—Have you heard about Cauchy? Chevalier asks.

He always steers the conversation back to mathematics. I know he does it for my own good, but it irritates me.

—Whose memoir has he dismissed this time?

—No one's; he left Paris last week to join the Royal family in exile.

—Like a dog at its master's heels.

—France has lost its best mathematician.

—Augustin-Louis Cauchy! I spit out his name. Coward! Self-serving egoist! There's no justice! How can someone like him possess genius? He hasn't got a trace of the magnanimity that genius ought to possess. Hedonist! He wouldn't sacrifice his breakfast, let alone his life, for the ideals of mathematics. He ought to feel ashamed whenever he utters the names of Pythagoras, Archimedes, Abel. And yet this egoist will probably contribute more to mathematics than the unfortunate Abel. Exile won't stop his stream of memoirs: He'll no doubt become even more prolific. In the meantime I'll have to deny my work in order to fight for freedom.

Two prostitutes smile in strolling past. A few months ago they were driven from the streets and public places by a Royal decree; now, in the wake of the Revolution, they are out in greater number than before.

—Liberty has its price, says Chevalier.

—Cauchy's no better than them, I retort, holding my breath against their perfume. What does your Saint-Simon say about creatures like that?

—Prostitution, drunkenness, poverty: They'll all be eradicated when mathematicians govern the state.

—Yes, but that ideal state of yours won't come about by wishful thinking. The final Revolution won't be won by academics shouting from their ivory towers. The people aren't interested in the square root of negative one. It's said the people followed even fresh-faced students, just because

263

they were in uniform and prepared to lead the way against muskets and cannons.

—Hell-bent on sacrificing your gift, aren't you?

—Better to face a musket than be like Cauchy.

As Paris put on its makeup after the orgy of destruction (cosmetics could not conceal the smell of death stifling the air, even though the mass graves had been cobbled over and strewn with flowers and wreaths), I continued attending meetings of disparate groups and societies, weighing one against the other, unable to decide which to join. One afternoon, on an oath of secrecy, I was taken to a gathering of anarchists at the back of a bakery. Despite the heat coming from the oven, the speaker wore a black frock coat buttoned to the neck. He was about twenty-five, thin, pale, with lips like a fish. He spoke in a lifeless voice, hands in pockets, not raising an eyebrow while advocating destruction and social chaos as the preconditions for a new order.

—Our first target must be Louis Philippe, he concluded in a confidential tone.

Casting furtive glances at the twenty or so young men with surly looks, I realized this group was not for me and left as the speaker asked for questions, his eyes glinting with suspicion. Outside, relieved to be alone, I tried to grasp the reason not just for my antipathy toward the anarchists, but for a feeling of revulsion that had welled up in me. Yes, I hated Louis Philippe intensely, I would also welcome his assassination, but not for the same reason as those anarchists. They were motivated by a perverse passion for destruction, not by the ideal of a Republic. Malcontents— that's what they were! They had turned to anarchy because they were either failed artists or megalomaniacs who, realizing they couldn't be Napoleons, were driven to destruction because of a feeling of spite and resentment. How many of them would have embraced anarchy if society had recognized their artistic talent, or if circumstances had allowed them to enter the public forum where megalomania can be expressed legitimately?

On another occasion I attended a talk on the ideas of Charles Fourier. Rushing to the basement meeting place, I collided with a dandy in yellow trousers, tapping the pavement with a silver-tipped walking stick. I arrived as the speaker, a young man with a sparse reddish beard, was answering questions.

— What's the essence of Fourier's utopia?

— The beehive: its order, proportion, harmony.

— Tell us more about this phalange.

— The present cult of the individual is a capitalist phenomenon, propagated to feed machines and benefit a few. In our system, each phalange will be situated on five hundred acres, accommodating two thousand people, where each person will contribute according to his or her talents and abilities. For instance, it's a universal fact that children enjoy playing in filth, so they won't mind cleaning the abattoirs and sewers.

— What's the role of mathematics in your system?

— There's no doubt that science is the door to a better future for mankind, and that mathematics is the key to that door. Our system is based on accurate graphs, logical proofs and axioms, detailed tables and calculations. Charles Fourier has found the solution to the problem of social organization and harmony.

The use of the word *mathematics* in such a setting rankled. What did they know about mathematics? It had nothing to do with politics and society: It was a pure study, pursued in solitude, with no material goal in mind. He was using the word to sound authoritative, to impress his listeners, to give Fourier's system respectability.

—Is it true that Fourier has studied the feasibility of harnessing ships to whales? lisped a fellow, precipitating a burst of laughter.

—And turning seawater into lemonade? chuckled another.

—And bricks to bread? heckled a third.

—They're metaphors, the speaker retaliated, flushed with indignation.

—What about his views on sexuality? asked another. It's said nothing is forbidden in the phalange: Young girls who misbehave will be given to elderly phalanx members, and all perversions will be catered for. Is that how it's to be?

—Your objection's a product of bourgeois conditioning, the speaker strained against laughter and derisive taunts. Once again Fourier is using metaphors to advocate a break with capitalist morality. He is in fact espousing complete freedom: spiritual, intellectual, physical.

I left the meeting seething with anger. How dare they use mathematics to promulgate such filth! Blaspheming against pure knowledge! If mathematics had little to do with organizing society, it had absolutely nothing to do with sexuality!

A few days later I was in the enormous hall of Pellier's riding school, where a crowd had gathered in oppressive

266

conditions to hear speakers of the newly formed Society of the Friends of the People. It had quickly established itself as the largest of the Republican societies, attracting many of those who fought in the streets. Looking around, I discerned a few who, judging by their appearance, were using the Society as a means to fame and greatness: the type who nurtured ambition in solitude, and who now saw their chance to rise above their own insignificance.

I listened to the speakers with interest. François-Vincent Raspail spoke softly, without rhetoric. A doctor in his mid-thirties, he advocated social reform, a moderate approach toward the monarchy, and proposed that each member of the Society become guardian and patron of a number of poor families. His speech was greeted coolly, with an occasional hiss of disapproval.

—What's your background, friend? asked a youth wearing the Polytechnic uniform.

—I'm a student at the Preparatory.

And suddenly the heat in the hall became unbearable, the air heavy with the smell of sweat and horse manure.

—You were locked in during the three glorious days, weren't you?

The question stung me, as though I had been slapped on the cheek. I turned from the youth, but wherever I looked I felt as though eyes were probing me, questioning my presence among people who had fought for freedom.

—I climbed over the wall, I said, summoning enough courage to meet his stare. I was out on the streets the whole time.

And to myself I defended the lie. After all, I tried desperately to contribute to the Revolution. I was there in spirit. If not for the Director's treachery, I would have been there in body too.

—Were you decorated? asked the youth.

Before I could ask what he meant, he pulled up his sleeve and displayed a scar along his forearm, still with fragments of crusty scab.

—A Swiss sword on the Rue St. Denis, he smiled.

My apprehension at being questioned on details of my involvement was allayed by the next speaker, who stepped confidently onto the platform and subdued the crowd by raising his arms. Pécheux d'Herbinville was about twenty-five, lean, tall, with a thick mustache and long hair. He kissed the tricolor and began by calling for a more radical constitution, one that would pave the way for a Republic. This was greeted with wild applause.

Standing on tiptoe to see over the shoulders of those in front, I was captivated by d'Herbinville's bearing and eloquence. I experienced a sense of belonging, as I had felt in the crowd at Father's funeral. This wasn't a nest of anarchists, which scurried about like rats in the dark and met in secret—there were two thousand people in this hall. I drew strength from the size of the gathering. This was a group that would make itself heard, that would draw even more followers, that would grow and become the great force for change.

—Monarchy is an evil that retards the growth of the human spirit. We must overcome it! Long live France! Long live the Republic!

Thunderous applause filled the hall. Yes! This was the Society I would join! It met all my requirements. I would serve it with passion. I had been prevented from fighting on the streets, but I would make up for it from now on. I would denounce the monarchy and Church and fight for the Republic. As I pushed through the throng to reach the section where members were assembled on the other side of a balustrade, I overheard a conversation.

—Our Pécheux has studied Robespierre well.

—Like him, he tends to be too much of an idealist.

—He loves fraternity in the abstract, but loathes it in the flesh.

—He's too dismissive of the vulgar and petty. One doesn't gain an understanding of the people from books, but from eating, drinking, laughing with them.

—Let's hope he avoids Robespierre's fate.

The words impelled me forward. d'Herbinville was a man after my own heart. I wanted to shake his hand and offer myself to the Society.

29

Since joining the Society of the Friends of the People I never miss an opportunity to berate the students who held back during the Revolution, calling on them to redeem their honor by supporting the Society and to speak out against the monarchy and the Director. The tricolor now flying in the courtyard will not save Guigniault: He didn't open the gates at the crucial time, he didn't support the Revolution. But many of the politically uncommitted students are still mistrustful of my austere manner, fearful of my fanaticism. Some even make jokes about me and laugh scornfully in my face. I will imbue them with my Republican fervor, though! The two-faced Director is my target: I must remove him from the school; that is the only way of winning over the students. If I can expose him for the coward he is, they will embrace the Republican cause.

—You seem to have found your place, commented Chevalier.

It was on the Sunday after I joined the Society, and we were strolling through the gardens of the Palais Royal, where crowds were milling about, hoping to see Louis Philippe and his family. The glow of the three glorious days had receded, the weather had become cold, and once again the city had wrapped itself in a grimy overcoat. Its knives and scissors sharpened, the north wind decimated the trees in the gardens and along the boulevards. Leaves scurried about like street urchins.

— The Society's going from strength to strength.

— And your studies?

— We're planning a big demonstration next week.

— Evariste . . . you're squandering your talent!

— In the name of freedom and equality.

— Equality? Do you really believe in that? We're all different, with different abilities. Is that old woman selling matches your equal, Evariste? Equality! Mathematics is the only place where you'll find equality: $e^{i\pi} + 1 = 0$! There's no natural equality between people. Yes, your Republic advocates universal suffrage: One person equals one vote. But what about talent? What about genius? Will your Republic acknowledge, encourage, reward those with talent?

— Let's face it, Evariste, human progress lies in encouraging and rewarding those with creative intelligence. This is precisely where Saint-Simon showed his understanding of human nature. He proposed that a subscription be established before Newton's tomb, and that everybody was to donate according to their means. Each contributor was then to name three mathematicians, physicians, chemists, physiologists, writers, painters, and musicians. The donations would be divided among those who received the highest vote, and the highest twenty would comprise the Council of Newton, with a mathematician as president. This Council would form a spiritual government, whose duty would be to direct all nations toward a common goal.

— Why the preeminence to mathematicians?

—Because they're able to rise above the human condition.

—I used to think like that too, I said, kicking a pile of leaves. Cauchy has opened my eyes, though: Even the best mathematicians can be petty and selfish.

—Think of noble Newton, not Cauchy. Think of yourself, Evariste. You can still become the kind of mathematician you once believed in.

—Are you flattering me, Auguste? Still trying to convert me to Saint-Simonism? Is that the reason for your interest in me? Is your friendship a pretext? I'm not naïve anymore. I've learned a lot since Father's death. You Saint-Simonists are living in a world of fantasy. The antics of your Bazard and Enfantin are nothing more than self-indulgence veiled in the smoky incense of a new religion. What were your leaders doing when people were dying in the streets? They were in their hazy temple, wearing their fezzes and gowns, preaching sexual freedom to dreamy disciples. Self-sacrifice, Auguste, not sensual gratification: That's how the human spirit will progress.

Chevalier's dark eyebrows fell, his features contracted. We walked in silence through a group of children who sprinkled us with star-shaped leaves. A patrol of the National Guard marched past on its civic duties around the city. They were also entrusted with protecting Louis Philippe, who needed all the protection he could get. There were anarchists and fanatical Republicans whose sole reason for existence was to kill him. Some were probably in the gardens right now, waiting for his daily appearance, which was nothing more than a ruse to endear himself to the people, to fool the gullible that he was in fact the Citizen

King. Who knows, I mused, the fellow smoking under that tree might well be an assassin—the murder weapon, a dagger, concealed in the walkingstick with which he poked the grass.

—Your cynicism is unfair, said Chevalier, snapping a twig. My friendship is no pretext! Let's end it here and now if you believe otherwise. You belong to mathematics, Evariste. I suppose I envy your talent and I can't bear to see you neglecting it. Who knows, my purpose in life might be to act as your voice of reason, to guide you back to mathematics.

I embraced him and apologized for my harsh words.

—I swear on Father's grave, Auguste, you will be the first to know if I decide to return to mathematics. But I must confess, my friend, sometimes I have grave doubts it will ever happen. Strange things are churning inside me. I seem to be possessed by hatred, anger, destructive urges. It's as if my heart now governs my head, and I don't know that I have the strength to reverse the situation.

Now, on this chilly December morning, in the library filled with thin sunlight, I look up from my reverie and reach for a journal lying on the table. Flicking through, I come across a letter by the Director, in which he claims to have supported the struggle against tyranny. Lies! Just what I need to expose him. Shaking, my words barely legible, I write a reply, accusing him of cowardice, of threatening students with police at a time when others were dying for liberty, of crass opportunism in that he was quick to decorate his hat with a tricolor brocade as the Revolution was being fought.

A week later my reply is published in the *Schools' Gazette*, signed simply, "a student of the Normal School"—the Preparatory's new name after the Revolution.

—You've gone too far this time, Galois, sneers a student, his green eyes keen as broken glass. Monsieur Guigniault wants to see you at once.

—I've written the truth.

—Not the way I saw it. He acted with our welfare in mind. You had no right to implicate others in your slanderous article. Who are the forty-six witnesses to support your rubbish? You would be lucky to find four.

—Coward! I was a fool to hope the Revolution would give you the courage to denounce him.

—We'll see how courageous you are, Galois. You've pushed him too far this time.

I knock sharply on the Director's door. He is sitting at his desk, head propped on his arms, a copy of the *Gazette* spread before him. The air is scented with the tang of pine. Flames twist and turn in the fireplace's black embrace.

—Sit down, Galois, he says in a subdued voice, indicating a chair with faded upholstery checked with crests and crowns.

His cordial manner surprises me, and takes the edge off my anger. Is this a ploy intended to disarm me before a furious attack? But there is something pathetic about him—a fatigue, a kind of resignation, that intimates he is incapable of a violent outburst. It may be the proximity, but he seems to have aged considerably since the Revolution. His eyelids are swollen, his nose has a purple tinge.

—Are you the author of this article?

—I had to respond to your letter in the *Lycée*, sir.

A log hisses and squeals, sap sizzles. The Director leans back in the chair, closes his eyes for a moment, and then gazes up at the lamps glowing above the desk.

— Perhaps I should have retired last year, he says, licking a faint smile. I've been teaching for forty-three years, but that's another story. I spoke to Monsieur Richard not long ago. He was very enthusiastic about your ability, said you had real talent.

He sighs and leans forward again, back hunched, elbows on the *Gazette*. I am uncertain of how to interpret his wistfulness. A log cracks, as though struck by an ax.

— I've often wondered why genius is given to youth. It seems unjust. After all, what has youth done to be blessed with such a gift? Genius should be the product of hard work, perseverance, experience. It should ripen in old age, as a reward for a lifetime of labor. What sweeter consolation than to taste the fruits of genius in old age, just before the end? It would validate forty-three years among musty textbooks, monotonous exercises, mute blackboards, mean-spirited students.

And he falls into a trance, as though the years are unwinding before him. Although perplexed by his confessional tone, I remain on my guard, determined not to allow his mawkishness to get the better of me, reminding myself that this is the man who denied me a part in the Revolution.

— I sympathize with your beliefs, Galois, he says, picking at a sunspot on the back of his hand. I'm also in favor of a Republic. I was very much against the Ordinances too. But these are my private views; they have nothing to do with my public responsibilities and the administration of this school. You must appreciate the delicacy of my situa-

275

tion, Galois. I tell you in all honesty, I anguished over the decision to lock the gates. And now, this.

He sighs, taps the *Gazette* with his fingernail, looks at me with moist eyes. I glance over his shoulder at the window behind him: Geese fly in V-formation across a leaden sky.

—You place me in an extremely delicate position, young man. But once again, I must suspend my personal beliefs and act in the best interests of the school. To remain Director and hold the respect of the student body, I have no choice but to expel you. I do this with great reluctance, Galois, despite your unkindness in the article. Your expulsion is effective immediately. The School Board will ratify my decision and you will be notified in due course.

The log in the fireplace snaps, spitting a few sparks.

PART THREE

30

Freedom, at last! My expulsion could not have come at a better time. Still living in Father's apartment I can now attend meetings of the Society whenever I please, indulge my passion for politics seven days a week, fight for the Republic at every opportunity. As I stride spring-heeled to a meeting, my spirit soars above the fog thickened by sulfurous smoke, fouled by vapors rising from the sewers, stirred only by the motion of carriages and pedestrians. When I arrive, d'Herbinville is already addressing the gathering, urging members to join the Artillery of the National Guard. He points out that the Artillery consists of four battalions, of which the second and third have a Republican majority. To protect their interests by controlling the National Guard, the bourgeois have precluded the poor from enlisting by imposing a 250-franc levy for the cost of uniform and equipment.

His words excite me, and I am ready to answer his call, to follow him into battle against the Royalists. Today, dressed in his Artillery officer's uniform, he looks more impressive than ever. I can't wait to see myself dressed like him—in a blue coat with red epaulettes, red-striped trousers, black boots. I listen intently, spellbound by his radiant face, clear blue eyes, imposing bearing. In a melodious voice, he gives details of how to join the Artillery, and follows this with a list of duties, which includes drilling twice a week from six to ten in the morning in front of the Louvre, and shooting practice once a week at Vincennes.

—We need control of the Artillery if we're to have any real power. Remember, the trial of Charles's ministers is set for the twenty-first. The people demand their heads, while Louis Philippe insists that they should be imprisoned for life. It's a situation made for another revolution. With numbers in the Artillery, we can lead the people forward, overthrow the monarchy, and declare a proper Republic.

Suddenly I want to get to know the handsome officer, look into his eyes, and declare my readiness to enlist. I have never experienced these emotions before: admiration mingled with excitement and apprehension. As I push through to the platform, the knot in my stomach tightens.

—My name is Galois, I say, barely uttering the words.

My hand wilts in his strong grip.

—I want to enlist.

He congratulates me and provides a few more details. I look down bashfully from his steady blue gaze and find his shining boots.

—And the money for the uniform? he smiles, running his fingers through a mane of fair hair.

—I'll get it.

The blue eyes hold me firmly for a moment, and then he asks for my first name.

—The Republic needs your enthusiasm, Evariste.

I want to reply, say something meaningful, but my

heart throbs in my throat. Not wanting to appear foolish, I quickly shake his hand (can he feel my sweaty palm?) and leave.

Outside the fog has condensed to a drizzle drifting obliquely across the city. Along the boulevard elms, black from dampness, reach out for sallow-faced pedestrians. I try to make sense of what I have just experienced, to account for this overpowering emotion. Is it due to d'Herbinville's uniform? Excitement at the fact that I will soon be wearing one? I had always felt inferior in the presence of students from the Polytechnic: They wore a military-type uniform, while uniforms were not worn at the Preparatory. No more, though! From now on I will be their equal, if not their superior. This, and maybe a sense of belonging to an identifiable group, might explain some of my excitement. But there is something else, something about d'Herbinville himself. Is it his bearing? His heroic stature? The thought of serving under him?

—A franc for you, sweetie, a whisper calls from the fog.

A woman in a shabby bonnet appears on the steps leading down to a rowdy tavern. A fox fur hangs carelessly over her shoulders: yellow claws on one breast, a red-eyed head on the other. Through the tavern's fogged windows I can just make out a young girl dancing on a table, wrapped in the tricolor.

—How much have you got? she asks, caressing the head, running a finger over its small teeth.

d'Herbinville flashes to mind and I run off, determined to get the 250 francs.

—No! said Mother, prodding the fire. You've lost all sense of reason. First expulsion, now this. No! I've had to sell the school. I can't support you any longer. You will just have to find work, Evariste. Perhaps your uncle might place you as a private tutor, or find a position as a legal copyist— your writing is good when you concentrate. Please, Evariste, I need your help.

—I need the money!

—Haven't you heard what I've just said?

—My life depends on it.

—I haven't got it. And even if I had . . .

d'Herbinville's image leaped from the flames.

—Give me half of next year's allowance, that's all. I won't ask for another *sou,* I promise. Look, I'll even sign a note disclaiming my inheritance. You will never have to concern yourself with me again. I'll have a home in the Artillery. I might even become an officer. It's my last chance. I want to make something of myself.

—Do it here, not in Paris.

She turned to the fire and clattered the grate with the poker.

d'Herbinville is addressing a contingent of artillerymen in the barracks of the Louvre, where the third battery has been posted for the day. It is a few days to Christmas, but my thoughts are not festivities.

Crowds are filling the squares, crying for the ministers' heads. They are waiting for the spark to ignite the revolt. If the House of Peers doesn't impose the death sentence, we will open the gates, arm the crowds, and lead them into battle.

Shouldering a musket, I stand at attention, ready to take on the world in my new uniform. Mother stood firm, even at the threat that my death would be on her conscience. I returned to Paris dejected, not knowing how to face d'Herbinville. But when we met a few days later, he embraced me with genuine feeling, listened sympathetically, and offered to pay my levy; he was certain I would serve the cause with honor. I promised to give my life for the Republic.

As the icy wind strengthens, my eyes water, ears sting. There is a smell of boot leather and gunpowder. The woolen trousers prickle, the musket's butt is smooth. d'Herbinville's strong voice and steady gaze fill me with courage and readiness for battle.

—Stay alert, he says. Wait for the signal. We're on the threshold of a revolution bigger than last July.

In the barracks an hour later, I am at the window with two other new recruits, watching the soldiers on duty in the courtyard, waiting for the signal. Father's death, my failure to enter the Polytechnic, my recent expulsion—everything will be avenged once the signal is given.

—Louis Philippe's days are numbered, says Duchâtelet, a law student who has suspended his studies for the cause.

—No more kings, says Lebon, smiling and chewing a dry fig.

—Long live the Republic, I add.

After an exchange of barbed whispers, two artillerymen in the back corner suddenly hurl abuse at each other.

—She's a worthless slut, shouts one.

—I'll cut your tongue out, retorts the other.

—I had her under the stairs.

—Liar!

They scramble up, grab their muskets, and thrust at each other. Their bayonets clatter until a few others intercede and draw them away to opposite ends of the barracks.

—They ought to be ashamed of themselves, I say. We're on the verge of making history, and they're squabbling over a woman.

—Tomorrow morning. Pistols. At twenty paces, shouts the shorter of the two.

As he struggles in the grip of those holding him back, two brass buttons snap from his coat: One flies into the mouth of the stove, the other rolls to my feet.

—Duel? Over her? Never!

—Shut up! Both of you! I shout, kicking away the button. If you're going to die, then die for the Republic, not for a woman!

The outburst stuns them. Scowling, the short one scrapes about on hands and knees, looking for his buttons, while the other swaggers to his bunk.

—Are they true Republicans? I whisper to Lebon.

—As much as you or I.

—How can they think of anything else at a time like this?

—Be tolerant, Evariste. There are many ways of serving the Republic. The journalist does it one way, the stonemason another, the prostitute on the street yet another.

They are not true Republicans. They would sooner die over a woman or a card game—that is the extent of their passion. Yes, I was passionate about mathematics, and maybe one day I will find that passion again. But mathematics is like the Republic: Both are ideals, both are grasped only by those who are prepared to forgo personal needs and ambitions for the sake of a universal truth. As voices hum and chamomile-scented steam rises from the kettle on the stove, I hone my reflection in the bayonet with a black whetstone.

—What are we waiting for? I ask Duchâtelet.

We have been in the courtyard three hours, freezing, standing in readiness, watching the vast crowd, and still no signal. When the verdict of life imprisonment was announced an hour ago, word got back to us that the ministers had been whisked away from the Luxembourg and locked in the prison of Vincennes, which was well protected by troops. Outraged at the verdict, the crowd has surged to the Louvre. But Louis Philippe is shrewder than I thought: As the crowd gathered, he ordered troops and the National Guard to surround the Louvre. The crowd was alarmed by the sight of so many soldiers. A tense standoff arose, and it has continued into the afternoon. An outer ring of troops faces the crowd, an inner is turned to the Louvre.

—They outnumber us ten to one, whispers Duchâtelet, his words vaporizing.

—We're not alone. Look at the size of the crowd— they're waiting for us. One shot, and they'll explode.

d'Herbinville marches past the lines and speaks to the men guarding the cannon. With steps crisp on the cold cobbles, he approaches my line.

—Stand firm, men.

Against the background of iron bars, troops, people, he is an imposing figure. My admiration for him has grown in recent weeks. Admiration? No, more like infatuation. His presence excites me, his eyes are full of the future, his look passes through me like lightning, dispersing the murkiness of recent months. If he gave the order, I would be the first to open the gates and lead the charge.

—We mustn't provoke them. Let them make the first move. The crowd will be more sympathetic to us.

The solstice night closes in upon the city, moving silently from tree to tree, lamppost to lamppost, bayonet to bayonet, spreading and filling the cannon's mouth, a tradesman's cap, the pupils of a red-cheeked recruit. As the darkness thickens and the air becomes chillier, my sense of expectation begins to subside. The sullen crowd begins drifting away, the troops seem more relaxed, fires are lit. Soon troops and civilians are fraternizing, brought together by the need to warm their hands. Snowflakes flutter lightly over my face, catch on my lashes, settle on the pyramidal arrangement of cannonballs. To occupy myself I calculate the number of spheres: There are ten rows in decreasing number, and the base is a square with ten spheres along one side. Is there a formula for the sum of square numbers starting with one?

We take short rests in the barracks during the long night. When my turn comes, I refuse to leave the courtyard. Lebon and Duchâtelet try to draw me away, but I insist I am not tired. They leave me, shaking their heads. How can I call myself a Republican if I cannot put up with cold and fatigue for the sake of the Revolution? Yes, the chances of anything happening tonight are small, but that is even more reason to keep vigil through the long night. I recall the night in the Garden of Gethsemane. Mother read that story many times, and every time I was disappointed that the disciples could not stay awake when so much depended on their vigilance. And now I see myself as a disciple of the Republic: For its sake I must overcome the cold nibbling at my face, the numbing feeling of hopelessness, this night vaster than the one that surrounded Gethsemane.

I am still pacing the courtyard as the night loosens its grip. Flocks of geese screech overhead. An artilleryman aims his musket and curses that he cannot bring one down for a Christmas roast. I stop and observe the situation on the other side of the fence. The crowd is building up again, and the troops have returned to their ring formation. But the atmosphere is now more relaxed, and it appears the crowd consists of people on their way to work, stopping out of curiosity rather than to start a revolt.

As the hours pass and the likelihood of a revolution recedes, the scene begins to resemble a carnival. Vendors of all kinds appear and mingle among the crowd. Children run and laugh, chasing each other between the troops.

My hopes suddenly rise at the sight of students from the Polytechnic. They will incite the crowd, as they did last July. Watching intently for a sign of unrest, I notice that a few vendors have slipped through the cordon of troops and made their way to the fence, where they are now trading briskly with the artillerymen. Following the vendors' lead, relatives and friends of the artillerymen are now conversing through the bars. To my dismay a group of people addressed by a Polytechnic student breaks up: Some go and shake hands with the troops, others are leaving the scene all together. Bewildered, I approach the fence, where lively trade and conversations are in progress.

—A *sou* apiece, shouts a vendor, almost jabbing me with a long skewer full of steaming sausages.

—What's happening out there? I ask, pushing the rod back between the bars. Why aren't they listening to the students?

—They are, says the vendor. I promise you, they're fresh. I slaughtered the pig myself only last week.

—Why are they leaving?

—The students are calling for restraint. They're saying Louis Philippe won't betray the people.

Stunned, I back away from the vendor.

—All right, three for two *sou*.

Within an hour the crowd has dispersed, the troops have marched away, and the gates of the Louvre are opened.

31

Chevalier and I stroll through the tangle of winter shadows along the Champs Elysées. It has been ten days since the failed revolt; days full of disappointment, darkened by a Royal decree which disbanded the Artillery division of the National Guard and prohibits members wearing the uniform. Nineteen officers and activists have been arraigned, among them d'Herbinville, on charges of fomenting unrest and conspiring to arm radicals with muskets and cannons.

— What are you going to do now? asks Chevalier.

— Louis Philippe will pay dearly, I reply.

A few well-dressed children are exploding firecrackers by pulling on a silk ribbon: leftovers from New Year's Eve party games. The chilly air smells of gunpowder. Pretending to be in a duel, two boys aim the firecrackers at each other and pull the ribbon.

— You're dead, shouts one.

— No, you are, protests the other.

With the family apartment now rented to a writer, I have been forced to return home, commuting daily to Paris in order to organize other accommodation. Before leaving this morning, I had a fiery exchange with Mother. Dismissing her suggestion that I find work as a private tutor, I went to my room and stood before my slightly distorted reflection in the wardrobe mirror. Despite the prohibition I have been wearing the uniform around the house, and I now admired it for a moment before taking it off. No sooner had the uniform given me meaning, hope, a sense of belonging, than it was stripped from me. I felt strong in it, as strong and confident as d'Herbinville. The boots, the full trousers, the coat's padded shoulders: All that added to my stature, made me appear robust. Now, in only my underwear, I was once again the thin youth with protruding shoulder bones, thin arms, and slightly bowed legs. I looked at myself from one side, then the other, even stood with my back to the mirror and looked over my shoulder: Whichever angle I took, I could not help comparing myself to d'Herbinville. If only I had his stature, his bearing. I put the uniform away, certain that the time would come when I would wear it on the streets of Paris again, when I would lead the crowd in what would be the final Revolution.

For a moment, my anger gave way to a feeling of pity for that pathetic little figure in the brown jacket with large collars and gray trousers. Nineteen, with cheeks still untouched by a razor, the girl-faced youth had no future, no place in society, barely a name on which to hang an identity. My anger returned, more fiercely than before. Suddenly I hated the youth in the mirror. I wanted to shatter him. A glass was already in my fist, but I was held back by the thought of multiplying him in a thousand fragments.

—Stop thinking of Louis Philippe, think of your future, says Chevalier.

—Maybe I ought to join the Saint-Simonists, take up residence with Enfantin, and indulge in the pleasures of free love. The way to the spirit through the excesses of the flesh. Isn't that what he advocates?

—I wish you wouldn't talk like that.

—Is it true or not?

—There's more to Saint-Simon than Enfantin's subjective interpretation of him. Ask your Republican publicists: They've adopted many of his ideas.

—What's happening at school? I ask in a conciliatory tone.

—Have you seen the latest issue of the *Schools' Gazette*?

—I haven't read a thing since my expulsion.

—It contains a letter, signed by the majority of students, that refutes your account of what happened last July. In fact, the students declare their support of Guigniault, of his actions in closing the gates and his decision to expel you.

—Boot-licking cowards!

As I pull up my collars against the chilly brilliance, a carriage with a line of horsemen on both sides clatters toward us. Men tip their hats, women wave embroidered handkerchiefs, children run noisily. Here and there people mutter about the rising price of food: Their words vaporize, fuse, rise as a single complaint. Inside the carriage, a head with rosy cheeks and muttonchop side-whiskers acknowledges the crowd.

—The Citizen King is out among his people, I say, holding a warm knife in the pocket of my overcoat.

—He's more popular than Charles.

—Just think, I whisper, holding Chevalier by the elbow. He stands between us and the Republic. A moment's daring, and . . .

291

—And you'll never see your Republic.

—Moses didn't get to see the Promised Land either.

—Stop talking nonsense, Evariste. Use your head for mathematics!

—Dear Auguste, voice of reason. But haven't you heard? We're living in an age that says reason is unfashionable. Out with order, let chaos rule! Romanticism and Revolution: Isn't that what our poets are writing? Our painters depicting? Our dramatists staging?

—Listen, Evariste, you're no longer a student or an artilleryman. Do something useful with your free time.

—And what do you propose?

—Give a series of public lectures on your mathematical work. Don't scowl! Listen—I'll help you organize it. My brother's editor of the *Globe*. We could advertise without charge. "Evariste Galois, mathematician, will present six lectures dealing with his investigations into algebra and his theory of equations." How does it sound? Who knows, the advertisement might attract a capable mathematician, someone who might study your findings, see their worth, and become your supporter, even a patron. What do you say?

The prospect excites me, but I remain surly.

—And where would these lectures take place?

—Michel has contacts, he'll help us find something.

Another cavalcade rumbles past, with cannons hitched to horses snorting out clouds of steam. I stare into the mouth of a receding cannon: It is the source of a great, black vowel, a concentration of darkness that destroys for the sake of creating a new order.

32

A brass bell above the door announces us as we enter Caillot's bookshop on the Rue de Sorbonne. Small, with low ceilings and dusty windows, the front room is crammed with books. The mustiness of old volumes mingles with the smell of recent publications. Books strain the shelves touching the ceiling, they are piled on the counter, they cover the floor in precarious towers. The smell reminds me of my childhood: autumn days in an oak grove not far from home, where the leaves lay damp and dark. I would always return from the grove with a sense of foreboding: a melancholy that not even Father's joviality could dispel. And now, stepping carefully between towers, I feel that melancholy stirring again, filling me with uneasiness. If not for Chevalier, I would turn around and walk out. Better the stink of an open sewer than this haunting smell of moldy pages.

I pick up a book from a row placed spine-up on the bench: *A Body of Work,* by Mathos Pechin. The yellow pages breathe over my face as I flick through them. Going by parts of the first page, it is a historical novel, set in Macedonia, printed in 1807, probably at the author's expense, for there is no imprint.

What did the author hope in writing this book? Fame?

Wealth? A literary career? The book has obviously failed. What if this were the last copy in existence? Mortified by the book's dismal reception, perhaps the author managed to retrieve the other copies and set them all alight. Perhaps he was so humiliated by the experience, he threw himself into the bonfire, taking the manuscript with him. And now, what if this last copy were also destroyed? Would that mean the obliteration of *A Body of Work?* Or would it somehow still exist, maybe in an ideal state, by virtue of the fact that it had been thought into existence?

Two hundred years from now another author might pick up the ideas and write the same novel, perhaps in a different language. And what of Pechin? Would he be raised from oblivion by the second author? Could the man's emotions, temperament, and intellect be recovered from the rewritten *A Body of Work?*

I transpose these questions to my own work. My findings might survive two hundred years, but what of Evariste Galois? If I were to die tomorrow, could my life be reconstructed from my mathematical work alone? Could I be reclaimed through my work? No, unlike words, mathematical symbols exclude personality. What if, say, in two hundred years, my work were esteemed and studied universally, while my life were a blank?

The idea of personal extinction alarms me. The presence of a future biographer becomes stronger. I take comfort in the knowledge that he is near, drawn even closer to me by the smell of these books, the taste of ink on the finger that turns the page. Stay close, biographer. Look over my shoulder, read my thoughts as the deaf read lips.

A plump middle-aged woman emerges from the back of the shop with an armful of books.

—Yes, gentlemen, she heaves.

And as she attempts to raise the books onto the counter, they spill from her smothering embrace, as though infants who, amply fed and warmed, break loose.

—Books! she exclaims with a sweep of her arm. And they continue pouring out of printing shops. A deluge each day. I have nightmares in which I'm drowning in an ocean covered in books, an ocean black from ink.

—Just look around you! Up to my neck in them. Not enough space to stand in, and that husband of mine keeps buying cartloads. I tell you, he's obsessed with them. And do you think we're able to sell them? People can't afford bread. Think they're going to buy books? We're facing terrible losses, and yet there's no stopping his ruinous passion. He's out day and night, scouring markets or buying the libraries of deceased estates, while I'm left here, in the gloom of this burial crypt for failed writers, trying to make ends meet.

Chevalier tries to interrupt her, but the torrent of words continues, as though it has accumulated in her fleshy, trembling throat. We exchange glances, resigned to waiting for the flow to ebb.

—Are you poets? Novelists? Beware!

She picks up two thick volumes and claps them together, sending up a cloud of dust.

—That's how his troubles began, gentlemen. At your age he also wanted to be a writer, but his want was greater than his ability. When the truth finally hit him, he got it into his head that if he couldn't write books, he would do the next best thing—collect and sell them! He has been a guardian of books ever since, a kind of foster father, bringing in every ragged, battered, water-stained orphan he can find, giving each one shelter, warmth, care—all without a thought for whether they can repay his kindness.

—We're not poets, I say. We're mathematicians. We've come for . . .

—Yes, mathematics! By all means! she grins, her lower jaw protruding beyond her upper, revealing two yellow canine teeth. Up there on the top shelf! Can I interest you in Euclid? All thirteen books in five leather-bound volumes. Genuine calfskin, mint condition. The Greek original facing the French translation. Pages of commentaries. You can have them all for seven francs, a steal for such classics. I flicked through one before shelving them the other day: beautiful, even though I know nothing about geometry. Two thousand years old, and still relevant. It takes real genius to write books like that.

—As for poetry and fiction—bah! Any writer of such rubbish can imagine he's a genius and that his work is an inspired masterpiece, whereas the only thing it inspires is a dying flame.

—We're here for the back room, Madame. My brother, Michel Chevalier, arranged it with Monsieur Caillot last week.

Perplexed for a moment, she turns from Chevalier to me, examines us from head to toe, then instructs us to follow her. A door lined with shelves opens to a room already prepared with rows of chairs and a blackboard mounted on

296

a tripod. Piles of books stand against the four walls. The stove in the corner wheezes.

— The room is to be used for mathematics, she huffs.

— You're welcome to stay and listen, says Chevalier.

— No politics. Nothing subversive. Understood?

The bell tingles frequently in the next half hour, and by six o'clock about thirty people have arrived, among them a few friends from the Artillery, including d'Herbinville, whose presence both surprises and flatters me. Does he have an interest in mathematics or is he here from Republican sentiment?

I notice several students from the Preparatory School. Charles Sturm is also here, sitting next to a Russian by the name of Ostrogradski, both capable mathematicians with whom I have discussed my work. I nod to them in recognition. As one of the editors of Férussac's *Bulletin*, Sturm has accepted a few of my articles for publication, for which I am grateful. It was through Sturm's work that I deceived Leroy, the mathematics teacher at the Preparatory. Reading from a sheet of paper, Leroy wrote the word *theorem* on the blackboard and proceeded to copy what he said was a new discovery in algebra made by a Swiss mathematician living in Paris called Sturm. He went on to point out the usefulness of the theorem, but said that a proof involved a level of algebra beyond our scope.

I had come to despise the way this teacher strutted around the room, using mathematics as a weapon to browbeat and humiliate students. He had no feeling for the subject: He simply used it to conceal his own lack of talent, and to lord it over students who struggled with the subject. I seized the moment.

—Some of us would be interested in the proof, I called out.

—It's too detailed, Leroy replied.

A whisper of anticipation buzzed around the room as the students sensed a confrontation.

—You might inspire a few of us to study it.

Leroy reddened. Shuffling a few papers on his desk, he ordered me to sit down, saying that new material would result in us falling behind the syllabus.

—But it's not that detailed, I continued. You could write it on the blackboard in a few minutes.

—Enough, Galois!

Some whispered that I had already worked out the proof in my head, and that Leroy's reluctance was due to his not knowing it. Others were betting that I was just showing off, that I did not know the proof. Encouraged by the whispers, I maintained the attack.

—An outline of the proof would be most helpful, I persisted.

And I pointed out that the proof would enhance our appreciation of the formal beauty of algebra. The living beauty of algebra was replacing the frigid beauty of classical geometry, and a new form of analysis was on the horizon, which would do to algebra what algebra had done to geometry. An analysis that would enable us to grasp the essential structures of problems and equations, a method applicable to entire classes of problems. How could we aspire to this new algebra if he refused to show us the latest proofs of the old algebra? Unless, of course, he was unable to do so, in which case I would be more than happy to demonstrate it.

—Very well, Galois, said Leroy, extending a stick of chalk. Let's see if you're able to reproduce Sturm's proof. I know exactly what it entails, so you had better get it right.

I erased the theorem and proceeded with the short proof, occasionally grating the chalk. Finishing, I struck a pointed full-stop, placed the chalk on the table, and clapped the dust from my palms. The whispers had grown to excited chatter. Leroy stood with arms crossed, creased forehead shining with perspiration, nodding at my work. I had him exactly where I wanted.

—Very good, Galois, he conceded. You've got the ability to be a fine mathematician, but you must restrain your haughty nature.

Several students applauded.

—Well, sighed Leroy, wiping his bushy brows which now drooped lower, almost concealing his eyes. Let's continue with our lesson.

As he reached for the eraser, I snatched it from the table and returned to the blackboard.

—I've just realized an obvious mistake, I said, wiping a line and inserting another. That's the proof, isn't it, Monsieur Leroy?

To this day I have kept to myself that I did not deduce the proof there and then. I had seen both the theorem and its proof weeks earlier at a meeting with Sturm. Now, waiting for Chevalier to finish his introduction, gazing out at haloed streetlamps swirling in concentric circles, as though painted on a black canvas by a feverish artist, I regret the incident. Like Leroy, I debased mathematics, used it as an instrument of power.

There! You know everything, brother-confessor-biographer. What will you make of this incident? How will you interpret it? I know you will be discreet, that is why I have chosen to confide in you and not in any one of a thousand others. Yes, there will be other biographers, I am sure—biographers who will portray me as a rebellious hero, a genius, misunderstood and thwarted by lesser minds. For such scholars this incident is the stuff of myths and legends: They will use it to depict a larger-than-life Galois, one capable of superhuman feats, of pursuing original work entirely in his head. But now, recalling this incident, I feel ashamed at having deceived Leroy.

I take out a few sheets, stand, and exchange looks with d'Herbinville, who winks in encouragement. My confidence in public-speaking has increased since joining the Society, where I have made several speeches outlining how best to organize and mobilize students. At the blackboard, I glance at Madame Caillot: She is standing plumply in the doorway, thick arms crossed at the wrist, obviously ready to bark at a mere hint of anything subversive.

—My lectures during the next six weeks will deal with my investigations in the field of analysis, in particular, my research into the theory of equations and integral functions. Before commencing with the technicalities of my work, I would like to preface it with a few remarks.

—First, when my work eventually appears as a book, it will not contain the name of any wealthy patron or distinguished member of the scientific community, like those names in big bold letters that dwarf the text itself. I have had no assistance from anybody in a position of influence; on the contrary, those who have been in a position to help have thwarted me at every step. It is no accident my manuscripts have been lost by honored members of the Academy. I expected better from them, in view of the fact that they have got Abel's death on their conscience. But enough of grievances. Let's begin.

In turning to the next sheet, I notice a fellow who has just entered and occupied a back seat. I haven't seen him before: He is about fifty, respectably dressed, with the pale complexion of one who spends a great deal of time indoors. I continue, surprised at the fluency of my thoughts and words.

—Progress in mathematics hasn't been due to our facility to perform lengthy algebraic calculations. With the work of Euler, who in a sense invented a new language, progress has been made through terse, precise exposition. In the last thirty years the algorithm, or the machine for working out results, has become so complex that it practically precludes any real advancement by such means. If we are to deduce anything from the fact that terseness and elegance are the avowed aims of most advanced mathematicians, then surely it's this: The creative, innovative mathematician is concerned with grasping several concepts at once, rather than stopping to look at particular details. But even the simplifications produced by terseness and elegance have their limits. The time will come when algebraic transformations *foreseen* by analysts will not be easily produced because they will require too much time. The mind of creative mathematicians must move by intuitive leaps, fearless of being revolutionary.

Feet shuffle, chairs creak. Madame Caillot, who has

been coming and going, glares at me from the doorway, her lower jaw ready to snap. Chevalier fills a glass of water for me.

—This is no time to retreat, I proceed with rising fervor. We're seeing the evolution of a new sensibility, a higher consciousness. Just look around: There's reaction everywhere. The marble-cold reason of Classicism is being challenged by the spirit of Romanticism. Look at Hugo's plays: The preface to his *Cromwell* outlines the new spirit. The poetry in his recent *Hernani* is worlds away from Racine and Molière; not only is the protagonist an outlaw from the lower classes, something Classicism would never have sanctioned, but the poetry itself speaks of life here and now, mixing the grotesque with the sublime. The language moves by emotional leaps, which often leaves reason behind. Who knows, twenty or thirty years from now a poet may emerge, someone of my age, who will write poetry more daring than Hugo's, who will leap in great arcs over reason, whose expression will be terse, concentrated, proceeding through a series of images moved by intuition, association, intimation.

Sipping the cold water, I feel it passing through me as naturally as the thought: Water is somehow the expression of gravity.

—Why am I using poetry to make my point? Like mathematics, poetry also strives for terseness and elegance. And what impact, if any, is Romanticism having on mathematics? Isn't the essence of mathematics evolution, not revolution? Doesn't it proceed by cool reason rather than flashes of intuition? No! Intuition leads, leaps from peak to peak, while reason follows behind, filling in the gaps, making the associations, constructing the bridges which enable mankind to move forward. Don't be misled by the popular notion that says mathematics moves smoothly, quietly assimilating, integrating past and present. More often than not it advances through radical, revolutionary ideas.

Thumping two books against each other, Madame Caillot prods me with a stern look.

—Allow me to remind you that the ancient Greeks were horrified when the concept of an irrational number began infiltrating their ordered world. There was no precedent for such numbers, which challenged and undermined their very beliefs. Initial opposition to these subversive entities was so strong, people were killed for daring to utter them. And even in more recent times the same outrage greeted the appearance of imaginary numbers, because they challenged the idea that number must have some correlation to the physical world. The great Gauss put it well when he said that the true meaning of the square root of negative one was vivid in his mind, though he found it difficult to express the meaning in words. This is precisely what I mean by the word *foreseen:* the intuitive, that which presently lacks an appropriate vocabulary. But just as the irrationals extended the scope of mathematics, so did the imaginaries, and today the fundamental theorem of algebra is defined in terms of these imaginaries.

—If you want another example of the revolutionary nature of mathematics, there's the development in Russia reported to us by Monsieur Ostrogradski. What better example of the reaction against Classicism than the work of Monsieur Lobachevsky, a professor at the University of Kazan? He has challenged the parallel-line postulate and proposed a new geometry, in which parallel lines meet and the three angles of a triangle do not sum to 180 degrees. It appears that this new geometry is based on the idea of curved space, instead of flat Euclidean surfaces. Despite Platonic idealism, the geometry of the ancient Greeks wasn't ideal at all, for it was founded on the false perception of a flat earth. I daresay this Lobachevsky would not have seen the limitations of classical geometry without intuition.

Looking up from my notes, I glance at d'Herbinville: He is fashionably dressed, wearing a purple cravat, sitting cross-legged, careful not to spoil the crease in his trousers.

—My work also proceeds from a tendency to think intuitively. Dispensing with details, I prefer to leap from foresight to idea to concept. New things might well emerge from analysis without this ability to foresee, but discoveries will be few and far between and mathematics will suffer from stagnation and eventual exhaustion. My approach has been to smash through the constraints of algorithms and calculations, to grasp and group operations, classify them according to their difficulty and not according to the deceptions of form. My approach must not be confused with that of people who avoid calculations, albeit superficially, only to express themselves in a lengthy, pompous manner, when terse algebra would better serve their purpose. My approach is nothing of the sort.

—I propose an analysis of analysis: a new, terser algebra, where the most elevated calculations will be considered as particular cases, useful to examine but which ultimately must be put aside for greater, more general investigations. There will be no lack of people to carry out the calculations envisaged by the new analysis. Just as the visions of prophets are the seeds which generations of theologians cultivate, so my foresights will be used by generations of mathematicians not only to solve particular problems but to advance new theories. Before using the blackboard to outline the technical nature of my researches, I propose a preview of my theory on the solution of equations.

Pausing for another drink, I try to gauge the level of interest among the listeners. Restless, some of the students are whispering; two youths wearing the Polytechnic uniform leave quietly. Having an intelligent look about him, the pale fellow still seems attentive. Has he followed everything? Or have I misread him? Maybe he has not understood a thing, maybe he is too shy and polite to leave, and his expression belies a mind set on supper or an evening with a mistress. Having rummaged in the back corner for some time, Madame Caillot now shuffles out, hugging another collection of orphans. Poised, sitting upright, d'Herbinville smiles at me. Is he here as a Republican? To report to the Society's leaders my effectiveness as a public speaker and my ability to draw students? Or as a friend? Whatever, I am flattered by his presence, in view of the fact that he has put aside his own impending trial in order to support me.

—My researches have concentrated on determining whether an equation can be solved by algebraic processes and the extraction of roots. The general quintic resisted attempts to reduce it to simpler equations, until Abel showed, using an algebraic proof by contradiction, that it could not be reduced, hence it could not be solved by radicals. I have taken Abel's finding farther. My theory is more general: It enables one to look at a particular quintic and say whether or not it can be solved by radicals, for we know there are countless quintics which can be solved by radicals. In fact, when my theory is applied to the general quintic, it validates Abel's finding.

—I must digress for a moment, I say, clearing my throat. I know that historians of mathematics will assert I owe a great deal to Abel. Who knows, perhaps an eager scholar will complete a doctorate arguing that my work is based on a close study of Abel. I want to state here and now, before you as my witnesses, that I was totally unaware of Abel's work when I made my first discoveries in this area. Furthermore, if one studies Abel's paper on the quintic, it will be obvious that our approaches are completely different. He uses algebra and long calculations of the sort I've just been arguing against. My approach, on the other hand, is based on the idea of a group.

Sturm and Ostrogradski exchange whispers. The Russian twists the end of his long beard.

—At this stage, before presenting a technical definition of a group, I'll just point out that once the group of an equation can be determined, then we need only examine the nature of this group in order to determine whether the equation can be solved by radicals. In this regard, the group is to the equation what the equation is to the trajectory of a cannonball. Just as an equation makes the physical world abstract, enabling us to determine the ball's maximum height and range without lighting the fuse, so a group abstracts an equation. A group is, if you like, an equation of an equation, what I referred to earlier as analysis of analysis. The group is also like a crystal ball: We look into it, analyze its structure, see whether the group can be resolved into smaller groups, and from this we can learn something about the essential nature of equations. If I may extend the analogy of the crystal: A group's like the prism that physicists use to determine the composition of the sun by analyzing the spectrum. Due to circumstances beyond my control, and my present commitment to the Republican cause, I haven't the time to apply the theory of groups to areas other than equations. But I'm certain it has wider applications. Perhaps wherever there is a situation that denies the mind direct access, groups may be used to model that situation and provide valuable insights. In this regard, groups may well provide a key to unlocking the secret of the universe. Through them we may be able to solve the universe's central mystery, or conclude that it has no solution.

After the lecture, a few people congratulate me, saying they found the material stimulating and look forward to next week's talk. d'Herbinville grasps my hand and expresses surprise at my talent. He wishes me well, adding he hopes I can accommodate both mathematics and the Republic. As I walk with Chevalier to the door, where Madame Caillot stands with arms crossed, inviting people to browse at the books, the middle-aged fellow approaches us and thrusts his hand toward me.

—I'm impressed by your ideas.

—Are you a mathematician, Monsieur . . . ? asks Chevalier.

—Beyle, Henri, he says, smiling and smoothing his thinning hair. I came to Paris years ago to study the subject at my father's insistence. In those days I was caught between love of algebra and passion for language. In the end literature prevailed, though I've managed to maintain an interest in mathematics.

Madame Caillot has erased the symbols from the blackboard and is now doing an arithmetical calculation.

—Do you write, Monsieur Beyle? I ask, disappointed.

—Yes, novels. In fact, your features, your physique, your intensity, the acuity of your mind—all remind me very much of the protagonist in my novel published last year.

—The title of your book, Monsieur? I ask.

—*Scarlet and Black*.

—I haven't come across it.

—Not many people have, he says, a tinge of red suffusing his cheeks. But it will be read in a hundred years from now, while many of today's popular works will disappear without trace.

—What makes you so sure?

—The very thing you mentioned in your talk: intuition.

—Are you a Romantic?

Picking a large moth from behind a pile of books, Madame Caillot holds the shuddering insect by one wing, rattles the stove, and drops it into the fire.

—Insofar as Romantics aren't constrained by preconceived ideas of art, and they stress the need for energy and vitality. At the same time, I'm against those Romantics who advocate reckless abandon or obscure mysticism. The head must control the heart at all times, that's my guiding principle. You see, my early schooling in mathematics has been invaluable. Who knows, one day I may write a novel in which the protagonist is a mathematician—a young man very much like you.

—And the name of the protagonist in your recent book?

A blue button is hanging by a thread on Beyle's bulging vest. The thought flashes to mind that it will fall before the night is out, probably as he walks along a dark street, fall and roll into the gutter without him hearing it. I am tempted to reach out, pluck it from the vest, and hand it to him.

—Julien Sorel, a young seminarian who secretly admires Napoleon and uses society women as a means to his ambitions.

—Why write about such a worthless fellow? I ask.

—To redeem him through art.

—What becomes of him?

—He dies on the scaffold.

Brushing soot and chalk dust from her hands, Madame Caillot approaches us and says she must close the shop. As we walk through the maze in the front room, Beyle accidentally elbows a tower of books, which falls onto another tower, and this onto another, and in the space of a few seconds the floor is covered in books, and Madame Caillot is rushing frantically to prevent other towers from collapsing, while shouting abuse at her husband.

33

Nothing tangible eventuated from the first lecture, but the response heartened me, and I was still optimistic that someone with position would attend subsequent lectures. After a night of hopeful plans interrupted by fitful dreams, I awoke the following morning still feeling excited, eager to rework my theory on the solution of equations.

Ten days earlier I had been summoned to appear before members of the Royal Council for Teaching, who were to ratify my expulsion from school. One of the members was Poisson, the mathematical physicist. After the proceedings, he spoke to me in the corridor and encouraged me to pursue my work, of which he had heard good things, and suggested I submit a memoir to the Academy. When I related how the Academy, through Cauchy and Fourier, had already lost two of my memoirs, he promised to take special interest in the paper and present it to the Academy personally. At the time I dismissed the offer as nothing more than kind but empty words, intended to assuage a young man's anger and an older man's conscience. But I felt differently the morning after the lecture.

Working with some of my former intensity, I finished the memoir in the afternoon and hurried off to test Poisson's sincerity. His study was littered with papers, pamphlets, books. He invited me to sit down, but he seemed preoccupied, as though his mind were teeming with problems and projects. I felt uncomfortable during the short visit: He hardly looked up from the pages on his desk, and the conversation gaped with long pauses. In the end he accepted my memoir and said he would submit it to the Academy at its sitting on January 17.

The next four lectures were not successful: Attendances fell by half on each occasion, so that by the fifth only Chevalier and I were there. But I was not overly disappointed: My hopes were buoyed by Poisson's promise.

It has been over a month since I submitted the memoir, and still nothing from the Academy, despite the fact that it has met on two occasions. Poisson has also been silent, even though he and Lacroix have been appointed by the Academy as referees of my work. Doubts have started to gnaw at me again. Abel's fate fills my mind, darkens my hopes. My despondency turns to bitterness at the thought that this memoir has met the same fate as the others.

Early yesterday morning I set out with a group of young Republicans to the church of St. Germain l'Auxerrois, to protest at a mass attended by Legitimists. Ostensibly the mass was to be a memorial to the Duc de Beri, Charles's younger brother assassinated eleven years ago; in fact, it was nothing more than a declaration of support for the Church and the exiled King. It was bitterly cold. Each brisk stride, each burst of vapor, stoked my hatred and anger. This was an opportunity to strike back at those responsible for Father's death. As we marched over a bridge, a few of the others shared crude jokes or boasted about

311

women. I grew angry at their laughter—it was unbecoming of true Republicans. Recalling Father's funeral, I felt the knife's edge in the pocket of my flapping overcoat.

—Incite the crowd, I said, as though thinking aloud. Smash the Church.

—You're too intense, Galois, one of them chuckled, tapping me on the shoulder. You'll have to come out with us one evening. Good wine, bad women—you'll see life in a different light.

I dashed off, eyes watering, ears stinging. A boisterous crowd in front of the church taunted, intimidated, abused those entering. People shouted that the mass was a sign of gross disrespect toward the memory of those patriots who died last July. I pushed through to a speaker: A young man in a black overcoat and yellow gloves urged the crowd to stop the Jesuits before they made a puppet of Louis Philippe, as they had done with Charles.

—Let's not be deceived, patriots! he declared, raising a fist. The Church serves and protects the interests of the rich. Let's destroy all churches. Let's use the stone to build hospitals, schools, orphanages for the children of those who died in July.

In an instant the crowd rushed toward the entrance of the church. I plunged into the torrent, conscious of nothing but a desire to avenge and destroy. At one with the swell bursting through the gates, I was no longer a mathematician, no longer even a Republican—more than the sum of individuals, the crowd imparted its momentum to each member, overwhelming the personal. And I experienced a sense of liberation in the chaos, in the dissolution of myself, in being swept forward by the driving force of the common

312

will. Joining the chorus of "Down with the Church," I could not hear my own voice, but that of a river roaring toward a waterfall. Pushing forward, I could not feel my thin body, but the implacable force of flesh as an instrument of history.

The coachmen in the courtyard were startled: Before they could save their vehicles from the rush, horses were screaming, rearing, breaking away. Empty carriages rumbled over the cobbles. Panic swept through the congregation as it struggled against the tide surging into the church. On the pulpit the elderly priest raised his hands, as though his palms would serve as a bulwark, but when the wave crashed against the altar, he leaped away and ran off with a sprightly step. Men with axes, picks, and sledgehammers smashed balustrades, statues, confessionals, pews, the pulpit, and then turned their fury on the marble altar. I ripped hymn books, tore down paintings and tapestries. I snatched a chalice (wine spilled onto my chest) and threw it at a slender stained-glass window, shattering a pale angel. In an instant all the windows spilled to the ground. Rioters broke into the back rooms and emerged with flagons of wine, vestments, staffs, crosiers. Smashing the bottles after drinking the wine, they put on cassocks, chasubles, hats, and challenged each other to greater acts of desecration.

I raised a marble cross with a silver Christ crucified to it and looked around for something on which to shatter it. Mother appeared: She held me with an imploring look and began reading from Revelation in a soft voice. Father took her place, unbuttoned his collar, and revealed a blue circle around his neck. I smashed the cross against the wall, and the silver statue snapped at the waist.

313

With the inside reduced to rubble, the cry to demolish the church became a wild chorus, and we scrambled outside. Encouraged by a roar of approval, those with tools began their savage onslaught against the columns and walls, until the roofbeams creaked, cracked, and the roof collapsed in a cloud of dust.

—To the Archbishop's mansion! a voice screamed.

In a frenzy we surged to the vicinity of the Notre Dame where, in the absence of opposition, we ransacked the Archbishop's residence, which had already been damaged in the July Revolution. As night palled the city, enormous fires were stoked with furniture, religious ornaments, clothes, and curtains. The flames flared on the dark Seine. People gathered in rings around the fires, singing the "Marseillaise," vowing to complete the demolition of the mansion in the morning. By midnight most of the crowd had dispersed. I remained with a group around the largest fire, which still burned vigorously. I was determined to stay and watch until the symbols of Father's murderers turned to ash. The flames crimsoned the faces and palms of those sitting on scraps of furniture, huddled against the piercing chill. A toothless fellow encouraged us in our vigil, saying this cold was nothing compared to the Russian winter, and he recounted stories of Napoleon's invasion. Reclining on a divan whose legs had been broken off, I looked up from the twisting flames: Through a maple's stark branches the stars were like the tips of icicles. A young man wearing an ecclesiastical robe to keep warm raised above the fire a large portrait depicting a bishop in scarlet, with black circular spectacles, clutching a book with one hand and the chair's lion-headed arm-rest with the other.

—Inquisitor! exclaimed the young man, his robe glittering in the restless light. This is where you belong!

And he threw the painting onto the burning pile. The canvas curled at once, the paint sizzled and smelled, the bishop was devoured by tongues of flame. As drowsiness filled my eyes, I gazed at the rectangular frame blistering and blackening. I imagined the frame as a golden section: a rectangle whose ratio of length to width was equal to the limiting ratio of consecutive terms of the Fibonacci sequence. And what if all rectangles were destroyed by fire? Would the golden section still exist as an innate sense of form and proportion? Perhaps it would be restored to its ideal state. If there was a God, He was not in those objects crackling in the fire. A process, God was restricted and diminished by objects. Fire was a metaphor of mind, and as such it restored God to His rightful place.

My head fell to the smell of wine on my chest, and I found myself witness to a great purging conflagration.

—The fire of the Apocalypse, announced Mother's voice.

—The fire of freedom, countered Father's.

This was the fire that would purge the accretions of matter clinging to the mind, and join mind and mathematics in a holy union. And my own flesh melted in the flames, and I became expansive, disembodied thought, zero and one, the ultimate pronumeral, an equation with infinitely many solutions, both real and imaginary . . .

I woke with a start: Someone had thrown a cassock

over me as I had slept. Sweeping it aside, I threw it on a pile of charred beams and smoldering rubble. It was dawn. The crowd was gathering again to complete what the night had interrupted.

—To the mansion! shouted a fellow wrapped in a velvet drape that had been torn down from a large window.

Yawning, shivering, I followed the crowd as it shouted, sang, swore, gradually working itself into a rage. Meeting no resistance, we forced open the gates, poured into the garden, and stormed the building, smashing and tearing as we went from room to room, from floor to floor. In one of the dining rooms, I was stopped by my reflection in an oval mirror hanging on the wall. I picked up a black marble sphere (an ornament from a clock which lay shattered in the fireplace) and shouted to a few men to get out of the way. A clearing opened between me and the mirror. Aiming at myself, I felt the sphere's smoothness, and the formula $^4/_3\pi r^3$ came to mind. But there was now nothing transcendental about π. The sphere was hard and dense, its gravity attracted an infinite number of decimal numbers, concentrated them, reduced them to the blackness before the first number, the great zero, of which the sphere was a physical representation. I threw it, shattering myself and the room into countless jagged fragments. The crowd cheered wildly. A young man leaped onto the mantelpiece, pulled the mirror frame off the wall, and held it up before an old man.

—A magic mirror! he laughed. It ages people in an instant!

—And restores youth to others, grinned the old man.

I looked for the sphere among the debris. I wanted to take it with me: There was something attractive about it, something I wanted to fathom in a quieter moment. Crunching over the chaos of the room multiplied countless times in the fragments on the floor, I was about to pick up the sphere but was pulled away and swept up to the next floor. As the rooms to the left and right were being pillaged and objects thrown from the windows, I followed a group to the double doors at the far end of the corridor, where a few were struggling with the doorknobs.

—Stand aside!

A passage was made for three men running with a large wooden cross ripped out of the refectory. A man at each arm and one at the foot, they rammed the head against the knobs: The doors flew apart, and we pressed in after the cross bearers, only to stop in our tracks. I looked around in disbelief: Everyone appeared overwhelmed by the impressive texts arranged in glass shelves, by colorful manuscripts in showcases, by rare Bibles. Most of the rioters were workers and laborers, probably illiterate. Was their reaction a kind of awe before the library's solemnity? The men now held the cross upright, all three supporting the vertical beam. Suddenly, a young man in black overcoat and yellow gloves leaped onto a writing desk and snatched an inkpot.

—Down with the Jesuits! he shouted, and in throwing the pot at a glass shelf, stained his gloves with green ink.

His call unleashed a whirlwind that shattered glass cases, toppled shelves, upturned desks and tables, ripped paintings and parchment scrolls. The initial awe now turned to a rage against books: Spines were broken, covers torn off, pages scattered in the air. Books in French, Latin, Greek, and Hebrew were thrown from the windows, and they fell in the courtyard, forming another tower of Babel.

A corner cabinet was smashed open and ancient Bibles thundered onto the floor. I picked up one in a silver jacket, inlaid with stones, fastened with a clasp. It was in Greek, with colored letters and drawings probably done by the careful hand of a monastic calligrapher. My initial reaction to tear out the parchment pages was checked by a large letter X at the top of a page: It was colored in purple, with vines coiling around it, surrounded by pastoral scenes, with the sun above it.

No! This was not the letter of life, not the symbol of liberation. Fear, enslavement, death: That was its secret meaning. It was for all those who feared death, who needed a sacrificial savior because they lacked courage to sacrifice themselves for their beliefs. This was the letter which killed Father because he dared to oppose it, which beguiled Mother with false promises. This letter had no place in the Republic. The symbol of the future was the x of pure mathematics. Just as faith in an unseen, unknown deity replaced the Egyptian pantheon of petrified gods — a faith that flesh was not able to sustain, and which eventually resulted in a personification — so the new x would be the symbol of a higher deity. The new x would have nothing to do with number, with objects, with flesh. Through it men would perform miracles, solve the great mysteries of the universe, overcome death. I ripped out the page, shredded the letter, tore the book from its jacket, and threw it from the window.

We spilled into the courtyard, now littered with furniture, books, vestments, sacred objects. As the final touch to our rampage, we threw everything over a parapet, into the Seine.

—Stop! For God's sake! Not in the river!

318

A tall, gaunt man was rushing about, trying desperately to prevent those with books from throwing them in the river. Caillot! The rioters dismissed him with a laugh or a rough shove. He picked up a few books, but they were knocked from him; he embraced a few others, they were torn from him, like children from his arms. Shrieking, he pushed through the taunting, jeering crowd and ran down the steps to the bank, where he knelt and reached out for books floating near the edge. His fingertips were on a large open volume, when a fellow with a red cap pushed him into the water. Uproarious laughter resounded from the parapet, where people had climbed to watch him thrashing about, up to his neck in books. He would have drowned but for a passing fisherman who hauled him into a skiff and rowed away from the commotion.

The residence reduced to rubble, we turned to Notre Dame, to unleash our fury there, when the National Guard appeared in force. Frustrated, though still excited by the pillaging and the wine from the Archbishop's cellar, a large section of the crowd turned from riot to revel. It was the middle of carnival season: People in costumes and masks were dancing and parading throughout the city. Making the most of the opportunity, some of the rioters dressed in ecclesiastical garments and, praying and chanting, joined the revelers.

I remained behind, disappointed by the turn of events, shivering in the cathedral's knife-edged shadow.

34

Two hundred Republicans have gathered in the restaurant Vendages de Bourgogne to celebrate the acquittal of the nineteen charged over the incident at the Louvre. Late-afternoon sunlight angles into the long room overlooking the garden. May has crayoned the flower beds, birds have found their pitch, the willows' limbs are visible through green negligees. Aroused by a week of warm spring weather, by young ladies promenading the boulevards in the latest fashions, by the band playing lively Republican melodies, by bottles of wine chinking back and forth—the gathering of mainly younger men is high-spirited and conversation buzzes. Probing a chicken breast with my knife, I am at a back table with a group of students. I have not said more than a few words since arriving. Despite the brighter days, my thoughts during the past month have become increasingly gloomy, due partly to the silence from the Academy, partly to the trial, which has reminded me of my own insignificance.

Two months ago I wrote to the Academy inquiring about my memoir: no reply. I had my pride, I was not going to grovel. They could all go to hell, including Poisson. As there were no other churches to be destroyed, I directed my anger at myself in small ways: sometimes by going without lunch or dinner, other times by neglecting my appearance. On April seventh, as the first swallows weaved around the house, I left early for the Palais de Justice. A vast crowd from all walks of life greeted the nineteen as they were escorted into the courtroom. I caught a glimpse of d'Herbinville: His clean-shaven face was particularly striking that morning, and there was an exalted look about him as he acknowledged well-wishers. Again I experienced that feeling of infatuation, though this time it was mingled with envy. I desperately wanted to be there with him, walking bravely into the courtroom, cheered by the crowd. I would have had this sort of attention in the mathematical world, if it were not for envious, incompetent academics; instead here I was, a nobody in the crowd. But a name could be made quickly in politics: One brave act, and I would be in the public eye. People would point me out as a true Republican, just as they were now admiring d'Herbinville.

I watched the proceedings from the back of the balcony. Cavaignac, Trelat, Guinard, and Pointis spoke with conviction and compassion for the poor, the sick, and the suffering. The gallery greeted their speeches with wild applause, while the President, Monsieur Hardoin, rapped the bench vigorously with his knuckles to restore order. When d'Herbinville took the stand, I pushed through to the front and stood beside a young woman, who accorded me a sharp glance from under prominently arched brows. A small gold disk inscribed with an *S* trembled from her ear as she turned to a female companion. I found her perfume pleasant, after the smell of those at the back who had come straight from the abattoirs.

—Isn't he handsome? she whispered to her companion.

d'Herbinville stood upright, gripping the surrounding banister, meeting the President's look with haughtiness verging on contempt.

—And how did you come by these weapons? asked Hardoin, pointing to a table with a collection of carbines, pistols, packets of cartridges.

—I want it known, Your Honor, that some were obtained during the three glorious days last July, when my comrades and I disarmed several posts for the sake of the people.

Cheers erupted, the gallery pressed forward. The young woman applauded, her gloved hands like butterflies.

—He risked his life for the people, she said.

And as she leaned over the balcony railing (as though straining to catch d'Herbinville's attention), I was struck by the hollow in the nape of her neck.

—Other weapons were bought at my own expense, Your Honor. I've had the good fortune to succeed in business, and I've used my income to equip young men who couldn't meet the expenses needed to serve in the Artillery.

—Handsome, brave, and generous, said the young woman's companion.

—Did you distribute arms?

—Yes, Your Honor.

The reply discharged a burst of commotion. As d'Herbinville was led from the stand, the young woman dropped her embroidered handkerchief, which fell in his path. He picked it up and nodded. I wasn't sure whether the nod was intended for me or her. He sat down with the other eighteen and their numerous advocates. Inhaling the young woman's perfume, I applauded, vowing to do something as brave and generous as d'Herbinville: an act to show everyone I was a true Republican.

I attended the trial for weeks, despite the fact that after each day my outlook darkened. My thoughts were especially gloomy when the jury acquitted the nineteen. I watched with growing envy as they were surrounded by a crowd of thousands in the Palais de Justice and the Quai aux Fleurs. I followed, rancor eating at me, as d'Herbinville and Trelat leaped into a carriage, only to have the horses unharnessed by the adoring crowd and the carriage pulled to Trelat's door.

Having picked the chicken to shreds, I look up at the main table. d'Herbinville is sipping wine, talking jovially, reaping attention with his flashing smile. This gathering is unbecoming of true Republicans: an expensive restaurant, while many people lived in dark hovels; fancy food, while others cannot provide bread for their children; wine, while water for drinking is polluted. What am I doing here? I should be out . . . I do not need wine for inspiration. I do not need its taste to stir me to action, nor its fumes to evoke visions of a Republic. Wine is for those who lack imagination and passion. I do not need it to speak my mind.

When the waiters clear the plates, the nineteen are congratulated and a toast is made in their honor, followed by speeches in honor of previous revolutions. They drink to Robespierre. To Raspail, who recently refused to accept the cross of the Legion of Honor because it offended his Republican ideals. And then Alexandre Dumas is called upon to make a speech. The writer, who has been scribbling in a

323

notebook during the speeches, stands and delivers an apology for the role of writers in revolutionary times. About thirty, well-groomed, he speaks confidently, pausing now and then to examine his left palm, as though it holds the text of his speech. After praising the actions of the nineteen, he proceeds to extol the virtues of poets, novelists, and particularly dramatists, who flesh their words and make them accessible to the masses.

The magnanimity of writers! I have heard it all before. They praise scientists and soldiers, while thinking themselves superior to both. But where were you, Dumas, during the Revolution? Wrapped in a smoking jacket, making notes on death and destruction?

—Long live Dumas! A toast to Dumas!

After the toast Dumas sits down and begins a conversation with a man on his left, one of Louis Philippe's comedians.

Parasite! That is what you are, Dumas. I clutch the handle of the knife concealed under my jacket. Consorting with the King's clown! You exploit the suffering of the illiterate in order to provide the bourgeois with amusement and diversion. You exploit those who give their blood for an ideal in order to satisfy your craving for wealth and fame. Very well, Dumas! I will give you something to write about—only make sure you describe the incident accurately, record my correct age, avoid the predilection you Romantics have for sensationalism.

—A toast! I announce, springing up.

—A toast, echoes the student next me.

The clamor and conversation continue. I take out the knife and raise it with the glass of wine I have not touched.

—To Louis Philippe!

After their initial bewilderment, those at my table urge me to sit down, while the student next to me tugs at my coat. Ignoring them, I climb on the chair and repeat the toast several times, in an increasingly louder voice, arousing surprise, concern, alarm. A few try to silence me with whistles and howls of disapproval.

—The dagger!

—He's mad!

—It's a threat!

—He'll jeopardize the Society!

—To Louise Philippe! I shout, stepping on the table.

The knife gleams in the lamplight. The room fills with commotion. Blanqui and his group of anarchists clap and cheer my toast. Shocked, Dumas and his party scrape back their chairs in protest and push their way through the room, knocking over glasses of wine which stain the tablecloths. Dumas darts me a reproving look, then leads his party through the open glass doors into the lamplit garden.

—Go! I yell. Coward! The Republic doesn't need writers of fiction. But if you must write for the bourgeois, then make sure you depict this evening as it is. Mention that I was drunk on ideals, not wine. Make sure you describe me as one of the most passionate of Republicans, prepared to give his life for his beliefs. Be truthful, Dumas! Don't tell your gullible readers you left the restaurant because the King's clown drew you away. We all know why you're leaving: You don't want to be compromised by my remarks!

The celebration quickly degenerates to wild whistling, applause, remonstrations. d'Herbinville strides to the table

325

and grips me by the ankle. My heart beats in expectation of approval and praise.

—That's enough, Evariste, he says. Get down before you spoil things for everyone.

Caution? At a time like this? And from him, of all people? Why is everyone afraid to speak up, to act on their beliefs? I have admired d'Herbinville above all other Republicans, been infatuated with him, perhaps even idolized him. Last February I would have obeyed his command to attack musket and cannon; now his call for restraint dismays me. Stepping down from the table, I am quickly surrounded by a group of younger Republicans who, slightly drunk, have taken up my threatening toast. Hurt by d'Herbinville, I turn from him and lead the group into the mild, blossom-scented night. Chanting "To Louis Philippe," we march to the square of Vendôme, where we continue the chorus, with some of them laughing and dancing around the central column.

I detach myself from the drunken group and sit on the steps. Laughter and wine will never realize the Republic.

35

After a brief hearing this afternoon, I was remanded in custody and brought here, Sainte-Pélagie prison, charged with threatening the life of Louis Philippe, King of France. I am in a wing housing political prisoners, in a room with about fifty others. Apart from Republicans, who are in the majority, there are also Legitimatists, Bonapartists, Saint-Simonists, Utopians, Communists, and Anarchists. Conditions here are not too harsh, and prisoners are allowed to move between their sleeping quarters, the courtyard, and a small canteen.

The curtain in my room was swept aside early yesterday morning. I sprang up from sleep to find a policeman on each side of the bed. Mother was in the doorway, protesting that a mistake had been made. Brilliant sunshine filled the room, colored the water in the jug, snuggled into my shoes, settled on my clothes thrown carelessly on the armchair. As one policeman read the warrant for my arrest, the other picked up the knife, tested the point on his palm, and nodded.

—Evariste! What have you done? cried Mother.

For an instant doubt undermined my defiance, evoked not by Mother's contorted face, but by a glimpse of my left shoe with its heel worn badly on one side. As the policemen escorted me along the gritty path to the wagon, Mother pleaded with me to take a small Bible. I did not reply until we reached the wagon, when I turned abruptly, snatched it from her, and threw it in a thorny rosebush, scattering a flock of sparrows. We glared at each other for an instant, long enough for me to be struck by how much I resembled her, especially around the cheekbones and eyes.

—You'll learn respect in prison, said the policeman who had read the warrant.

They pushed me inside and bolted the door. As the wagon rumbled off, I could see her through the small grilled window: She was bent over the rosebush, picking lightly through a tangle of branches.

After the first week here my initial bitterness turned to resignation; after the second, resignation has turned into a kind of joyful acceptance. The irony of it all! I was denied entry to the Polytechnic, where I hoped to find the spirit of the Republic; now I sense that spirit here, among true Republicans, people who have sacrificed liberty for their beliefs. Prison is a necessary experience in my development as a true Republican. The prophets were exiled or went voluntarily into the wilderness, where, away from comfort and distraction, they strengthened their faith, purified their voice, and returned to preach of a new world. Prison will be my wilderness: a place to test and prepare myself, from which I will emerge with a clearer vision of the Republic, a stronger voice for imparting my message.

Word of my audacious toast has spread, endearing me to many of the older Republicans, filling me with a sense of belonging to a brotherhood. Flattered by their attention and acceptance, I am determined to spend time with them, to speak to them, to get to know as many as possible. Up to now the Republicans I have mixed with have been largely students and professionals; here I mix with tradesmen, workers, and those from the growing class of the unemployed. These men are "the people," they won the July Revolution—"the people" admired by many professional Republicans but only in the abstract. They are my brothers, blood brothers if need be, as much as Raspail, d'Herbinville, and the others. Their language is coarse, their manner abrupt. They drink in the canteen, swear profusely, and sing bawdy songs. I try to be tolerant—true Republicans should be judged by their actions, not their language.

—What's it to you what I've done? retorts a pugnacious fellow with a naked woman tattooed on the inside of his forearm. Are you one of them spies they send here from time to time?

I apologize, but the fellow winks and places his arm over my shoulder. Extending his other arm, he flexes the muscles of his forearm: A sinew between the woman's legs twitches. The fellow laughs, tightening his grip on my shoulder. He is a Republican, I tell myself, struggling to overcome a feeling of revulsion.

On my first walk in the courtyard I was surprised to see children wandering around, playing games, conversing with the prisoners. They were the gamins, I was told. The orphaned, the abandoned, the homeless who roamed Paris like feral animals, begging, stealing, in some cases becoming hardened criminals before the age of twelve. The authorities had calculated it was cheaper on the public purse to round them up and house them in an annex here than have them on the streets. They were kept here until the age of thirteen, when they were considered old enough to know the law and fend for themselves.

Each afternoon I make a point of watching as about twenty children gather in a corner of the yard, sit cross-legged on the ground, and listen attentively to a scruffy, bearded fellow, whose taciturn manner appears to have isolated him from the other prisoners. Was he entertaining them with tales and legends? Stories of Napoleon? Or was he a teacher giving them lessons? If so, I might assist him by offering lessons in arithmetic.

One blue afternoon, as drunken laughter spills from the canteen, curiosity gets the better of me. The ideal Republic in prison, I muse, approaching the fellow as the children scatter after another session.

—They listened to every word, I remark.

Sitting on a bench, the fellow turns slowly and gathers me with a languid look.

—You're the one who threatened the King.

—I had to remind a few Republicans that the July Revolution hasn't fulfilled our hopes. Our leaders are making concessions to the King, forgetting the sacrifices made by the people.

He nods, combs his beard, examines the ashen strands caught between his fingers, and blows them away with a light breath.

—I've been telling them about paradise, he says.

—Religious fairy tales? I ask, disappointed.

—Not at all, he replies, forcing a smile through his

thick beard. Republic, Utopia, paradise—call it what you will. The best possible world for them.

With a forefinger severed at the middle joint he points to a few girls hopping on numbered squares.

—Paris must burn for paradise to arise, he says, becoming more animated, the whites of his eyes streaked with red. I'm an anarchist, and the children are my disciples. Providence has brought us together. I preached the purity of fire outside, but nobody would listen. They laughed, threw slops, set their dogs on me. In the end they locked me in here. But it's been a blessing, friend, a real blessing. The children aren't infected by bourgeois morality. They're empty vessels, friend, vessels I fill with stories of paradise, of a world with love and material comfort. And they listen when I tell them the way to paradise is through anarchy. Yes, they listen, and look upon me as the loving father they never had. My ideas have taken root in their little bodies. When they leave this place, they'll carry the poppies of anarchy in their hearts and the vision of paradise in their minds. And do you know, friend, some of my little disciples can't wait to leave, to burn Notre Dame as the first step toward paradise on earth.

He looks away for a moment, chewing a thumbnail bitten to the quick, then turns his back and chuckles in a way that suggests he is not quite right in the head.

Later in the afternoon I approach a girl from the group. She throws a white pebble, which clatters and stops in a square numbered four. Grinning mischievously, she tells me that Ogin is crazy, and the only reason they listen to him is because of the bonbons he gives after each talk. Is she telling the truth? Is paradise nothing more than a sweet? Or is that sweet a way of misleading the authorities? A way of protecting father Ogin?

d'Herbinville has visited me a number of times and arranged, at his own expense, for an advocate to represent me in court. I am flattered by his concern, though not without some reservation. After all, he is five or six years older than me, he has made a small fortune from manufacturing party firecrackers, he has good connections; why is he taking such a personal interest in me? What can he possibly hope to gain?

At our first meeting, the advocate suggests we use intoxication as our defense, but I insist I was sober, that I cannot bear the smell of wine. Bemused, the advocate scrapes his shoes on the floorboards in the visiting room.

—But that's our only real defense, he protests. Wine was plentiful on the evening, people were celebrating, words were said under the influence.

—I wasn't drunk, I repeat.

—There's no other defense, he says firmly. Remember: The incident may have been quite harmless, but the Orleanist papers have described it as the first threat against the King. We must win the jury by appealing to their sense of compassion. I intend to portray you as a passionate, though somewhat foolish young man who drank too much and spoke without thinking.

d'Herbinville accompanies the advocate on his visit the day before the trial. As we walk to the table, a swallow flits into the room through a broken window and darts to a simmering nest.

—Have you considered my advice? asks the advocate.

—I wasn't drunk.

—Be reasonable, Evariste, says d'Herbinville. You're more used to the Society outside than in here.

—Reasonable! What credibility will I have with the students when the papers spread the story that I was drunk?

—Very well, then, says d'Herbinville, sitting more upright, his head and shoulders now in sunlight. Let's at least qualify your threat. There are people who would testify they heard: "To Louis Philippe, if he betrays the people." They would also swear that the qualification was drowned by the noise.

—Perfect! exclaims the advocate. Such a qualification changes the meaning and the intent.

—We're planning marches and demonstrations for Bastille Day, adds d'Herbinville. We want you out to lead the younger Republicans.

Unlike a month ago for the trial of the nineteen, the courtroom is now somber, the balcony empty. There are no young ladies with handkerchiefs, no fierce supporters: Most of those present appear uninterested in the proceedings. I feel cheated, disappointed. I imagined this as my opportunity to display my Republican passion, to outdo d'Herbinville, but the size and mood of the gallery dispirit me. Alfred is sitting at the back, looking overawed by the courtroom's solemnity. Chevalier is also present. He visited me in prison several times, and each time urged me to concentrate on mathematics in order to make the conditions more bearable. I thanked him for his kind thoughts, but pointed out that I needed to associate with real patriots, that I felt at home among them, and that, at the moment, mathematics was a barrier between me and the Republic.

d'Herbinville is at the front table with the advocate, whispering to him from time to time, flashing optimistic smiles toward me. Sitting in the dock, listening to the advocate defending me with the qualifying clause, followed by several witnesses testifying on my behalf, I feel my spirits sinking. I wanted to use the stand as d'Herbinville had, but now it seems pointless and all I can do is stare at my tessellated shadow on the tiled floor, or at the juryman who has been scratching at a scab on his forehead during the proceedings.

Ten minutes after the advocate's concluding remarks, the jury reappears and announces a verdict of not guilty.

36

As we leave my attic room in a boardinghouse on Rue des Bernadins, Chevalier asks how I intend to make ends meet without Mother's support. I have been living here since my acquittal ten days ago. I could not possibly return to Bourg-la-Reine, not after the last incident with Mother on the morning of my arrest. She betrayed Father, and she would sell her own son for the sake of the Jesuits. Alfred and Nathalie visited me in prison on two occasions, and they informed me that Mother demanded an unconditional apology. I refused, saying I was quite happy never to speak to her again. According to Alfred, she was just as determined to sever herself from me.

— d'Herbinville is paying for the room, I reply, as we make way for a cart filled with carcasses from a boning room.

— He's taking a special interest in you.

— He knows I'm committed to the cause.

— I don't trust him, Evariste.

— Condemn your lecherous Enfantin before you denigrate good Republicans! What do you want from me anyway? Are you still trying to recruit me? Am I ripe now that I'm free and without prospects?

335

—I want to steer you back to mathematics.

—You always do this, Auguste. Just as I begin to feel mathematics dying within me, you come along and stir the embers.

—I believe in you, Evariste.

—Your belief's misplaced! It's best for those embers to become the ash of a burned book.

—Have you heard from Poisson?

—Four months, and not a word!

—He's a busy man. He might need a prod. Pay him a visit.

—Busy? Like Fourier and Cauchy?

—It may be your last chance. A favorable report from him would open a few doors.

—You'll have me clutching at straws again.

—Better straws than pistols.

Chevalier has managed to coax me to attend the Salon, where artists are displaying their latest paintings in an annual exhibition. On the way I feel the embers flickering again. He may be right: Poisson might well be my last chance. I should visit him as soon as possible.

—All Paris is talking about it, says Chevalier.

—Talking about what?

—Delacroix's painting of *Liberty Leading the People*. They say he has captured the courageous spirit of the July Revolution, and that not only his subject matter, but his very composition and color are said to be Romantic and Revolutionary.

—Is he a Republican?

—It seems so.

336

—Was he at the barricades?

—One critic has already attacked him for not having experienced what he has painted.

—Then he is a parasite, exploiting the Revolution, the death and suffering of the people, for his own advancement. When he sells the painting, will he give the proceeds to the widows and orphans? No! He'll live well, dress fashionably, mix with those who can afford to buy paintings. The high life at the expense of those who died! It's obscene, Auguste!

—They say Louis Philippe will buy it for the Palace.

I spit into a murky canal. In a nearby workshop a man is chiseling a triangle on the upper section of a rectangular slab of marble.

—Louis Philippe's no fool: He is determined to cultivate the idea of the Citizen King. He'll buy it to impress the people. Delacroix's an opportunist. A true Republican wouldn't allow his work to enter the Palace, not until the Palace becomes a public museum.

Among the hundreds of paintings in the Salon, Delacroix's enormous canvas with its larger-than-life figures attracts the greatest bustle and excitement. We push past rustling dresses, through a cloud of cigar smoke, between mixed reactions.

—It wasn't like that at the barricades, protests a stubbled man with hands the size of shovels. It's us tradesmen that were the heroes of the Revolution. Monsieur Delacroix should have left the safety of his atelier. If he'd seen the fighting with his own eyes he wouldn't have painted that top-hatted bourgeois as the hero of the moment. Shame on him! He's cheated the people! And the greater shame is that his painting will give future generations a false account of those three glorious days.

—Sensationalism! exclaims another, with a bright red cravat to match the color of his face. These Romantics have lost all sense of harmony! They're obsessed with death and destruction. Just look at that figure.

Raising a silver-tipped cane, he points to a man lying in the left foreground, naked from the waist down.

—Why is he there, in that state? There were corpses, many of them, on both sides, but were any stripped naked like that? What is Monsieur Delacroix's intention? Does he wish to shock? Does he wish to display his virtuosity in depicting the naked body? Well, he fails: The figure's face intimates a peaceful sleep, while the nakedness undermines the work's authenticity.

—Monsieur Delacroix will no doubt create a myth around the gamin, comments another, in a black frock coat buttoned to his chin. He'll have future generations believe that the Revolution was led by street urchins. Look at that rascal: a pistol in each hand! There's nothing noble or innocent in those little savages. It's an outrage to glorify them like that! I know what the little devil must be thinking —Thank you, Monsieur Delacroix, for putting these pistols in my hands. Let your audience believe I'm risking my life for the cause. The truth is, I took these pistols and this bag strapped over my shoulder from a fallen officer. I'm going to run down the first lane I come to and pawn them at the first opportunity. Vermin! That's what they are! Always pestering and picking the pockets of honest citizens. I'm forever driving the scavengers from my pastry shop.

—What do you think of it, Evariste?

The tricolor is raised in Liberty's right hand, a musket in her left. She is broad-hipped, with a red waistband fluttering in the forward rush, her rouged face profiled, forehead and nose in a straight line, her breasts full and firm. Her presence in the midst of the Revolution angers me. I know my Greek: Liberty is the ancient Eleftheria, a feminine noun. I know her function in the painting is symbolic, metaphorical, a personification of freedom; despite this, I feel she does not belong there. I have come here expecting to experience something of the Revolution, to see a faithful representation of those daring days, use my imagination to project myself into events from which I was excluded by circumstances. But this is nothing more than caricature! It lacks feeling for the people, sympathy for their suffering. There is no place for symbols and female personification in a moment when men were charging to their death.

—Delacroix hasn't overcome his Classicism, has he, Auguste? Look at Liberty: a mixture of the ancient Nike, a Christian angel, and a Raphael Madonna. And what's his intention in showing her breasts? Are they needed to arouse the passions of the men around her? Doesn't he know there are men who can be inspired by ideals, who don't have to be led by a woman's body? No doubt a prostitute was his model for Liberty; a slut leading the people given center stage, together with her protégé, the gamin, while one of the true heroes of those glorious days, the student of the Polytechnic, is reduced almost to shadowy insignificance.

My anger contracts to two fists. I know from the chef's account that the students fought in the front ranks, fearlessly leading groups of workers. This student has been depicted wearing the Polytechnic's red-and-blue peaked hat, with a saber raised in his hand, but there is no glorious light around him. Quite the opposite. A small, frail figure, he is staring wide-eyed at the groin of a dead man, as though deliberating whether he should scramble over a pile of broken beams, rubble, bodies. He has been represented as a coward, while the prostitute, who was probably entertaining clients during those days, is elevated to a goddess.

The painting should be destroyed. Delacroix has overlooked the fact that the students were the real heroes of the Revolution. The workers were driven to fight in order to improve their desperate lot; the tradesmen, against high taxes; the bourgeois, to maintain their comfortable lifestyle; while the students fought for nothing other than the idea of a Republic.

— He has debased the Revolution with that slut.

— It's only a painting.

— The student should have been in her place.

— Speaking of the student, Chevalier smiles, you didn't pose for Delacroix, did you, Evariste?

— What do you mean?

— He bears a striking resemblance to you.

Staring at the face whose anxiety is sharpened by long well-defined eyebrows, I experience a fleeting sense of self-recognition, accompanied by a feeling of déjà vu.

— Don't you think so?

— Perhaps a little.

— Maybe Delacroix made a sketch of you while you were unaware. Artists are always sketching faces to use in future works.

And I recall an occasion in the coach on the way to

340

Bourg-la-Reine, when a frail-looking fellow was sketching and darting glances at me. Was that Delacroix? What if that student is based on me? Delacroix has unwittingly placed me in a situation I longed to be in, from which I was kept by Guigniault. Under different circumstances that student in the painting might well have been me: the Evariste Galois who passed the examination on the second attempt, who entered the Polytechnic, and who fought in the Revolution. There is neither uncertainty nor fear in the eyes of my look-alike: He is waiting for the moment to spring from the rubble, leap over the naked body, vanquish the monarchy, and race light-footed to a shining future. Unlike the other four main characters, my look-alike takes no direction from the flag-waving slut: He will act when the Republic beckons, not at the sight of a pair of breasts. That is the Evariste Galois who, after the rise of the Republic, will enter the Polytechnic and devote the remainder of his life to mathematics.

37

During a lull in the Society's activities, I spend long stretches of time in my room, without prospects, drawn to the precipice of despair, though saved from the edge by . . . a flash of the Republic, the flutter of an x, the flit of a daydream. As a coal carrier groans and thunders up the stairs, I find myself thinking about Chevalier's advice, and soon a desperate hope rekindles the embers I wanted to extinguish. In an instant I am on the stairs, blackening my shirt in squeezing past the carrier, on my way to the Academy, to discover the fate of the memoir I submitted six months ago.

It is a hot, still morning in early July. Almost a year since the Revolution, the city has been restored to order. The treacherous holes where cobbles were picked for the barricades have been paved over. Saplings have been planted where trees were felled, and their light-green leaves are small tongues licking the sun. Shopfronts, windows, and signs have all been repaired, and business is brisk. Broken streetlamps have been replaced, and they now gleam for the dark. Apart from the odd tricolor hanging limply from a building, there is little to indicate that the Revolution achieved anything. I recall the ant nests I used to prod with a stick as a boy: They would scatter frantically in the freedom of chaos, only to regroup a short time later, reestablish their order, safe in the certainty of their lines. Looking around, I see the city in the same way: The people, even the most rebellious, appear to have succumbed to the old order. A more violent revolution is needed to create a new order. Maybe the Republic has to arise from the rubble of this society. Maybe Blanqui and the anarchists are right.

—Evariste!

An open-topped carriage traveling in the opposite direction stops beside me.

—Where are you going? asks d'Herbinville.

I glance at his companion and recognize her at once: the young woman on the balcony during the trial of the nineteen.

—To the Academy.

—We'll take you there, he says, smiling and opening the door.

The young woman turns to a bandstand in the shadows of the elms, where a dozen different brass instruments blend to produce a mellow tune.

—It's not far, I say, and walk off abruptly.

Why has the brief encounter disturbed me? The music is still brewing in my ears. I imagined that, like myself, he lived only for the Republic. The sight of him with that woman, riding happily around Paris as though the Republic has been won, is unbecoming of a true patriot. I feel hurt, disappointed, as though he has betrayed me personally. I thought him a kindred spirit, someone who subdued his instincts for the sake of an ideal. It now seems I was mistaken. If he were a true Republican brother, he would have instructed the driver to take the woman home, leaped out of the carriage, and accompanied me to the Academy, discussing as we went how best to realize the final Revolution.

When I enter the Secretary of the Academy's office, a man with padded elbows looks up from stirring a white solution and grimaces.

—Yes? he asks in a brusque manner.

As I explain the reason for my visit, the man adds another teaspoon of sugar or salt to the glass and stirs it vigorously.

—An abscess, he says, as though I have asked the cause of his distress.

—Has Poisson presented my memoir to the Academy?

—How does it look?

He twists his neck, tilts his head, and stretches open his mouth with a hooked forefinger. The back of his lower gum is ulcerated white.

—Been like that for a week, he mumbles.

—What about my . . .

The man drinks a mouthful of the solution, swishes it by puffing his cheeks, and expels it in a bucket under the desk.

—Salt, he says, reaching for the glass.

I prevent him from taking another mouthful by asking for my memoir in a sharp tone. Pressing his cheek, the man stands and goes to a grid of shelves at the back of the room, saying he is only the assistant, not the Secretary. After shuffling papers in several partitions, he pulls out what looks like a memoir, disturbing a moth which flutters in his face. Brushed away, it scatters and drops into the bucket, where it shudders convulsively.

—Galois, Evariste, he announces, grimacing, garbling the name. Your memoir was examined by Messieurs Poisson and Lacroix, who presented it to the Academy last week, the fourth of July.

—What do they say?

He shoots a glance at me. Is he smiling wryly, grimacing in pain, or using the memoir to agitate me? The moth ripples frantically in the bucket.

—May I read their comments? I ask, annoyed by the way the fellow embraces my work.

He explains that protocol in these matters requires a copy of the report to be made, the copy filed, and the report sent to the author. As a copy has not been made, and as he is not the Secretary, that position held by Monsieur Arago, he has no authority to show original reports to anyone, including the author.

—I want to see it, I demand, checking an impulse to snatch it and run.

And he steps around the desk, glancing into the bucket, where his reflection is fragmented by the moth's death throes.

—Protocol!

Is he playing on my obvious impatience and curiosity? Or playing games to distract himself from his discomfort? Tucking the memoir under his arm, he reaches for the salt solution when I pull out a knife, flick it open, and spring behind the desk.

—Give it to me!

Terrified, the assistant places the memoir on the desk and backs away. There is complete stillness in the minute or so it takes to read the report; even the moth stops struggling. Lowering the knife, I drop the memoir and leave without a word.

Outside, I walk in a daze, my thoughts and feelings in turmoil. If only my memoir had vanished like the others. I see the report again, and the signatures of Poisson and Lacroix, and their comments: "unintelligible," "incomprehensible," "vague," "further expansion and clarification necessary," "doubtful results." Cutting as these judgments are, I can at least attribute them to the shortsightedness of the referees. My terse manner of exposition requires a certain kind of mind, a certain kind of reading. Poisson and Lacroix are both plodders, unable to follow my ideas because they are burdened with all the excess baggage of present mathematical exposition.

What cuts me to the bone, what twists my insides, is Poisson's suggestion of plagiarism. Plagiarism! He even has the gall to quote passages from Abel's work and point out the similarities. Envious fool! Can't he see the two approaches are totally different?

Plagiarism! I did not know the name Abel when I submitted my first memoir to the Academy, and the present one is simply an elaboration of those initial findings. Besides, Poisson's quote from Abel comes from letters the Norwegian wrote to Crelle and Legendre concerning discoveries he made shortly before his death, some of which dealt with the theory of equations. Yes, I have read those letters, though not in Crelle's *Journal*, where they were first published at the end of last year, but in Férussac's *Bulletin*, published *after* I submitted my memoir to Poisson.

Plagiarism! Let any serious, unbiased scholar examine my findings and compare them to Abel's. The truth will emerge at once. Poisson! A mathematical physicist! He is insensitive to the spirit of pure mathematics, the spirit that inspired Newton and Leibniz to discover the differential calculus independently of each other, that moved Lobachevsky and Bolyai to challenge Euclid, one from Russia, the other from Hungary, the spirit that imbued Abel and me.

By the time I return to my room, the feeling of dejection has hardened to anger. No more hopes, I vow, standing before the Artillery uniform hanging from a nail on the wall. This is the last time the Academy will deceive me.

Poisson and Lacroix! Their very names intimate collusion with the Jesuits!

From the bottom drawer of the cupboard I take out one of a pair of unloaded pistols given to me by d'Herbinville. No more mathematics, no more false hopes. I go to the open window, cock the hammer, and aim at a broad-hipped woman plodding across the square with a bucket of water in each hand. I squeeze the trigger: The hammer strikes, sharp as a cracking knuckle. The woman stops beneath the window and complains to a neighbor about the stinking water.

I pace the narrow room, then stop before the uniform. In all the silver buttons on the jacket, I see the same thing: the distorted room, a small figure, a pistol pointing at his temple. If a corpse were needed to start the Revolution I would . . .

Father appears, beckoning me with arms outspread, a

silver star on his chest, the one Grandfather received from Napoleon. And then Mother slips into all the buttons, pressing a Bible to her breast. The hammer cracks.

A week later, secure in my uniform, I am standing at the window, counting a bell clanging against the gray morning. I slept fitfully: The night was humid, the mosquitoes persistent, my dreams unsettling. The day's activities were planned yesterday. Duchâtelet and I would lead a group of fifty disbanded artillerymen to the Grève, where a ceremony was to be conducted in honor of Bastille Day. d'Herbinville supported me against some of the more conservative members, who argued that wearing the illegal uniform would be too provocative. The Society had become too cautious, I countered, cheered by the younger members. Action was needed to stoke the people's emotions. A man with a gold chain across his vest jumped up and said that the Society's survival depended on caution, or it would be banned, driven underground, lose the support of the people.

The veins in his neck swollen, d'Herbinville pointed out that the Society ran the risk of making speeches and nothing else, and that they would lose the people's confidence if they did not act from time to time. His call for action dispelled my misgivings about him. Perhaps the woman in the carriage had been nothing more than an acquaintance, perhaps she meant nothing to him, and his real passion was for the Republic. The admiration I had felt for him returned. For an instant, as our eyes met in mutual understanding, I was moved by a feeling of fraternal love.

At the sixth clang several policemen appear in the

square below, marching grimly toward the courtyard of my building. Equipping myself with two pistols, a knife, and a short-barreled rifle, I run up a flight of stairs to the roof, where I crouch beside a chimney. I recognize the caretaker's lisp as he shows them to my room. A fist thumps the door.

— Evariste Galois, calls a chesty voice. This is the commissioner of police for the district of Saint Victor. I order you to open at once.

— What's he done? asks the caretaker.

— We are here for your own welfare, Monsieur Galois. We know about today's demonstration. You'll be detained until tomorrow, then released. I give you my word.

As they scramble about in my room, I press the rifle's cold barrel against my forehead, hardly breathing. Two blue-gray pigeons swoop down not far from me and perform a courtship dance.

— The candle wax is still warm, remarks the commissioner.

— Must've left before I got up, says the caretaker.

When voices and footsteps recede down the stairwell, I straighten up and, raising the rifle, scatter the pigeons coupling in a flurry of feathers.

38

A week since Bastille Day and my arrest on the Pont Neuf, and the authorities have yet to charge me with a specific crime. Duchâtelet and I were leading a group of young patriots to a demonstration when the police confronted us. Ignoring my call for calm, the group dispersed. Duchâtelet and I were surrounded, apprehended, disarmed, and taken to police headquarters. A preventative measure, that was all they said and continue to say. Unlike the previous occasion, when I saw imprisonment as a preparation for greater Republican involvement, when I mixed freely with the others, the days now weigh heavily on me. I have become somber, gloomy, taciturn. Duchâtelet has explained the legal situation: The authorities want a conviction, and for this they need a charge that will warrant a trial by judge, not jury, which is likely to be sympathetic, as it was in my previous trial.

Yesterday's events are still swirling in my head. I feel ashamed just thinking about them. I should have shown more restraint: I am no better than those I despise. Seems I have forgotten Pythagoras's teachings. And once again I see myself in the courtyard, pacing, glancing at Ogin and his little disciples, feeling a hopelessness invade my thoughts,

seep into my being like a dark vapor—a hopelessness arising partly from the deliberate vagueness of the prison
authorities, partly from having nothing, not even mathematics, with which to support myself and make this confinement bearable.

There was nothing exciting about prison this time. It
was not like my first incarceration, when my vision of a
Republic was bright, and there was still a glimmer of hope
the Academy would recognize my talent. Poisson's harsh
rejection had killed that hope, and this in turn darkened my
vision.

—The sun's scrambled his brain!

Laughter filled the courtyard from the canteen's
window.

—Thinks he's too good for us!

—We don't need highbrow patriots!

—A friend of the people drinks with the people!

Driven by a need to be alone, I now shunned the prisoners whose company I had welcomed only a month ago,
and they in turn reacted sharply, turning on me with savage
sarcasm.

—Don't take too much notice of them.

Raspail took me by the arm to a stone bench in the
shade. Arrested shortly before me, he was charged with
publishing subversive pamphlets. I admired him: He was a
true scientist—a man of ideas who kept his emotions under
control and the Republic clearly in mind. He brushed his
stringy hair behind his ears and gathered me in an affec-
tionate look, with eyes that always seem to be brimming
with tears.

—That canteen is nothing but trouble, he said. It

351

wouldn't be so bad without alcohol, but the prisoner running it is greasing the superintendent's palm.

—They're animals, François.

—Don't lose sight of the Republic.

—They don't deserve one.

—Have you forgotten the oath you made when joining the Society? Who do you think the people are? Mathematicians and scientists, like you and me? Be a little more accommodating, Evariste. Make your heart a Republic first. Don't be so aloof. They taunt you because you're too serious. Get closer to them, speak to them, learn from them.

—They can't teach me a thing!

After some coaxing, he persuaded me to go with him to the canteen for a game of chess. The place was like a restaurant, providing everything from caviar to coffee, from spirits to sweets. Respectful of Raspail, the prisoners who taunted me looked up from their card game, winking and snickering among themselves. We sat at a table beside a window overlooking the courtyard. Arranging our pieces, I glanced out: His disciples gone, the shaggy-haired, barefooted Ogin was limping in a strip of shade, deep in thought.

We had not made four or five moves when an attractive woman entered the canteen, embracing a pair of knee-high riding boots. The prisoners became excited. Her husband, the canteen-keeper, greeted her with a kiss.

—Right on time, chuckled an old fellow, who had been sweeping the floor. See the way she hugs her lovely twins.

He stood beside us and rested his stubbled chin on the broom handle.

—Them boots might be thin-soled, but they'd fill the devil himself with spirit.

The canteen-keeper took the boots, placed them on the counter, and, as though performing a magic trick, began pulling out bottles of brandy. At each bottle the prisoners shouted for more. When he pulled out the last one, plunging his arm shoulder-deep in the boot, he returned the boots to his wife, who went behind the counter, filled them with empty bottles, and left. The prisoners gathered around the keeper and bought several bottles.

—A toast to the Republic! announced a swarthy man.

Invited to join them, the old sweeper shuffled to an extended glass.

—And you, patriots? he asked.

I stared fixedly at my black bishop. Raspail accepted the invitation.

—Are you a patriot or not? prodded the toast-maker.

—More than you will ever be! I retorted.

—What's that? he snarled, turning truculently.

—Forget him, his companions shouted. A toast!

—To the Republic!

I leaped to my feet, swept the chess pieces off the board, and dashed off to the courtyard. Ogin was still there, sitting in a patch of cobbled shade, arms around his legs, head on his knees. I stopped beside the flagpole. It had been recently painted white, and its shadow cut across the yard. Soon the tricolor would be brought out for the evening flag-raising ceremony, when the prisoners gathered in the court-yard and sang the "Marseillaise" in solemn tones, and the children followed with their own patriotic verses. It was a moving moment, and everyone seemed transformed, elevated. Why weren't they always like that? How could they be so idealistic on one occasion, so base on another?

—What's he doing? one of them shouted from the window.

I remained fixed to the spot, my back to them.

—He's thinking about numbers, taunted another.

—Numbers? Of what? asked the swarthy one.

—Numbers of nothing. Just numbers.

—What do you mean, numbers of nothing? I bet he's counting the number of days to his release.

—Or the number of lays he's missed.

—Or the number he's going to have.

—That's enough, I heard Raspail say.

—He thinks the Republic's going to hatch from his head!

—Hey, genius! You're more likely to see the Republic in a glass of brandy.

—Or in a whore's eyes.

—Enough, Raspail demanded.

—What's he done for the Republic? shouted the swarthy fellow. They can't find a charge to pin on him. He'll probably be out in a week. Republican, my arse! I could've been a writer, another Hugo or Dumas. But I've used my talents for nobler things. I wrote and printed pamphlets for the workers, not porridge for the bourgeois. But they tracked me down, smashed my presses, and gave me three years for subversion. Hear that? Three years!

—Haven't you all said enough? Raspail protested.

—Republicans gamble!

—We get drunk!

—We lay whores!

—The Republic needs men!

I struggled to contain my anger, first by concentrating on my shadow, then by repeating over and over one of the theorems in my last memoir: An irreducible equation of prime degree is solvable by radicals if all its roots are rational functions of any two of them—this is a necessary and sufficient condition. But the last taunt was like a barb. I turned, flew past Ogin, who did not look up from reading the lines on his palm, and bounded up the stairs into the canteen.

—Animals! I shouted, shaking.

Springing up, two of them threw aside their chairs. Raspail rushed from the window and restrained me, but I broke loose and my words shot out like sparks.

—Republic! You don't know the meaning of the word! It has nothing to do with your filthy desires. A true Republican has the mind and soul of Archimedes, who gave his life for a circle! Only those prepared to sacrifice their lives for an idea are worthy of the Republic.

—Who's been drinking, him or us?

—Animals! It's easy to be brave after a bottle of brandy.

—Take a drink if it's so easy.

—Prove you're a man.

Pushing past Raspail, who tried to hold me back, I snatched the bottle from the swarthy fellow and took a long drink. The others chanted: More! More! Raspail pulled the bottle away from me.

—I'll drink it all, I shouted, tears in my eyes.

And I grabbed the bottle from Raspail, drank again,

and threw it at the swarthy fellow, who just managed a sidestep, so that it shattered against the wall. Raspail caught me in a tight embrace.

—I despise them.

My chest burned, my stomach was on fire. All the right angles in the canteen were breaking apart. I thrashed violently in Raspail's arms, yelling insults and abuse, raving about the Republic and mathematics. The canteen began reeling, the ceiling was falling, the floor was sinking. I was about to collapse when the old cleaner propped me up from one side, Raspail from the other, and together they dragged me out, my shoes scraping the stairs, the cobbles, as I babbled and sobbed all the way to my cell.

—François, dear François. You're a better Republican than me. You don't get drunk, you're always high-minded, you're a true friend of the poor. I like you, François, now more than ever. What's happening to me, my friend? There are two forces in my puny body: One's for order, the other for destruction. The pity is, I know which one's going to win. I'm too impatient, too excitable. I loathe alcohol, but at a word from those animals I drink a whole bottle. I don't like women, but I'll probably die in a duel because of some coquette. Why, François? Why?

Raspail's face hovered above me, the cell was swaying, nausea was rising.

—The stairs! The stairs! That's where my salvation lies!

I writhed and kicked, but Raspail held me down by the shoulders until my body slackened again.

—What do I lack, François? I'll tell you, my friend. More than mathematics, more than the Republic, I need someone to love. Can you understand that? I loved my father, François. But he's dead, and nobody has filled the vacuum he left in my being. Laugh, François! I'm a miserable creature. But you're not like the others. You're a doctor, you know all about suffering. What a filthy hole we're in! I want to get out!

I sprang up again, shaking, grasping Raspail's arms, raving.

—I will love again, François. Someone will fill the vacuum left by Father. And then I'll be happy again. I'll have the peace of mind to work on my mathematics. It will be a pure love, François. Love without . . . you understand. Purity, François. That's what I've sought all my life. Mathematics without matter, a Republic without possessions, love without flesh. It's possible, François. Purity, like the angelic voices of the castrati. Why not? The body's the source of all that's base and vile! Oh Father! Father!

I tore myself from Raspail's grip and snatched a pair of scissors left on a chair by a prisoner who had just finished cutting his toenails. A few others scrambled to assist Raspail.

—Let me go, I screamed, as they twisted the scissors from my fist. Look! They're a cross, an x, salvation.

The scissors clattered on the stone floor. I retched, heaved, spewed on the bed. The prisoners leaped aside. Another torrent splattered on the floor. I looked at Raspail supporting me by the arm, his kind face dissolving in my hot tears.

39

The bolt rams into my skull, the narrow sliding panel in the door is a guillotine across my nerves. Here I am, alone in a windowless cell, between the flame honed to a point by the stillness and a bucket stinking in the corner. Two days of solitary confinement! Sapped of strength by the violent outburst in the canteen last week, I have been unable to subdue a feeling of vulnerability, an anxiety that threatens to overwhelm me. I would not be in here if I weren't so physically weak. Maybe I would have shown more restraint in my confrontation with the prison superintendent.

The prison was buzzing with ideas of how best to celebrate the first anniversary of the July Revolution: Ideas ranged from open revolt to a silent vigil around a catafalque to be placed in the courtyard. For days there had been mutterings, grumblings, forebodings. Then, yesterday at lockup time, as a few of us were talking in the cell, a shot cracked the evening and the prisoner nearest the window slumped to the floor. As we fell to our hands and knees, I noticed a figure with a musket dart from the window across the street. The prisoner wasn't badly hurt: a grazed forehead.

We took him to the superintendent, who listened with increasing dismay as he examined the prisoner's injury.

—The assassin should be arrested at once, I demanded.

—Assassin?

—The shot came from the guards' quarters.

—Nonsense, Galois!

—It was intended for me.

—That's absurd!

—Will you act or not?

—How dare you! Ah, I know your game. The anniversary! You've contrived the whole thing in order to ignite a riot? After all, he wasn't struck by the bullet, but conveniently gashed his head in falling.

—You're behind it all! I shouted.

A plump rat scurries along the stone floor and slips out through a crack in the corner. Lying on the bunk, I attempt to calm myself the only way I know: mathematics. A shiver passes through me. Surrounded in stone, there is nothing to distract me, nothing to stir my irascible passions.

Here, I am no longer a Republican. What is the minimum number required for a Republic? I am no longer Evariste Galois—a name is needed only in the presence of others; no longer a prisoner—this crypt has freed me. I roll onto my side and blow out the flame. Now there is even more freedom. Archimedes needed sand for his work, I need nothing but a blackboard of darkness. Perhaps the purest mathematics can only be done in a cell like this.

Gradually a feeling of peace infuses my being. The

humid darkness embraces me, seeps into me, dissolves me. It is like the peace and security I experienced as a child, warm in Father's arms. Father and mathematics: the only things I have ever loved. One is now a memory, the other a state of mind I find more and more difficult to summon. There is no telling how much longer my imprisonment will last. I must not squander my strength on debilitating anger.

Mathematics—without it I will go mad. More than ever my survival in this hellhole depends on focusing my thoughts on mathematics.

A cool late-October breeze shakes summer from the poplars outside the prison walls as the police wagon rumbles through the gates. Duchâtelet and I are inside, returning from the courtroom, where we have just been tried on charges of wearing a banned uniform and illegally carrying arms. The authorities played their cards well this time: The trial, by judge alone, was over quickly. We were both found guilty. Duchâtelet was sentenced to three months on top of what he has already served, while I was given a further six months. The sentence crushed me. I did not have the strength to protest at the fact that my sentence was twice Duchâtelet's. Instead I bowed in resignation as my defense counsel—paid for once again by d'Herbinville—vowed to appeal against the severity of the sentence. My crime was no worse than Duchâtelet's, he protested; in fact, my accomplice had an added charge of drawing the decapitated head of Louis Philippe.

The appeal is set for the third of December in the Royal Court of Paris. In the meantime, my health has deteriorated and I have become more withdrawn. Confronted by my emaciated appearance, the prisoners who taunted me now look away or cast pitiful glances.

My only comfort is mathematics. I spend hours thinking in the courtyard, facing the knife-edged wind, shuffling among dry leaves dancing around me, pacing through misty rain. But even with mathematics my moods vacillate: At times my enthusiasm shoots up like a steep asymptote, and everything is possible; other times, my spirit plummets into an asymptotic abyss, and everything becomes meaningless. In moments of optimism, there is still time to further develop my ideas, put them in a book, make a name as a mathematician. Recently, in such a mood, I revised two papers on pure analysis—one being the memoir Poisson had rejected, which was finally returned to me in prison.

I also managed to write a four-page preface to the book that would contain my collected work, putting in ink much of what I had said in my first lecture in the bookshop. As with the lecture, I denounced patronage and attacked the Academy for losing my manuscripts in the article. This was followed by a summary of the two papers I had reworked. I accepted the criticism that both were short treatises, containing as much French as algebra. But I sought to go beyond algebra. Yes, I could have increased the number of equations by successively substituting all the letters of the alphabet in each equation, and then numbering them in order. This would have the effect of multiplying indefinitely the number of equations, for after the Latin alphabet there was the Greek, and others . . . But this was not my aim.

I then went on to denounce Poisson and the examiners at the Polytechnic. Even though I had reason to believe the scientific fraternity would greet my work with a condescending smile, I persisted in trying to have my work published. I did this so that my few friends might know I was still alive; and so that my work might fall to capable men, and direct them toward a new analysis. And by this I meant pure analysis.

Finally, I tackled the question of why readers found my work so difficult, even incomprehensible, and concluded it was due to my inclination to dispense with formalisms and calculations. Given this new area of research, I had often encountered difficulties which I could not overcome. Even in these two papers, I had explicitly stated that I did not know certain things, knowing full well I was exposing myself to the laughter of fools. But the most worthwhile books were those whose authors declared openly matters they did not know, refusing to mislead readers by concealing a difficulty. Yes, when egotism was banished from mathematics, when people associated with one another for study and not to send sealed parcels to the Academies, honesty would prevail and people would be eager to publish even small findings, as long as these findings were new, concluding they did not know the rest.

Strange, on completing the preface I had to overcome an urge to tear it up.

Nathalie visited me shortly before the appeal. She was alarmed by my haggard look and the state of my health. Noticing a wedding ring on her left hand, I congratulated her. She was now Madame Chantelot.

—Why have you come?

A hoarse cough convulsed me, crumpled me like paper.

—Do you need anything? Food? Blankets? Money?

—No, I replied, recognizing my voice in that hollow sound.

—Mother's worried about you.

—Then why hasn't she come to see me?

—You've hurt her, Evariste. She's waiting for an apology.

The old animosity rose for an instant, then sank in a swamp of apathy.

—Tell her . . .

Another violent cough shook me. She reached out as I struggled to smother it with my hands.

—Have you seen a doctor?

—It's the damp in here.

—Try to keep your spirits up. We'll do all we can to have you home for Christmas.

Winter tightens its grip on the prison and on my lungs: My cough has become chronic, causing the others in my cell to complain. I avoid them whenever possible, choosing to pace the courtyard, despite the cold. Another two months, I think, walking under a slate sky, almost lost in an oversized overcoat given to me by Chevalier. But the thought hardly perturbs me. Two months ago I was devastated by the rejection of my appeal, but that has passed and I am now numb to the monotony, the privations, the cold. I will survive this until my release at the end of April, and then . . . What? Return home? Never! Seven months, and she has made no effort to visit me. I have my pride, too.

The Republic? Politics needs passion. Not so long ago I would have given my life for the very idea of a Republic, but that passion has been extinguished as much by my declining health as by the proximity of people I loathe—the so-called true Republicans of the canteen. Will freedom reignite that passion? Perhaps not. They say the Society is becoming increasingly divided, and that there is a real danger it may fragment, perhaps cease to exist by the time I am released.

And mathematics? The thought of publishing my two works sparked some hope and produced the preface, but that was before the appeal. Now even Chevalier's encouragement fails to so much as stir me.

—You're destroying yourself, Evariste, he said on a visit last week. Raspail and d'Herbinville don't care about your mathematical genius, or they would have kept you from this place. The Society is doomed, Evariste. Come with us. We'll provide you with a clean, quiet room where you'll be able to continue your work.

I hardly said a word, but sat with head bowed, scratching the table with a dirty fingernail, occasionally looking out of the barred window. Rain was falling obliquely and a steeple was just visible through the black branches on the other side of the prison wall. He said his brother had contacts, he would find a position for me, help publish my work. Excited, he reached across the table and grasped my wrist. When the visit ended I found that I had absentmindedly scratched a diagonal cross on the table.

Ogin appears in the courtyard. Wrapped in a tattered blanket, he sits on his bench and pulls it over his head. In walking past him I hear sniffling, whimpering.

—We're all doomed, he sobs, raising his shaggy head. My little angels will never see paradise.

I am puzzled by his lugubrious tone. On the few occasions we have spoken I have been impressed by the fervor with which he has expressed his beatific vision of a new world: a heaven on earth brought about by his little angels.

—What are you talking about?

—The pestilence, it's coming. It will destroy me, you, my little angels. Paris will become a vast graveyard.

He wipes his glistening moustache with the back of his hand. Has he cracked? Has the role of a prophet got the better of him? Has he been reading Revelation?

—What kind of pestilence?

—*Cholera morbus*, he grimaces, forehead creasing as he looks skyward with eyes opened wide. It's come from the Ganges, a river teeming with religion and pollution. It's devastated Russia and Poland. Only last week the first victims were reported in London. We're next, brother, there's no escape. Better to take one's life than suffer the agony of that pestilence. I've spoken to sailors who've seen its ravages. Its victims are like the living dead, they say. A person's healthy one day, skin and bone the next. They say the flesh turns inky blue and the eyes shrivel to half their size. Oh, you'll know it in yourself, brother. They say it begins with a loss of balance, with the sound of bees hiving in your ears. Then you feel an iciness, first in the fingers and toes, then it spreads through the entire body. Depending on the victim's constitution death comes in several hours or a few days. There's no escape, brother. No cure. Death's a blessing once you've got it.

As though seized by dread, Ogin darts from the bench and runs across the courtyard, the blanket flapping around his legs.

I am haunted by Ogin's prophecy. The day after we spoke, he threw himself down a stairwell and died on the spot. My cough has turned into a hacking bark, and I become alarmed when I feel a chill in my fingers or toes, or when I start from murky dreams to find myself short of breath and damp with sweat, or when I catch a glimpse of my hollow sockets in a mirror. My alarm turns to dread as the word *cholera* spreads through the prison. It must be more than just a rumor: The authorities have increased the quantity and quality of food and distributed warmer clothing and blankets. Perhaps as a result of these fears preying on my mind, my health has deteriorated to the point where I am confined to bed.

— Evariste, are you asleep?

Raspail is bowed over me with a book under his arm. The mid-March sun glistens the gold letters on the spine, but my vision is blurred and I am unable to make out the words.

— Can you hear me? You're leaving this place tomorrow. I told the superintendent he would have a riot on his hands if anything became of you. d'Herbinville has arranged for your transfer to a sanatorium on the Rue l'Oursine. You'll be on parole, but with enough freedom to come and go as you please. Don't lose heart, friend. Spring will breathe new life into your body.

40

We sit opposite each other in his carriage, knees touching at each jolt, d'Herbinville's cologne blending with the smell of boot polish. He was saying that Faultrier sanatorium was among the best in Paris. I would have my own room, nourishing food, and the services of his good friend Dr. Dumotel, who was the resident physician. But why is he going to so much trouble and expense, paying from his own pocket for what will be a two-month stay at the sanatorium? I am too weak and tired to pursue the question, and turn to the window. The sun is an eraser clearing the sky of chalky clouds, the city has cast off its gray overcoat, sparrows hop excitedly in the branches of an apricot tree breaking out in blossom. After eight months of grim, morose faces, the people on the streets seem cheerful, their movements lively. I ought to be happy leaving Sainte-Pélagie: My parole will be almost like freedom, and yet I cannot overcome a feeling of numbness. Has prison crushed my spirit to such an extent that even freedom is a matter of indifference?

A shopfront sign alarms me: I can barely read the name of the proprietor, even though it is written in large red letters. I look at more distant signs: They are all blurred. My eyesight has never been good, but I could at least make out signs at twenty-five or thirty paces. Is the deterioration due to my general weakness? The hacking cough? Will my sight be restored with an improvement in my health? I recall with a shudder Ogin's description of a cholera victim's eyes.

—That's the fourth new fountain I've seen today, says d'Herbinville, pointing to a few stonemasons working in a corner of a square. Fresh water is vital in preventing cholera.

—Is it true there's no cure for it?

—Opinions differ. The authorities have issued a document informing people how best to avoid the disease. It suggests they remain composed, avoid overexertion and emotional upheavals, abstain from all forms of excess, introduce sunlight into their homes, take tepid baths, eat food that's easily digestible, safeguard against chills, and avoid sleeping too many in a room. Splendid measures for those who can afford them, but what of the masses of poor?

The carriage stops in front of a three-story building situated behind an imposing stone wall. The numbers 84 and 86 are flaking in the marble plaque above the entrance. As we cross the front courtyard, d'Herbinville nods to a young woman waving from the first-floor window in a wing to the left of the main building.

—Mademoiselle Stéphanie, he says, and after a moment's reflection adds: Dr. Dumotel's daughter.

Having introduced me to the doctor, d'Herbinville accompanies me to a small room on the third floor, where he places my belongings on a table, embraces me with affection, and promises to visit regularly. I am alone for the first time since my solitary confinement months ago. The floorboards wince as I go to the window overlooking the courtyard. The room fills with clean sunlight as I open the shutters. Swallows flit above the yard with bits and pieces in their beaks. One arcs past the window with a length of black string. The front door of the wing opens and the young woman appears. Standing on the front steps with arms folded, she seems to be admiring the swallows. My vision slightly blurred, I attempt to focus on her features. I have seen her before, but I cannot quite grasp her face distinctly. One with its shadow, a black cat flows up the steps, arches its back, and caresses her ankles. She does not appear to mind the cat's attention, until d'Herbinville appears in the courtyard, when she pushes it away with her foot. His boots gleaming, he strides across the yard and kisses her hand.

Is it her? The young woman who was with him in the carriage? The one on the balcony during his trial? As they walk arm in arm toward the entrance, my heart quickens for the first time in months, the way it used to for mathematics, for the Republic.

Here a week, and I now feel strong enough to leave the sanatorium and go for a walk through the city. A small mirror cracks my reflection: I appear less gaunt, my eyes are not so sunken, haunted by fewer shadows. Despite feeling better, Ogin's words continue to trouble me. I still start in the middle of the night, drenched in sweat. The last vestiges of fever and fatigue, the doctor has reassured me. But even this cannot fully dispel my fear of cholera.

Passing through the gate, head bowed in thought, I collide with the doctor's daughter. Her cylindrical cardboard box falls to the ground. Before I can overcome my confusion, she picks it up and brushes the black bow on the lid.

—I'm sorry, she smiles. I didn't see you coming.

I am flustered by the sweetness of her apology, disarmed by her lilac-scented perfume, confused by her eyes, green as spring leaves. My heart hammers, as though driving a nail into . . . I look down at the tips of her pointed shoes peeping from the hem of her dress.

—Aren't you Monsieur Galois?

My name has never been said like this: the *g* pronounced with such tenderness, the *l* so liltingly, the second syllable so wonderfully, and all embodied by such a minty breath. In glancing up and nodding, I notice for the first time that she is about my age.

—I am Stéphanie Dumotel.

A crow calls raucously from a sooty chimney.

—Monsieur d'Herbinville has told me about you. He says you have sacrificed a promising mathematical career for the Republic.

I see Ogin's shaggy features in a patch where a chunk of render has fallen from the wall.

—You must visit us with Monsieur d'Herbinville, she says, picking at a button between her breasts.

I nod again and leave abruptly, pulse pounding in my ears, steps light, unsteady. I try to compose myself by breathing deeply the mild breeze scented with blossom.

The day is more like late April than late March. Dark, damp, the last two months in prison have frozen my emotions: I longed for nothing, looked forward to nothing. Mathematics and the Republic became chilly mists. Now, strolling between massive overlapping elms, sensing the powerful stirring of sap driving upward, pushing through to the tips of the highest branches, I feel my emotions beginning to thaw. Today the sun's touch is friendlier than it has ever been: I welcome it on the back of my hands, on my forehead, my eyelids. And all the time I cannot get her features out of my mind: Her smile as she said my name has dispelled the brooding Ogin. No woman has ever made me feel like this. I have never been susceptible to this emotion before, caught up as I was in mathematics and politics. Now, in my present loneliness, in my uncertainty and anxiety about the future, she appears, bright and warm as the spring sun.

I try to fathom this new feeling. I recall the gypsy in the almond grove and the way I resisted her, finally dismissed her. But I cannot summon that rancor against Stéphanie: not only because I am too weak, too empty, but because . . . well, because . . . I do not want to dismiss her.

What is her relationship to d'Herbinville? Is he a family friend? Or is there something more between them? And what if there is? Why have I allowed myself to be affected like this?

I find myself in the Place de Grève: the square I set out for eight months ago to plant trees of liberty. Cobbles have been dislodged for tall saplings decorated with red, white, and blue ribbons. The square is teeming with activity: grinning faces, grotesque masks, vendors hawking their wares, musicians playing against each other, entertainers in costumes. A juggler walks a tightrope stretched just above the ground: Five knives flash in describing precise parabolas and circles, each held for only a fraction of a second. I

371

could once juggle mathematical concepts like that: permutate the coefficients of equations, create groups, distinguish between groups, determine the solvability of equations, all completely in my head. Will I ever regain that mental dexterity? People gape at the juggler, yet my talent attracted no attention, my memoirs were ignored or lost.

Stéphanie—her name rhymes sweetly with geometry. Stéphanie—my inner voice has never sounded like this. Are you here, biographer? How strange! After years of telling you everything, I am suddenly embarrassed to talk to you. But I must . . . where sinners confess for the sake of redemption and an afterlife, I must confide in you in the hope of rising from the coffin and living forever in a book. One cannot be coy when it comes to immortality.

Come closer, friend, closer. Listen to my whisper; better still, read my thoughts. Stéphanie: Her name, her face, her lilac-scented perfume, everything about her dispels the disappointment that has festered in me for so long. For the first time since Father's death I feel the stirring of . . . hope. No, more than hope.

—*Cholera morbus! Cholera morbus!*

A clown parts a section of the crowd.

—Cho-le-ra! Cho-le-ra!

Running and laughing, children pick up the cry and turn it into a singsong chorus.

—Has it reached Paris? I ask the masked clown.

—Claimed its first victim, replies a woman's voice.

—Where?

—Rue Mazarine. Horrible.

Ogin's prophecy comes to mind, together with Mother's apocalyptic invectives against Paris. And yet the grim news does not alarm me: Stéphanie's bright face scatters the vision of darkness and devastation.

My feelings for her have grown in proportion to the horrors ravaging the city. I am now full of optimism. Two days ago, in a burst of inspiration, I dashed off a follow-up to the preface I wrote in prison. It was a discussion on the progress of pure analysis. Of all the areas of human knowledge pure analysis is the most abstract, the most logical, the only one that does not rely on the evidence of the senses. From these facts many conclude that it is the most methodical and best-coordinated subject. This is not the case. A glance at an algebra book, whether a textbook or some original work, reveals nothing but a confused accumulation of propositions, whose individual logical structures contrast with the disorder of the work as a whole. All this would greatly astonish the man on the street, who generally takes the word *mathematics* to be a synonym for logical organization.

It is astonishing to reflect that mathematics is the work of the human mind, which is destined to study rather than to know, to seek the truth rather than to find it. A mind that has the power to perceive at a glance all mathematical truths—not just those presently known but all that would ever be known—can also deduce them methodically and mechanically from a few principles by a uniform method. But then there would be no obstacles, nor any of those difficulties—so often imaginary—encountered by scholars. In fact, there would be no role for the scholar. This, however, is not the way things are. If the scholar's task is more difficult and nobler, the progress of mathematics is also less methodical, with chance playing more than a small role. Mathematics is inorganic, its growth resembling that of crystals. Analysts do not deduce, they combine, agglomerate. When they arrive at the truth, it is by virtue of groping around the sides of the hole into which they have fallen.

I went on to outline my conception of analysis and why I had ventured in this area of research. I followed this with the role of the critic in mathematics, arguing that in less abstract subjects—in works of art—it was ridiculous to precede a critical discussion with one's work. It would be a naïve admission of what is almost always true: the tendency to make one's self the standard of comparison. But here it was not a question of an objective, completed work, but of the most abstract ideas conceivable by man. Here criticism and discussion were synonymous, and to discuss was to throw one's ideas into the arena with the ideas of others.

The disease has spread rapidly since the first case ten days ago, and the papers are now reporting a thousand deaths a day. Despite this, on my walks I observe that people's springtime enthusiasm has not been dampened by the epidemic: The theaters are still full of patrons, entertainers are everywhere in boulevards and streets, shop windows with figures and paintings depicting aspects of the epidemic are surrounded by crowds who laugh, jeer, make faces at the disease. My health too, has improved greatly, the cough has cleared, but I lack the confidence to approach Stéphanie in the courtyard, to visit her with d'Herbinville, so I spend hours at the window each day, watching, waiting for a glimpse, daydreaming of the opportune moment to meet her again.

Its black draping lifted by the inquisitive breeze, a wagon grinds past the sanatorium, heavy with its freight of corpses from last night. I have been standing at the open window in a shaft of mellow light for the past hour, trying to summon enough courage to wait in the courtyard for her return.

How ironic! I would not have thought twice about giving my life for the Republic, and now here I am, unable to act, my insides knotted, and all because of a girl.

Knowing how miserable I would feel if I allowed another day to pass without speaking to her, I take one of my memoirs and hurry out. I position myself strategically at the entrance to the courtyard. The instant she appears down the street, I set off in her direction, driven by a pounding heart.

—Good morning, Mademoiselle Dumotel.

She looks up, surprised. My greeting was too abrupt. There is no turning back now: Courage must overcome caution.

—Monsieur Galois! Are you going walking again?

—Prison has given me an appetite for the sun.

—Be careful, the disease is spreading.

—It's not contagious, I say, encouraged by her concern.

—You'd do much better to join me in a cup of cocoa at home.

My heart leaps like a hare, my words falter in accepting her invitation.

As we climb the steps to her front door, my senses tingle at the rustle of her dress, her slender white-stockinged ankles. I remind myself of the need for restraint, and that I must not reveal my feelings too soon, not until I know how things stand between her and d'Herbinville.

She returns to the sitting room with a tray and two cups. A wealth of golden hair spills in springy curls onto her shoulders. Sitting directly opposite me, she tells me that she is studying the piano and hopes someday to be able to teach it. I tell her about my mathematics. She listens with sympathy at my rejections and misfortunes.

— Music and mathematics go hand in hand, she smiles, looking searchingly into my eyes.

My cup and saucer rattle as I turn to the piano brooding in the corner. What does she mean? Is it a hint of . . . No! I must not jump to conclusions. Restraint.

— A dreadful disease, she says. And no telling how long it will last. You say it's not contagious, but Father has heard of a case where a young man transmitted the disease to his fiancée through the act of kissing. How horrible! A moment of such tenderness to be the cause of misery and certain death. And it's so unpredictable: afflicting the young and the old, the strong and weak, the rich and poor. And not only is little known about the disease, but the methods of treatment vary, though Father believes it's best treated by opiates and systematic bloodletting.

Despite the morbid nature of our conversation, I feel buoyant in her presence, my doubts and fears are dispelled by her clear, rhythmic voice. She asks if I would like to hear her play the piano. I barely manage a yes. Is this a sign? Would she extend my visit if she were not comfortable in my presence? Surely it is more than politeness? And I can tell from the tone of her voice that she is not a frivolous flirt. She has been touched by the suffering of others, her character has been deepened, she sees through the trappings of beauty, prestige, wealth. She can empathize with those who live for ideals, who suffer, who are scorned and rejected by society. This solemn tune is further proof of her high-minded nature: She is not playing a toe-tapping polonaise or polka, but a slow, almost melancholy piece in the lower register.

Yes, she knows from my eyes that I have suffered, and that is why she has chosen to play this tune. Suddenly I want to be caressed by her sunlit fingers, by the velvet notes. I want to rest my head on her lap, to be carried away.

Restraint. What about d'Herbinville? Why hasn't she mentioned him during the course of our conversation? Surely if there were something between them, she would have made it known in order to dampen my interest, which must be evident to her by now? Why the silence? Is he nothing more than a family friend? And if he is courting her, then her silence can mean only one thing: She is not interested in him. There is no denying his handsome looks, his charm, his wealth: He is the ideal man for most women. But there is a glint of conceit in his blue eyes, a mark of arrogance in his robust appearance. He has never suffered for his ideals, which Stéphanie knows, and that is why she could never love him.

She stops on a deep reverberating chord which fills the room and passes through me. I stand, rolling the memoir and shoving it in my pocket. She closes the piano lid.

— That was very moving.

— Thank you, she smiles, taking the chattering cup and saucer from me.

Our fingertips touch. I summon all my courage to look into her eyes. There I am, circumscribed by her pupils. And in that instant π reveals its perfect proportion and is reduced to a chaos of digits, the Republic is created and destroyed, I am extinguished and reborn. My ardent look must have disconcerted her, for she blushes and turns to the table. Restraint. There is plenty of time. I thank her for the cocoa, tell her how much I have enjoyed the afternoon, and ask if I may visit again.

— Whenever you wish, she says. Monsieur d'Herbinville will be away for a month.

— A month? Where has he gone?

— London. To negotiate the purchase of gunpowder.

— For the Society? I ask, taken aback by the thought that perhaps another revolution is being organized for this summer.

— No. She laughs, reaching out and touching my memoir. For his business. Firecrackers are in great demand.

I laugh as well. I cannot recall the last time I was so happy. It is as though I hear the sound of my own laughter for the first time: a voice no longer closed and suspicious, no longer confessing to an invisible biographer, but free and open as the spring sun filling this room.

41

My sentence ended yesterday. This morning, the first of May, I am free to leave the sanatorium, to settle anywhere in Paris, return to Bourg-la-Reine if I choose. Certain that the epidemic will abate with the warmer weather, Dr. Dumotel has advised me to remain for another month as a matter of precaution. As for the expenses, he was sure that d'Herbinville would take care of everything.

There was no need to coax. I want to be close to Stéphanie, to see her as often as possible, to watch her from this window, just like now, as she steps lightly across the courtyard on her way to her piano lesson. My heart racing after her, I recall our meeting a few days ago. Why did she smile like that in telling me that d'Herbinville would be delayed in London until the middle of the month? I must find an opportunity to tell her how I feel before his return.

Is it right? Happiness in the midst of the suffering caused by cholera? I am happy just being with her: walking with her, listening to her play the piano, sitting with her, even when one or both of her parents are present. Not so long ago I looked down on the trivial conversations of others; now I am interested in whatever she talks about: the new spring fashions, Hugo's current play, the novel she has been reading. Last week she finished *Scarlet and Black*. I told her of my meeting with Beyle, of the fellow's opinion of his own work; she looked a little disappointed when I described the author as plump, bald, and overweight, but she spoke highly of the book, praised the author's perspicuity in matters of love, and insisted that I read it.

Was this another indication of her feelings for me? Of course I took the book, even though I do not like novels. It would give me another subject for conversation, a topic on both our minds: love. I tried reading the book, but could not get beyond the first few chapters: Aside from being too absorbed in my emotions to concentrate on the written word, I just could not relate to the main character.

I know better than to walk through the quarters surrounding the Hôtel de Ville, where the epidemic is rampant. Yet I am drawn here almost against my will, drawn not by perverse curiosity, but a need to test the validity of my happiness, to see whether it can withstand the city's misery. I shudder as victims are carried to hospital on litters and mattresses, the spring sun on their livid faces, blossom-scent mingling with the stench of diarrhea. I hold my breath in passing through a square crisscrossed by swallows, pungent with the chlorine that some believe clears the air of pestilence.

At the outbreak of the disease there were not enough hearses to carry the dead, so the authorities resorted to Artillery wagons, but these proved too loud and cumbersome: Their rattling chains terrified people, their lack of springs resulted in coffins jolting and bouncing dangerously. On one occasion I was walking behind one of those rumbling juggernauts when it struck a cobble, and a few coffins crashed to the ground, spilling their corpses on the street. It was through sheer reflex I avoided tripping over them. Fortunately most of those wagons have been replaced by this quieter cart in front of me. The warm breeze frolicking through the city rustles the dresses of mourners, stirs the horses' manes, lifts the funereal drape shrouding the cart, revealing sixteen coffins exuding the fragrance of pine.

Stéphanie's face is a beacon through this dismal purgatory, her gentle voice rises above mourners crying and wailing, her musical hands are a source of hope in the midst of so much horror. Dispelling the city's suffering, she leads me forward to a better world, a place where happiness is inviolable.

Torment, tantalizing, a week of it, and finally I am alone with her. It is Sunday afternoon and we are in the gardens of the Louvre. Strollers are caressed by the sun, assuaged for the months of misery. The glorious day marks an easing of the epidemic: The morning papers have reported fewer deaths, though warning against complacency. A cautious hope shows on everyone's face: from the fellow grinding away on a wheezing organ to the woman wearing that enormous hat trimmed with feathers and bows.

We walk close together, shoulders almost touching, our merged shadows gliding before us. She is describing Hugo's latest play, but my thoughts are on summoning enough courage for what I must say. Reaching out for a black butterfly fluttering across our path, the back of her hand brushes mine, and last night's dream flashes before me. I am in a grove of towering pines, lost in the dark-green gloom. The thought of a pebbled path checks my anxiety, and I begin brushing aside pine needles, first with my shoes, then with bare hands. Mother appears, ringing two small silver bells. Still no sign of the path. When I look up again, the gypsy has taken Mother's place. Her hands are working deftly, braiding a rope of black hair. Tossing the rope over her shoulder, she picks up a pine needle and writes with it on her palm. Drawn by curiosity, I am suddenly beside her, staring at a cross within a circle. When I look up, Stéphanie is there, leaning against the pine's massive trunk, completely naked. I look around for something to cover her. If only these trees were maples. I cannot hide a thing with needles. She reaches out for me. I look away from the crimson circles around her nipples, the black triangle beneath her navel. I remove my jacket and cover her with it, whispering that I want her more than mathematics and the Republic. We look tenderly at each other and she is about to say something when a familiar voice calls me from behind. Father appears from the thick shadows, with a purple crépe ribbon tied around his neck and a flue on his shoulder. Stéphanie whispers, for me to stay, but Father calls me again, in a louder voice, scraping soot into his palm and extending it to me. The pebbled path appears, draws me from Stéphanie's whispers, and leads me to Father. On the way I am struck by how cold the pebbles are under my bare feet.

Stéphanie and I now come to a bench under a pine tree whose tangy fragrance fills the air. My heart is beating wildly, and there seems to be a hive of bees in my ears. I must seize the moment. Encouraged by everything around me, I throw myself into the unknown.

—Stéphanie, I say, taking her hand.

Surprised, perhaps alarmed, she tries to pull away, but I tighten my grip. A surge of emotion disorients me, scrambles my words.

—You must know how I . . . The last month . . . I've never been happier. My life's been a difficult equation. You're the solution, Stéphanie. I feel complete, at peace with myself and the world when we are together.

She pulls away with a look of consternation. A hangnail on my thumb catches on her lace glove.

—Don't say any more, Evariste, she says, springing up.

—I can't silence my feelings.

—You must, she snaps, crunching the sand with her heel.

—But . . . I . . .

—No, Evariste! she flashes. We're friends! There'll never be anything more between us.

The long arch of her golden eyebrows falls with a kind of finality. A sheet of glass shatters within me. Thoughts and emotions swirl senselessly. I grasp at words from the confusion that threatens to overwhelm me.

—But . . . the last month . . . our happiness . . .

—If Monsieur d'Herbinville's friendship means anything to you, then please stop.

—d'Herbinville!

—We're getting engaged. A crow swaying on a nearby tree cries a few times then springs away, causing a shower of white blossom.

—You love d'Herbinville? I ask, as if the words are bitter seeds.

—Yes!

—He's not right for you, Stéphanie, I plead, desperate

383

to save the situation. He's vain and arrogant. He'll never love you as I do. He'll take you for granted, mistreat you, have affairs with other women.

—He's a fine man, generous to a fault. He's paying for your stay at the sanatorium, and you dare make such accusations! Not only that, he asked me to spend time with you in his absence, to entertain you so you wouldn't brood.

I walk away in a daze, past a water vendor tapping a metal cup, past the Louvre, to the poorer districts where the epidemic has been most devastating. I wander the side streets aimlessly, and all the time her face mocks me, her words echo in my ears. A church bell tolls, and I find myself in a square. A crowd has gathered around a rubbish cart, listening to a scavenger sermonizing from the pile of refuse in it.

—It's a plot to destroy the poor, he shouts. There's no cholera. It's all the work of the authorities. The deaths are due to poison! I tell you, cholera's just a ruse! At this very moment there are people prowling the city, stalking the markets, the premises of wine sellers, our very drinking fountains. People carrying vials and packets of poison to contaminate our food and drink. Paris is overpopulated, the authorities want to rid the streets of us. What better way than by pretending there's a cholera epidemic?

—Beware! Take nothing for granted! Examine what you eat and drink. Are you in a public house? Make sure the wine you order hasn't been laced with poison. Are you at the fish market? Make sure the trout hasn't been given a dose of something lethal. It happened before my very eyes at the butcher's stall this morning: A fellow sprinkled pink

384

powder on a tray of sheep tongues. No sooner was he caught than he broke loose and disappeared, but not before he was identified by a few people as a police informer. So, I say to you, trust nobody. If you see anyone acting suspiciously, you owe it to your family and friends to act. Look at that youth over there. He's been leaning on the well for some time. What's he up to? What's he got in his pockets?

When I realize that he is referring to me, I am surrounded by snarling faces. He leaps from the cart and confronts me with his unbearable stench.

—What are you up to? he smirks.

The crowd has been stirred to the point of panic. Despite the gravity of the situation, I reply almost disinterestedly that I have stopped to rest on my way home.

—People these days don't rest next to fountains and wells, unless they're taking a drink. Just yesterday a fellow not much older than you was set upon and torn to pieces by a mob on the Rue Ponceau. Why? Because he stopped to look into a wine shop. Was he a poisoner? Or did he stop to check the time? The mob didn't ask.

The thought that I might meet the same end passes through me without a ripple, as though all my emotions have been deadened by Stéphanie's words.

—If he's got nothing to hide, he won't mind being searched, says the scavenger, nodding to the others.

I comply, extending my arms sideways.

—On your way, growls the scavenger. Next time you mightn't be so lucky. Last week a man was killed in the Faubourg St. Germain for carrying a bag of white powder which turned out to be nothing more than camphor.

I blow out the lamp and go to the window. A wagon of death rumbles past in the dark, its heavy chains dragging along the cobbles. Here and there at crossroads, in court-yards, on streets, fires are flourishing, lit to purge the atmo-sphere of pestilence. Shadows flit like bats, hurrying either to avoid death or to make arrangements for the dead.

Is it possible I mistook everything? Her smile, her openness toward me: Was it all nothing but pity? The af-fection one would give a sick child or an injured animal? Or was she just flirting with me all along? A coquette, taking advantage of d'Herbinville's absence to amuse herself. I focus on a red lantern above a gaping doorway where shad-ows flock.

No! Her feelings cannot possibly be due to pity or pet-tiness. If there is something between her and d'Herbinville, why didn't she at least intimate it during the course of the month? Why? Maybe her feelings for him changed as she got to know me better. Maybe she realized I loved her as her fiancé could never do. Why then did she say she loves him? He is due to return in a few days. Maybe she is afraid of him. She does not want to upset her parents. She is be-having honorably, denying her new, true emotions for the sake of appearances. I must speak to her again, before d'Herbinville's return. I must tell her not to be afraid of her true emotions, that I will defend her against d'Herbinville or anybody else who dares to intimidate her.

The cloud that gathered over me in the garden begins dispersing. All is not lost. There is still a lantern of hope in the dreadful dark.

* * *

I have been pacing the courtyard all morning, but not a sign of her, not even in the window. Her cat, which has become fond of me from my visits, claws its way down the trunk of a blossoming plum tree in the corner of the yard. I kneel and caress its glistening fur, pick a few flakes of blossom from its back, and gaze into its black slits. As the cat arches and curves its tail into a question mark, I spring up decisively and knock on the front door. Her mother opens and tells me in a peremptory manner that Stéphanie is confined to bed with a headache. Speechless, thoughts in turmoil, I stand on the bottom step as the cat purrs in circles around my ankles.

I run up to my room and write her a letter in which I pour out my feelings.

—Monsieur Galois! huffs the mother when she answers the door.

—Would you please pass this to Mademoiselle?

—But, sir, I . . .

—I won't leave until I get a reply.

I sit on the warm step. From a chimney across the street, a rope of black smoke unwinds and spreads against the blue. The front door opens and her mother extends an envelope.

—Stéphanie wishes no further disturbance.

Resisting the temptation to tear open the envelope, I return to my room, where I desist from opening it, savoring the fragrance of her perfume, the vision of her delicate hand writing my name. Finally, sitting on the edge of the bed, I read it once. *We can no longer see each other under the circumstances of the previous month,* she writes. *All private correspondence between us must stop.* In the future she will try to

387

converse with me in a friendly manner, as she did before this impossible situation. I should not think of things which did not exist, which never could have existed.

I fall back onto the pillow as though struck between the eyes. Does she mean those words? I gaze at the hook behind the door. Stung as much by anger as uncertainty, I bolt upright, tear the letter, and throw the shreds into the fireplace.

Two days later, I am back in my room after a morning in the poorer quarters, where I wandered among mourners, funeral processions, the screams of the dying, all of which seemed to assuage the ache in my heart. I now watch from my window as a carriage stops at the entrance and a well-dressed fellow of about thirty strides across the yard. Opening the door, Stéphanie's mother greets him with a smile and a kiss. He looks familiar, but it is not until a few minutes later, when he steps out with Stéphanie, that I recognize him as a friend of d'Herbinville's from the Society. They stop at the entrance, where the fellow speaks with a serious expression, accentuating his words with sharp gestures. Stéphanie listens with a sad look, nodding from time to time. He kisses her on each cheek and leaves. Walking back pensively, she glances up at my window.

Scarlet and Black in my hands, I knock on the door. Stéphanie opens guardedly.

—Your book, I say, passing it through the narrow opening.

She accepts it without a word.

—Can I see you, Stéphanie? For a few minutes?

—There's nothing more to say.

—Who was your visitor?

—Mother's younger brother.

—He saddened you. Why?

—Please go, she says.

—He's going to tell d'Herbinville about me, isn't he?

—I don't want any trouble. Your health is better. Leave before he returns. You know how hot-tempered he is. Please, go. Mother will be back soon. She'll tell Uncle you've been here, and things will become worse.

—Tell me it wasn't pity you felt, Stéphanie.

She attempts to close the door, but I stop it with my foot.

—It wasn't pity! she flashes. I was flirting with you, leading you on, just like a schoolboy. I was using you to ... to make my future fiancé jealous. There! You've got the truth! Now go!

42

If only I could silence this inner voice.

Leave me alone, biographer! Now that I do not want you, your presence is stronger than ever. Like a vulture spiraling on a dying creature, you are hovering above my head, keen to pick my thoughts before it is too late. I do not want you to write about me anymore.

I am tired of my miserable life, tired of projecting it to you. It is not worth writing about. Go and find another subject, someone whose life might serve as an example to others. But you won't leave, will you? Death is in the air, and that is what you biographers live on, isn't it? I could lie to you, misrepresent this evening, conceal myself in subterfuge.

How can you be sure I have not already done that? There's something for you to think about. You know me well by now, don't you? Know that I have been unable to tell a lie, even when my life depended on it. That was the idealistic Galois, but he is nothing but a memory now. Surely you have noticed the change in me over the past few months. I am a different person from that idealistic youth. I have become bitter, spiteful, vengeful, though no longer at society but toward myself. Life is meaningless, an equation without real or imaginary solutions, something that should be torn and thrown in the fire.

If only I could stop thinking! Who knows, you might disappear in the absence of thought. But while I am still breathing, I persist in this habit of verbalizing my life. Perhaps there is only one way of severing this bond that exists between us.

I have been staring at this blank sheet for an hour, and now my attention is caught by the ghostly watermark. Raising it to the window, I can just discern what looks like a woman's profile. What is today's date? The twenty-fourth? No. It has been exactly one week since I last saw her: seven days, each waxing more golden than the last; seven nights, each contracting, becoming denser than the last. The sum? They have canceled each other out, become a meaningless gray. It is the twenty-fifth. May is almost over, too.

I must reply to Chevalier's letter of a few days ago. It is a kind letter, full of noble sentiments and encouragement. Sitting at the small table, pen poised to pierce passing thoughts, I want to empty my heart, unburden myself of the weeklong anguish. I want to tell him . . . What do I want to say? That there is a kind of sweetness in being miserable? Yes, but only if one can at least hope for consolation.

How am I to console myself? In the space of a month I have exhausted the greatest happiness possible to man. Exhausted it without happiness, without hope. I want to tell Chevalier that after what I have just experienced, his fine words about peace and harmony sound hollow, bookish. This is a time for blood, not books. No peace! No pity!

No harmony! Hatred, that is what I now feel. An all-consuming hatred. But how can I tell Chevalier, how can I tell anyone, that this hatred is as much hatred of myself as hatred of the world? Hatred for having fallen in love, for having been deceived by a coquette? How could I have allowed it to happen? I, who disliked women, who prided myself on my intellect. I am not the Evariste Galois of two years ago, the one whose intellect burned fiercely, freely, who spurned the gypsy and saw all women as snares.

Hatred! That is what I feel most. And with this, anger. All the anger I once directed toward the Academy, toward Louis Philippe, toward the Church—all this I now focus on myself. And this anger hurts. It twists my heart, squeezes tears from my eyes.

How am I to convey this to Chevalier? Better not to alarm my faithful friend. Better to tell him that those who do not feel a deep hatred for the present will never feel a true love for the future. The future! Yes, that will allay him, give him the impression that his unfortunate friend still hopes for a better future, conceal from him the dark void to which his poor friend is being irresistibly drawn. I want to tell him that I approve of violence. (How often we have disagreed on this point! He has always upheld the Saint-Simonist view of a peaceful, spiritual revolution.) Violence—not of the mind, but of the heart. I want to tell him that I am determined to get even with those who thwarted me, and that I want to avenge my father's death. But I must conceal from him and others what I really want—my own destruction. My own extinction.

Dear Chevalier! Always imploring me to join the Saint-Simonists, saying there were people who cared for me, people who loved me. Love! The very word prods my hatred, stokes my anger. But I will not tell him any of this. Why hurt his feelings? He has been closer to me than a brother, never failed to remind me of my gift for mathematics. He writes of a premonition that I will possibly never do mathematical work again. I know him—this is intended to spur me toward mathematics.

Mathematics? Impossible! My heart has completely rebelled against my head, and yet I do not feel the pity of it, as Chevalier added to his fearful premonition. I must not alarm him, though. Write that we will see each other on the first of June, after leaving the sanatorium. Yes, we will see each other often, especially in the first two weeks of June, before I leave for Dauphine on the fifteenth, where I hope to recuperate fully, regain my vitality.

She is playing a lively melody on the piano. The trickling notes are painful as I cross the courtyard on my way to post Chevalier's letter. Again I go through the poorer quarters where the cholera has been most devastating, and on the way I am absorbed by thoughts of being infected by the disease. In a day I would be nothing but skin and bone; in two, the death cart would rattle me off to some ditch. Why not? What is there to live for? I turn to the sound of women crying. Is my life more important than the person who has just died or is dying in that room up there?

Death by cholera, the records will show, one of the tens of thousands who fell to the epidemic. One, absorbed by a black nothing, multiplication by zero. Isn't this preferable to what Father went through? At least the handful of people who care for me will not blame themselves for anything. Did Father feel as empty and hopeless? Now more than ever I can empathize with the anguish he must have experienced, and accept that his death might have been suicide and not the work of assassins.

— Father, Father, I say aloud, brushing my eyes.

I am at an intersection of several narrow streets. The air is laced with the smells of chlorine, pine from branches heaped on a furious fire, refuse spilling from carts. Some say the epidemic is due to contaminated water. Perhaps if I drink from that fountain? In one of the rubbish carts, knee-deep in refuse, a scavenger is delivering a foaming protest to a group of heavy-eyed onlookers.

— We've got to live, don't we? he spits his words. They want to clean up the city by using new carts, ones that'll make it impossible for us to pick through. How are we going to make a living? We won't stand for it. This plague's not caused by refuse. I've been picking through rubbish all my life, and look at me — fitter and stronger than all those lily-livered ministers put together. We've got a right to live, haven't we? It's not our fault we haven't got an education or a trade. If they use the new carts we'll smash them, burn them, throw them in the river.

At the fountain I rattle a metal bowl attached to a chain. Dazzled by the sunlight glancing off the water in the bowl, I close my eyes and drink.

Is it the twenty-eighth or the twenty-ninth? My mind is a swamp. I have not left the sanatorium in the last few days. Three sharp knocks on the door, and the present invades. I open the shutters. The morning sun is pale, its circle indistinct behind a gauze of clouds. d'Herbinville stands before me at the door, more imposing than ever, and behind him, her uncle, whom he introduces in a grave tone.

—Sit down, I say, placing another chair at the table.

—This isn't a social call, says d'Herbinville.

There is now a gray glint in his eyes, and his jaw is set like a trap. They move to the table as I sit on the bed.

—Your behavior toward my niece is unacceptable, says the uncle. You took advantage of Pécheux's absence to make those slanderous remarks about him.

—I didn't expect this from you, Evariste.

—Stéphanie told you she was practically engaged to Pécheux, and you continued tormenting her.

—Have you anything to say? asks d'Herbinville.

And as he steps in front of the window his shadow covers me like a fine veil. Looking up, I feel my affection for him stirring once again. I am about to tell him that she behaved coquettishly, played with my emotions, but I hold back. What will it achieve? Alleviate my self-hatred? No! I know why they are here. Let circumstances take their course.

—I can't allow those insults to go unanswered, says d'Herbinville. What is it to be, Evariste? Pistols at twenty-five paces?

I nod, almost indifferently, as though an observer to an affair that involves somebody else.

—Tomorrow morning at six, says the uncle.

They have already arranged everything, including seconds, weapons, and a sufficiently remote spot in the Gentilly district: a pine grove beside Lake Glaciere. They will send a carriage for me in the morning, together with an appointed second. Of course, as a gentleman and a fellow

Republican, I must not tell anyone of the duel. I nod to everything they propose. I shake hands first with the uncle, then with d'Herbinville, whose hand is warm from being in his pocket. Our eyes meet, pupil to pupil, circle coinciding with circle, and for a fleeting instant, I feel again that strange combination of admiration and infatuation. I want to embrace him, ask his forgiveness, kiss him on the cheek the way I would a brother, though not to avoid the duel—there is no avoiding that—but to ease his mind, for it appears that he is going through this against his will, at the uncle's instigation. In the end, however, all I manage is a slight nod and a promise to be ready for the carriage.

Stretched out on the bed, covered in a sheet of clean sunlight from head to foot, I am certain of the duel's outcome: d'Herbinville is a good marksman, he will not miss from twenty-five paces. My equanimity surprises me: Death is a certainty tomorrow, and I lie here, following a fly humming clockwise above my face, and when it stops and preens its transparent wings on the back of my hand, I still have the presence of mind to swipe at it. I remain in this position for some time, musing, daydreaming, projecting tomorrow's events in the patch of plaster on the ceiling. The carriage will come early, before sunrise, rattling against the twitter of excited swallows. The appointed second will enter, fresh-faced from the crisp morning, and explain in a pleasant voice the points of protocol. I will make conversation in the carriage. Discuss the recent death from cholera of Chief Minister Perier, and how the Republican cause would benefit from it. He might even offer me a dry fig or a sweet. The carriage will clatter away from the gray city

396

just beginning to stir, through green wheat fields spotted with poppies, to the misty silence of the pine grove. There, no matter how I arrange and rearrange the scene of the duel, how I group the given elements and position the characters relative to the sun splintering through the pines, no matter whether a duck tows an expanding *V* on the lake's smooth surface or a cuckoo counts by twos—whichever permutation I consider, the outcome is always the same: d'Herbinville finds his mark.

43

—Clothes! Clothes! Bought and sold!

A woman's voice rises dolefully from the street outside the sanatorium. Twilight consumes the afternoon, fills my room, covers me in crimson here on the bed. I still have my Artillery uniform. Why not sell it to her? Chevalier could pass on the money to Mother, to help with the cost of my burial. Or I could return it to d'Herbinville, who bought it for me. It would be no good to anyone bloodstained, with a bullet hole in the chest. I might as well salvage something from this mess. I take out the uniform and spread it on the bed. It smells musty, the epaulettes have faded, the buttons have lost their shine. I have not worn it since my arrest ten months ago. I admire it for a moment, then smooth out the wrinkles.

I am not destined to wear it fighting for the Republic. There was talk of another revolution, bigger than the one last July, but nothing eventuated. Sell it? Get a few francs? What is the use? It might look good on me tomorrow. After all, a duel is a battle of sorts, even though it is to be between fellow Republicans. I have not regained all the weight I lost in prison: The trousers are baggy, the jacket loose, the padded shoulders droop.

Boots! That is what I lack: a shining pair to complement the uniform. If I am not destined to die a hero in a revolution, I might as well look the part in the morning. My shoes are in the corner. How long have I had them? Alfred bought them for me just after my imprisonment. They are a part of me. Skin and hide. Clothes wear out in the same way for most people, but shoes are worn and shaped by the individual, by one's weight, habits, manner of walking. I feel sorry for myself at their sad condition. Pigeon-toed, badly scuffed, crushed above the heel, full of darkness. Does it matter? Such thoughts at a time like this! Shining boots or shabby shoes—it makes no difference in the end. I place the square mirror on the table, against the lamp, and examine myself from several angles—what a comical figure! d'Herbinville will smile ironically when he sees me.

The profile of an ancient mathematician emerges from the outline of a cloud, reminding me of an image in a recent dream: a cylinder circumscribed in a spherical eye. Strange, if I weren't at the window, or if the cloud were shaped differently, I might never have recalled the image. It would have been lost forever, as though it had never been.

Two hours have passed and I am still at the window. Someone coughs hoarsely below. Dishes are being washed in the sanatorium's kitchen. I slap at a mosquito that has been annoying me for some time. There is a small spot of blood on my palm: the price for proximity to flesh.

I take my mathematical papers from their satchel and spread them on the table. What do I fear? The duel? No. The bullet will destroy a world I loathe, a world corrupt to the core. No. This panic, this anxiety, is for my papers. My soul lies in them. They are the part of me that has not been corrupted by the world. Now, staring at this spot of blood, I realize with startling clarity that the Republic I have dreamed of exists only in mathematics.

Chevalier, dear Chevalier. I should have listened to you. You are the only friend I have ever had—you and Father.

What should I do? What time is it? I do not care about this puny body—let the bullet destroy it—but the findings in these papers—my very soul—how can I save them from the grave?

Soul? No, not the ghostly thing weighed on the Christian scales of good and evil. Nor the Pythagorean entity. I admire the ancient brotherhood for their asceticism and the manner in which they initiated the worthy into the mysteries of mathematics. I admire the beauty of Pythagoras's Theorem—always a curse to students who could not grasp the incommensurability of a line with obvious beginning and end. A theorem which probably has far more validity in the imaginary world after death than in the physical plane, where a right-angled triangle is always imperfect by the very reality of the lines that define it. Despite the virtues of the Pythagoreans I cannot accept their belief that says a body can be reincarnated into a dog or a fish, while the soul remains invariant under this transformation.

Soul? Maybe another word for the truth in my papers, the essence that survives death, the x in an equation that has no real solutions. Soul? Maybe Swedenborg's meaning of the word, as far as I understand from what I have picked up during the odd visit to a Salon. It is the best approximation to my conception of a soul. At fifty-seven, in a Pascalian turnaround, he walked away from mathematics and science, and spent the next twenty-seven years investigating heaven, hell, and life after death. It is said he conversed with angels for thirteen years, from whom he received his authority. According to him the first stage after death was neither heaven nor hell, but a preparation for one or the other. In this realm, an entity is supposed to take the form that expresses the affections and intellectual preoccupations of its human predecessor, and the entities, or souls, of like-minded humans are attracted to each other. This last point attracts me. Yes, his model of the afterlife is appealing—and it is a model, just as Kepler's equations fit a model. What better heaven than to be eternally with like-minded souls? All pure mathematicians!

I read the memoir Poisson rejected. Calmed by the mathematics, I lapse into a reverie over my former hopes and dreams. A bell tolls six times. I find that I have been scribbling on the backs of the manuscripts, in the margins, over the work itself. I am shocked by a sketch of a grotesque face with hair swept off his forehead in a wave, a long upturned nose, a beard, and wearing female shoes. Above this I have written my name, and to one side words I have absentmindedly written and obliterated—words and symbols which now I cannot decipher. On another page, among the mathematics, I have scribbled the word *pistol* on one side and *d'Herbinville* on the other, the last few letters of the name faint, trailing away to blankness.

Gathering the scattered papers in a pile, I turn to the fireplace. Why not tear them up and burn them? Through the liberating flame inspiration would return to inspiration, ash to ash. But a rising feeling of fondness for my work checks this impulse, and I am struck by the thought that

401

the real Evariste Galois exists somewhere in here, among these proofs, theorems, propositions: the Galois of uncompromising idealism, who did not succumb to lust, whose spirit was as pure as mathematics. And what about this person at the table, with a scar on the back of his hand from a childhood accident? His life is worthless, miserable, nothing in comparison to the flashes of insight in these papers. In twelve hours the carriage will come for him, in thirteen he will be dead. His puny body must die for the real Evariste Galois to be set free. Repeating this, I carefully arrange the papers in chronological order.

How is the real Galois to be saved from extinction? The question jolts me, fills me with anxiety. Suddenly everything depends on these papers. I must bequeath them to someone who believes in my work, who will bring them to the attention of a capable mathematician.

Chevalier! I must write to him at once! A last will and testament. I must summarize my findings, stress their importance, and entrust Chevalier with the rest. It is my last chance to save my true self. I dip the pen into the inkpot. Empty! I snatch a small bottle and dash out. Without thinking, I knock on her door. Her mother answers. I plead for a little ink, swear that it is a matter of life or death. Bewildered, she threatens to call the police and shuts the door in my face. I race out of the sanatorium like a madman. If only she knew! I swallow back my tears. I was prepared to spill my blood for the Republic and she would not give me a drop of ink.

Twilight is turning ash-gray. I weave through the crowd, bottle in hand. Ink is now more important than my own blood—ink for my last will and testament, for my work to be recognized. Ink as the source of immortality. The shopkeeper is preparing to close. He refuses to serve me. Breathless, I plead that my life depends on it. Complaining of varicose veins in his legs, he takes the bottle with a suspicious look and fills it from a small barrel. I strain over the counter, listening to the liquid's black trickle. He glances over his beefy shoulder. If only the fellow knew the ink staining his stubby fingers is to be the source of my immortality!

On the street again, the hour tolls, heavy, doleful, each toll an expanding circle of brass that spreads over the city, gathering everything. The seventh toll takes in the entire city, the earth, the night numbered with stars. This is the great circle, the primal nought, the mysterious zero from which the universe has arisen, to which it will eventually contract. These scintillating thoughts surprise me with their spontaneity: They illuminate deep ideas, highlight new associations, reveal truths seen only dimly before. Proximity to death! Strange things happen. The mind is said to move at the speed of lightning. I sidestep a hawker who tries to entice me into a theater.

—It's the best play in town, he barks. Our theater's spotless. Not one of our patrons has fallen to the plague.

Turning into a darker lane, where the smell of onions frying garnishes the sound of music and laughter, I become entangled in a group of youths emerging from a basement tavern. Boisterous, reeking of smoke and wine, they enclose me in a ring.

—What's your hurry, friend?

—Don't listen to the authorities. Excitement's the only way to avoid the plague.

—It's no good running away from it.

—Wine and women! That's the only remedy.

—Spit in the plague's ugly face. Enjoy today, and it can have tomorrow.

—What are you afraid of, friend?

—Live for the moment!

—If cholera doesn't get you, consumption will.

—If not consumption, the clap.

Laughter thick with wine bursts from them as they sing and dance around me.

—What's that in his hand?

They stop in a circle.

—What's inside?

—Ink, I reply, my voice cracking, heart racing like a clock out of control, thoughts on my last will and testament.

—Forget your studies, friend.

—Dip your wick instead of your pen.

—Clap's less painful than cholera.

—And how do we know it's ink?

The circle contracts.

—Might be poison.

—You might be going around poisoning public places.

—What are you running from?

—What have you poisoned?

—It's full of ink, I protest, opening the bottle.

In extending it from one to the other, I am struck by the thought they might tear me to pieces over a bottle of ink, in a lane smelling of onions, with that woman looking down peacefully from that third-floor window, holding an infant to her breast.

—Drink it!

—Drink it! chorus the others, skipping around me.

I attempt to reason with them, but their laughter turns threatening. I raise the bottle and swallow a mouthful of bitterness.

—Let's go, boys.

—We've got wicks to dip.

—Want to join us, little scholar?

—I'm going to see a dying friend, I say, tasting the ink. He wants me to write his last will and testament.

The circle opens and they send me off with a chorus of sympathy for the dying friend and exhortations to live for the moment.

In closing the shutters, I see them walking across the courtyard, arm in arm, probably off to the theater. d'Herbinville glances up at the window. She looks directly ahead. There is not much oil in the lamp. I light the flame, keeping it low—it will have to see me through the night. A small spider wriggles on a fine line hanging from the lamp. Spinning frantically, it descends onto one of my memoirs and remains motionless above an x, as though intrigued by its mystery. Twitching back to life, it crawls down the page and stops again, this time on an equality sign, where it shudders, as though not knowing whether to move right, toward the waiting mouth of zero, or left into the maze of an nth-degree polynomial equation. It crawls right, reaches a blank, contracts its legs as though pulled from within, and dies as a spot no bigger than a period.

I walk around the table. My mind is spinning, sparking thoughts. But how am I to grasp these flashes and translate them into words? I glance at the mirror: My lips are still black, even though I have rinsed my mouth several times. I must start writing. It is already past seven. Eleven hours to save the better part of myself from oblivion.

I have been scribbling again, this time on the back of a memoir. The mind is capable of all sorts of things in moments of distraction. I destroyed her letter weeks ago, and now, to my amazement, I have written it out almost word for word, down to her name and date. But the transcription is obscure, maybe deliberately so. Here and there I have unwittingly left gaps and omitted compromising words. If these papers find their way to Chevalier, what will he make of this cryptic note? And if they fall into the hands of a biographer? Will he attempt to reconstruct the last days of my life from scraps like this? With two thick black lines I obliterate her name. Will some future researcher uncover what lies under those black lines? Discover the name of the woman responsible for my death?

I begin, but not with mathematics. I am not yet in the right state of mind. It is a letter. I address it to all Republicans, choosing my words carefully, so that nobody will ever suspect I went to my death willingly. I ask friends to forgive me for dying in this manner. I wanted to give my life for the Republic, but I am the victim of a coquette and there is no way out. And here, to avert suspicion, to make it appear I really wanted no part of this duel, I add a touch of pathos and ask: Why am I destined to die for such a trivial reason? For something so contemptible? And I follow this with further proof of my unwillingness to duel, writing that I succumbed only after a great deal of pressure was exerted by my adversaries. I am not afraid, I write. I have always stood up for the truth, and I go to my grave with a clear conscience and hands unstained by patriots' blood. In closing, I ask forgiveness for those who will kill me, adding that they are good Republicans, though unfortunate victims of the coquette.

I address this to Gervais, a prominent member of the Society, and commence another, to my Republican friends Lebon and Delaunay. I ask their forgiveness for not having told them of the duel—my adversaries have put me on my word of honor not to inform any patriot. Furthermore, I ask them to prove that I went through with this against my will, having exhausted all possible means of reconciliation. Finally, I want them to make it known to all that I was incapable of lying, even in the most trivial matters.

An anxious face returns my look from the inkpot. Incapable of lying? Why not tell them all I welcome death? No. I must die in a way that preserves the real Evariste Galois, that will raise him from all this sordidness and project him into the future, and if that means telling a lie or two, so be it.

Will my friends succeed in proving to others that I went to my death unwillingly? Is such a proof any different from a mathematical proof? In the end a person's life can be reduced to events a, b, c and these events may be grouped, arranged, and rearranged to reconstruct a life totally different from the one that was actually lived, but sufficiently compelling to become the life accepted by posterity. Isn't this how biographers work? Isn't this how mathematics works? There may be many proofs of a theorem, all correct, and yet one will emerge as the most correct, the most compelling, because it is the most concise, the most elegant, the purest. And that is what I now ask of my friends: to extricate the pure Evariste Galois from the one who succumbed to a worthless woman.

Unable to focus on my last will and testament, I have been absentmindedly scribbling, sketching, scratching on a sheet. A bell sounds, muffled by the humid darkness. In the silence after the eleventh and last toll, I am surprised by the chaos on the sheet: mathematical symbols, words, initials, letters coupled to form strange characters, conjunctions of *e*'s and *ʃ*'s. Here I wrote *a woman* and then obliterated *woman*; there *logarithm*, elsewhere *indivisible* and even *death*.

From this confusion, a passage from Homer's *Odyssey* leaps to mind: twenty or thirty lines memorized in Greek as a student at Louis-le-Grand. Upon going ashore to the place foretold by the witch Circe, Ulysses excavated a pit, slew the ram and black ewe she had provided, and watched as their blood fused and filled the gaping hole. Suddenly the shades of the underworld began stirring, rustling, twittering, crying, finally clamoring to approach the pit and drink from the warm pool, which would enable them to converse with Ulysses.

I pour a pool of ink onto a blank sheet and watch it spread as it is absorbed by the textured paper, its perimeter changing from a circle to a ragged coastline. Figures and faces begin stirring in the black island.

The knot in my stomach tightens. Another seven hours, and then a separation from my hands, my shadow, the sound of my name. I will be reduced to zero.

The flesh will be entombed
In zero's all-embracing womb.

Couplets! At a time like this! Father's facility for impromptu verse comes to mind, and then his death in that
room. Asphyxiation or a bullet: It is all the same in the end.
They say life flashes past in the instant of death: a red ribbon carefully rolled all one's life, only to slip from one's
hands and become a tangle on the floor.

Is death like that? A return to the beginning? I and
nothing, one and zero, Archimedes and the Roman.

—Archimedes, I say aloud. As though summoned, the
bearded face of the old Greek appears in the ink stain. Inspire me with your courage. You were nearly eighty when
the Romans came, I'm only twenty. Does that difference of
sixty years account for your equanimity and my fear? Fill
me with the spirit of mathematics, give me the strength to
overcome the fear of the sword, to write my last will and
testament, to catapult my name into the distant future.

The bearded face appears to nod before receding into
the ink. It is an affirmative nod, full of encouragement, as if
to say the sword has no edge when one is filled with the
spirit of pure mathematics. A throb, and I feel the spirit
stirring, struggling against my fears. Another face emerges,
this one in profile. Indistinct at first, it moves closer hesi-
tantly, until I recognize the round forehead, the bony prominent nose, the thin neck.

—Pascal! You've come to show me the way. You never
really renounced mathematics for the cross, did you? When
you were tortured by a toothache, you weren't assuaged
by your faith, were you? The Holy Spirit of mathematics
possessed you for two weeks, eased your pain, and revealed
to you those wonderful properties of the cycloid. For two

weeks mathematics raised you above your miserable body and gave you glimpses of eternity. Pascal, I feel as abject and worthless as that rotting tooth of yours. Help me rise above my suffering and save my eternal soul through mathematics.

Pascal's profile loses its definition and fades like a circle on a dark pond. I am about to put aside the stained sheet when a third figure stirs. It remains nothing more than a point in the distance for some time, and it may not have moved forward at all but for my silent invocation. The point grows and assumes the features of a pale young man, who approaches with obvious diffidence.

—Abel! I call, noticing his battered black boots. Come closer, please.

But he remains in the shadow, as though preferring obscurity.

—Show me the way. You managed to work under the most appalling poverty, and even the consumption that crushed your chest couldn't extinguish the fire of your mind. Martyr Abel, may we become brothers in this sacred ink! I had no knowledge of your work when I wrote my first paper on equations. The remarkable similarity of our ideas is no coincidence: We were moved by the same spirit. Guide me through this terrible night toward the Evariste Galois who was as pure and noble as you.

At the sound of a bell's single toll, Abel recedes, becomes ink once again. I start from the reverie. Another death cart rattles past, drawing me to the window. It has not come for me, though. This one carries cholera victims. Such carts creak out in the dead of night, so their sight will not exacerbate people's anxiety, and yet the sound of their

410

chains sends a chill through me. Here and there at cross-roads, in courtyards, fires are flourishing, meant to purge the air of pestilence. Shadows flit like bats, hurrying either to avoid death, tend to the dying, or make arrangements for the dead. Across the street a red lantern shines above a gaping doorway.

44

Past midnight, and the smell of burning oil is becoming stronger. How much longer will the flame last? Time unwinds in a thread of black smoke. They were in the courtyard a few hours ago, saying good night. Her laughter rose above the scatter of horseshoes. d'Herbinville is probably asleep now. He will wake in the morning fresh, sharp, and ready.

And I?

The flame stirs. Is it my breath? Or is there another presence in the room? Biographer, is that you again? Have I inadvertently summoned you? Or have you summoned me? The transcendence of thought! Here we are, in this coffin of a room, on this warm May night, and yet physically we are probably centuries apart, perhaps living in different languages.

My last will and testament. I must start it. Focus my thoughts on mathematics. Division by zero: the great taboo in arithmetic. Forbidden because it undermines $1 + 1 = 2$. And yet using this taboo, one can prove that $1 = 2$, or $1 = $ anything. What am I when divided by zero? Multiplication by zero reduces everything to zero. And death? Is it multiplication or division by zero? From a graphical point of view, division by zero represents a singular point, a paradox, an instant when a function may be both negative and positive infinity. Perhaps death is a singular point in an otherwise continuous function of being. And when the small round sphere finds its mark tomorrow? My being might well be divided by zero. Is that what death is? An instant when consciousness becomes transcendent, when the mind expands and reconciles contradictions, when being overcomes both space and time?

My dear friend, I write, and look up. Faithful Chevalier! I will be something like the square root of negative one by the time he reads this. I won't write everything in my heart, though, not from shame or secrecy, but because it is now all so trivial compared to what is in my mind. He knows me well. He will read between the lines and deduce what I leave unsaid. He never failed to offer sincere friendship and encouragement in times of adversity; now I regret I did not always respond to that friendship. But he will know I trusted him more than anyone. He will accept the role of executor of this will and help save my soul, these papers, from oblivion.

I have made a few new discoveries in analysis, I resume writing. Some are concerned with the theory of equations; others with integral functions. In my theory of equations I have endeavored to find the conditions necessary for equations to be solvable by radicals. My work in this area has given me the opportunity to study the theory and to describe all the possible transformations on an equation even when it is not solvable by radicals. It will be possible to make three memoirs of all this. The first is written. Despite Poisson's comments, I still think it is important, and I have made a few corrections to it. The second contains some applications of the theory of equations.

I stare at Poisson's name. If his mind were nimbler, he would have understood my work, and all this would not have been necessary. May history condemn him for his judgment on me. No time for ifs and buts! Who knows, someday an algebra may arise predicated not on certainty, but on ifs and buts.

My writing is fluent, effortless, as though I have slipped back into my rightful element. Like the seals at the zoological gardens: cumbersome, dragging themselves forward over the rocks, but wonderfully graceful once they slip into the water. I am now imbued with the spirit that moved Archimedes, Pascal, Abel. I no longer feel my emaciated body, nor the pain between the shoulder blades nor the tightness in my chest due to the prolonged cough. And now, I see even death in terms of mathematics. Why not? If mathematics is able to explain the phenomena of light and gravity, why not life, consciousness, death? If consciousness is a function of life, and life a function of time, then perhaps consciousness might be considered a rational function of time. How freely mathematics flows out of me, as naturally as blood from a wound. My writing is almost automatic, spontaneous, like the writings of mediums who claim they are possessed by the spirit of dead writers.

The third memoir, I continue, concerns integrals. We know that a sum of terms of the same elliptic function always reduces to a single term, plus algebraic and logarithmic quantities.

What do I mean by this? I could have expressed it better. What I mean is: The sum of elliptic integrals of the same type. Ideas—they have always been too quick for my hand. The mind so swift, the body so sluggish. Leave it as a challenge to future editors of my work. A test to determine whether they are capable of following my thoughts.

No other functions possess this property, though integrals of algebraic functions exhibit absolutely analogous properties. We treat at one time every integral whose differential is a function of a variable and of the same irrational function of the variable, whether this irrationality is radical or not, or whether it is expressible by means of radicals or not. We find that the number of distinct periods of the most general integral relative to a given irrationality is always an even number. If 2n is this number, we have the following theorem: Any sum of terms whatever reduces to n terms, plus algebraic and logarithmic quantities. The functions of the first type are those for which the algebraic and logarithmic parts are zero. There are n distinct functions of this type. The functions of the second type are those for which the complementary part is purely algebraic. There are n distinct functions of the second type.

Intuition? A sixth sense? I read the last sentence again. What exactly is this faculty I possess? In an idea lasting no more than a fraction of a second, tremulous as a soap bubble reflecting the world, I have apprehended the full beauty and significance of elliptic integrals, even though they are relatively new and little is known about them. If only I had the time, the language, the symbols to express this insight. Thought and expression: At times the two are separated by a gulf of silence. At present this type of integral is nothing more than a seedling, and yet I have glimpsed the wonderful fruit it will produce. Who knows, it may take another twenty or thirty years before somebody comes along and, quite independently of my work, plucks the ripe fruit.

I tilt my head back, twist it this way and that until the bones in the nape of my neck crack. A clock strikes once, twice. Number and time. The two combine powerfully in matters of life and death. How many more times will the clock strike before they come for me? Eighteen! And each like a nail in my coffin. Death is no longer a dark figure in a fog. It is fixed in time and place: tomorrow, just after six, beside the quiet lake in Gentilly. Four hours, and their hearse will be here. After the chaos of the past year, after the madness of the last month, I am once again in the temple of mathematics. The lamp on the table casts a halo on the ceiling. The flame is pointed, watchful, the sole witness to this spring night.

My Gethsemane! The dark moth of anxiety flutters again. The oil in the lamp is falling; there is no more than a couple of hours of light in it, and I am still a long way from finishing my testament. There is no time, no time. Avoid digressions, Evariste.

You know, my dear Auguste, that these subjects are not the only ones I have explored. For some time now my efforts have been directed principally to the application of the theory of ambiguity to transcendental functions.

I would have expressed the last sentence more fully under different circumstances. As it stands, I have used a handful of words to convey an entirely new field of mathematics. Maybe a little difficulty is not such a bad thing. It will force those who are genuinely interested to work for my meaning. After all, following a mathematical argument is not like reading a novel: The reader must be active, prepared to enter the writer's mind.

It is desirable to see a priori in a relation among quantities of transcendental functions which transformations one may make, which quantities one may substitute for the given quantities, without the relation ceasing to be valid. This enables us to recognize at once the impossibility of many expressions which we might seek.

Ah, if only I applied this theory to the function of my life! I might have known a priori to avoid the impossible: Those hopes and dreams that could never be realized, those paths that led to dead ends. Perhaps life and theory are mutually exclusive. The spirit of mathematics will always be closer to ink than blood.

The flame begins twitching. Only a sliver of oil left. Will that pointed tip ward off the encroaching night for me to finish my last will and testament? The light and the text. Does light find its fulfillment in the text? Staring at the anxious flame, I see the duel, just as I foresaw and related to Raspail that I would probably die over some worthless woman, just as I grasped in a flash of intuition the entire theory of equations. The early-morning sun darts curious glances through the pine trees. Yes, there will be a pine grove, of this I am certain. As I step out of the carriage, a finch begins honing its song on the silence. Fennel growing on the banks of the lake scents the crisp air. Dew glitters on the grass. The seconds explain the rules, load the pistols, mark out the distances. But one of the pistols is faulty—the hammer will not stay back. We agree to use one pistol, taking turns at firing. Who will shoot first? We decide to throw fingers, starting the count from d'Herbinville. If the sum falls on him he will go first. I throw zero, knowing this will maximize the chances of the sum falling on him. He throws five. It all happens quickly, as though it were a game, a mock duel like those I played as a child. At twenty-five paces d'Herbinville looks more charming than ever. He is well groomed, clean shaven, and his boots are polished. I am slightly embarrassed at the shabbiness of my Artillery uniform. He strides briskly, boots rustling over the crisp pine needles, reaches the inner marker, aims, and fires.

But I have no time (I write, struggling to summon Chevalier's features against the compelling vision of tomorrow) and my ideas are not developed in this field, which is immense. Print this in the *Encyclopaedic Revue*. I have often dared to advance propositions of which I was uncertain, but all that I have written here has been in my head for nearly a year. Besides, I cannot afford to deceive myself by pretending that I have never been suspected of announcing theorems for which I did not have a complete proof.

In reading the last paragraph, I insert *in my life* between the *often* and *dared*. The flame is quivering, as though straining to detach itself from the wick, to fly from this dismal room. There is no time for elegance; meaning will come through to those who bother to read the text carefully.

The small hot sphere of lead will claim me, draw my consciousness with its gravity. Division by zero, I muse, falling forward, left cheek on the bristling needles, the smell of earth mingling with gunpowder, a sharp pain shooting through my left side. Later, when they perform an autopsy at the Cochin hospital, they will find that the bullet punc-

418

tured my left lung, passed through intestines, and lodged itself in my right buttock. What will they make of this detail in the future? Perhaps from the bullet's trajectory through my body they will be able to reconstruct the scene of the duel. Meanwhile I lie there for some time, perhaps an hour or two, unable to move, feeling the cool darkness coursing through my veins. Has my second deserted me? Has he gone to find a doctor? Or, seeing the extent of the wound, has he fled with the others? A peasant in an army overcoat lifts me into a horse-drawn cart and sets off with a loud cry. I am on my back, the fellow's coat under my head, the pain in my side exacerbated by each jolt. The sky is strewn with white clouds, and on the way to the hospital I lull myself with the words: the calculus of clouds.

The hospital room is distorted in the conical stethoscope pressed to my chest: The windows are trapezoidal, the spherical lamp bowl ellipsoid, the triangular stirrup above my head defies Euclid. The nurse's starched skirt rustles like crisp paper. Alfred appears, sobbing over me. Only Alfred, neither Nathalie nor Mother. Why hasn't Nathalie come? She came to see me in prison. Perhaps it is better like this. And Mother? I have not seen her since . . . Alfred's eyes are red and he appears to be drifting away from me, even though he squeezes my hand. I tell him not to cry, that I need all my courage to die at twenty. But I regret my words. Alfred sobs uncontrollably as the nurse takes him away.

Ask Jacobi or Gauss, I scribble, to publish their opinions, not as to the truth, but as to the importance of these theorems.

Again the cold stethoscope. The bearded doctor's

warm breath is scented with chamomile. Holding my wrist, he concentrates on my fading pulse. But my heart has already given up its lifelong count, its collaboration with natural numbers. The only numbers it is now susceptible to are the imaginaries: It can grasp the meaning of the square root of negative one, feel the presence of the elusive i. By tonight, it will renounce these for the transcendental, the mystical, π. And by tomorrow it will renounce even these for the holy zero. Black footsteps on the marble tiles. A priest leans over me and places his bag on the sunlit bed. A pin of light darts from the silver cross swaying from his neck. His fingers are crossed in a tight knot. The golden hairs on the back of his hands disturb me. Perspiration glistens on his lined brow. Flicking the bag open, he asks if I am ready to receive absolution. Summoning what little strength I still possess, I refuse with a harsh no. This is the last word I breathe. I focus on the priest's collar. Christ or x? The room becomes dark. A cuckoo is counting clearly in the distance. I am in a white circle of light, prostrate along a vertical diameter, arms stretched horizontally along a chord, fingertips on the circumference.

. . . After this I hope there will be some people who find it profitable to decipher this mess. I embrace you affectionately.

E. Galois. 29 May 1832.

Finished: my last will and testament. There was enough time after all. And I thought I might have to plead with them for another hour. But it is all done. I have managed to extract my soul from an otherwise worthless life that will soon be thrown into a nameless hole. Let them come—I am not afraid. Besides, they are not coming for Evariste Galois the mathematician, but for the reflection in the mirror. How distant he now seems, that youth in the Artillery uniform! It is as though he and I are connected by nothing more than a thread of faint light.

Immortality—in a feather from a dead crow. We live in each other's death. I blow on my name and date. This is more than the breath of life. I gather the pages scattered over the table, tap them in a neat pile, and count them. Eleven—a prime, good. I embrace them. The halo on the ceiling trembles. The flame is now fluttering. It cannot be long before dawn. Absorbed in writing, I have not heard the bell tolling the hour. Let them come. All is in order. Chevalier will not let me down. He will have these pages published. The great Gauss will see at once the importance of my work, and the mind, the soul, the essence of Evariste Galois, will be rescued from oblivion.

And this flesh and bone? The person who suffered, who encountered so many obstacles? Who, on the eve of his death, stared at a blue vein throbbing in his thin wrist?

The truth of the work will survive, while the chaos of my life will . . . Isn't that how it should be? Truth and beauty: In the end they are all that matter.

And for the rest? The life that produced it?

Still here, biographer? I have not managed to shake you off, have I? No, you are now closer than before: I can almost sense you in the fading lamplight. Well, I suppose there will be others who will attempt to reconstruct my miserable life.

Do you want to know me truly, biographer? Then forget everything I have told you. It has all been nothing but fiction. Go, study my work and resurrect the real Evariste Galois.

The flame is now in its death throes. I do not need light anymore. My work is done. I draw the lamp and put out the flame with a breath. It will happen to me just as naturally. At ten twenty-three on the morning after the duel (I can see the pointed hands waiting to embrace me), the hospital room will darken and the clock will stop counting its way into the future, like the walking stick of a blind person before a precipice.

And I am a child again, running happily toward Mother, eager to tell her that I have learned to count backward to zero.

The discoveries of Evariste Galois (1811–32) have given rise to an important branch of modern mathematics known as Group Theory, whose application extends to fields such as nuclear physics and genetic engineering.

Selected References

These books and articles are a selection of the more important sources used in the research for the Master of Arts.

Edward Temple Bell, *Men of Mathematics* (Middlesex: Pelican Books, 1953).

Louis Blanc, *The History of Ten Years 1830–40* (London: Chapman & Hall, 1844).*

R. Bourgne and J. P. Azra, *Ecrits et memoires mathematiques d'Evariste Galois* (Paris: Gauthiers-Villars, 1962).*

Paul Dupuy, *La Vie d'Evariste Galois* (Paris: Ann. de l'Ecole Norm. Sup., 1896).

H. A. C. Hollingham, *The July Monarchy: A Political History of France from 1830–48* (London: Longman, 1988).

A. Infantozzi, *Sur la mort d'Evariste Galois* (Paris: Revue d'Histoire des Sciences, 1968).

Leopold Infeld, *Whom the Gods Love* (New York: Whittlesey House, 1948).

T. Rothman, "The Short Life of Evariste Galois," *Scientific American,* April 1982.

T. Rothman, "The Fictionalization of Evariste Galois," *American Mathematical Monthly,* vol. 89, February 1982.

George Sarton, "Evariste Galois," *Osiris,* vol. 3, 1937.

D. E. Smith, *A Source Book in Mathematics* (New York:

Dover, 1929). See pp. 278–85 for a translation of Galois's final document.*

R. Taton, "Evariste Galois and His Contemporaries," *Bulletin of the London Mathematical Society,* 15, 1983.

*These titles are especially acknowledged for valuable material that was adapted in the writing of this book.